BASIC HARMONIC PROGRESSIONS

By the authors of
*Scales, Intervals, Keys,
Triads, Rhythm, and Meter*

Norton Programed Texts in Music Theory

Basic Harmonic Progressions

A Self-Instruction Program

JOHN CLOUGH
Slee Professor of Music Theory, State University of New York at Buffalo

JOYCE CONLEY
The University of Michigan, Ann Arbor

W • W • NORTON & COMPANY
New York • London

EB

The text of this book is composed in Times Roman, with display type set in Helvetica.
Composition by JGH Composition, Inc.
Manufacturing by The Murray Printing Company.

First Edition

Library of Congress Cataloging in Publication Data

Clough, John (John L.)
   Basic harmonic progressions.

   (Norton programed texts in music theory)
   1. Harmony--Programmed instruction. I. Conley, Joyce.
II. Title. III. Series.
MT50.C65 1984   781.3'07'7   83-25391

W.W. Norton & Company, Inc., 500 Fifth Avenue, New York, N.Y. 10110
W.W. Norton & Company Ltd., 37 Great Russell Street, London WC1B 3NU

ISBN 0-393-95372-6

1 2 3 4 5 6 7 8 9 0

CONTENTS

INTRODUCTION
To the Instructor

Designed to follow our more elementary programed text *Scales, Intervals, Keys, Triads, Rhythm, and Meter* (referred to as *Scales . . .* below), this book approaches the study of diatonic harmony through a four-stage paradigm which we call the *basic harmonic progression*. In Part 1, the progression I V$^{(7)}$ I, which was introduced toward the end of *Scales . . .*, is expanded to the four-stage model: opening tonic—pre-dominant—dominant—closing tonic. Everything in Parts 2–7 is built on this model, as the student is taken step by step from simple to more elaborate progressions involving prolongations of various harmonic functions, alternative chords within a harmonic function, linkage of one harmonic function to another, and finally simple modulatory progression.

Together with its antecedent text *Scales . . .*, the present book is intended as a primary text for first-year college courses in music theory. Where counterpoint or other topics are taken up before or concurrently with harmony, the usage of the two volumes may very well span three semesters. Most instructors will wish to adopt an appropriate anthology for use along with *Basic Harmonic Progressions*. Depending upon the orientation and breadth of the course, some instructors may also wish to adopt a standard-format text in conjunction with this book.

When we began planning a companion volume to *Scales . . .*, we decided immediately to continue the strategy of the earlier book, in which each topic is treated in a quantity and variety of exercises sufficient to ensure its thorough grasp on the part of the student working independently, and topics not well suited to the programed approach are excluded altogether. The result, validated by extensive trials, is a program through which students can be expected to achieve mastery of part-writing fundamentals and understanding of the basic concepts of harmonic progression with a minimum of guidance from the instructor, thus freeing large amounts of class time for pursuits that take full advantage of the classroom situation.

More specifically, there are basically three ways, listed below, in which class time may be utilized concurrently with work in this text. The choice among these is a matter of instructional style, and may vary from one part of the book to another according to the difficulty of the material and other factors.

1. Students work through the material essentially on their own, with little or no guidance or classroom discussion. Dates by which each part of the book must be completed may be given; meanwhile, class time is devoted primarily to topics outside the scope of the book, such as melody, texture, and form.

2. The instructor introduces each topic and gives an overview as appropriate; students do sets as homework assignments (in most cases a single set is roughly commensurate to the average homework assignment, in time required) followed by class discussion of any problems and supplementary activities—analysis of pieces and excerpts, composition, aural perception, etc.

3. Students are assigned sets (without introduction by the instructor) and complete them as homework. After completion of each set or group of sets, class time is devoted to reinforcing and supplementary activities.

For the average class, here is a suggested schedule for the completion of *Scales . . .* and *Basic Harmonic Progressions* within one year, to be treated flexibly as the objectives and context of the particular course may dictate:

Quarter/Trimester System

1. *Scales . . .*
2. *BHP*, Parts 1–4
3. *BHP*, Parts 5–7 plus substantial amount of work in anthology

Semester System

1. *Scales . . .; BHP*, Parts 1–2
2. *BHP*, Parts 3–7 plus substantial amount of work in anthology

As indicated earlier, a few topics in harmony are omitted altogether or mentioned only in passing because, in our judgment, they are not intrinsically well suited to programed format, or they could not be successfully programed within a space commensurate with their importance. These include sequence, harmonic rhythm, less frequent non-dominant seventh chords, ninth chords, less frequent and more advanced usages of raised $\hat{6}$ and lowered $\hat{7}$ in minor, phrase and cadence structure, and non-chord tones (except as they help to define certain prolongational chord patterns). We also decided to forego entirely the use of quoted excerpts and pieces, feeling that such materials could be more productively treated in conventional instructional modes concurrent with or following work in this text.

As in *Scales . . .*, we have adopted a lean set of voice leading rules, in order to avoid an unwieldy array of exceptions, exceptions to exceptions, etc. We feel that this has been accomplished without sacrifice of essential musical concept. Many instructors will wish to supply more lengthy exercises for which the given set of rules may be fine-tuned as deemed appropriate. Also as in the previous text, we have strictly defined the term *diatonic* as applied to the minor mode, to embrace chords derived from the harmonic minor scale only. In the theoretical literature, more than a little fuzziness attaches to this term as applied to the minor mode; our definition appears to have some advantages, including serviceability in the selection of pivot chords.

Obviously, this book does not address the need for aural and keyboard work. However, we strongly urge that such work accompany the study of harmony here, as it should any study of harmony. In particular, the part-writing illustrations and exercises in each set could be played to good advantage after the set is completed.

Although in no sense a text in Schenkerian theory, or even a Schenkerian theory text, this book does have its locus somewhere in the wave of pedagogical activity following the assimilation of Schenkerian theory (or the readiness to assimilate that theory) on the part of large numbers of the music-theoretical community. Of the materials issuing from this movement, the authors have been particularly influenced by Aldwell and Schachter's *Harmony and Voice Leading*.

The four-stage model of harmonic progression is one of those ideas which seems to have been "in the wind" for a long time but whose formal and explicit statement was long delayed. That important accomplishment belongs initially to Marion Guck in her article "The Functional Relation of Chords: A Theory of Musical Intuitions" (*In Theory Only* 4/6, Nov./Dec. 1978).

A particular debt is owed students at the University of Michigan School of Music, who worked through versions of Parts 1–6 of the program as it underwent revision and offered many helpful comments. Similar thanks are due students in the Department of Music, State University of New York at Buffalo, who worked through Part 7.

We are grateful to our editor, Claire Brook, for her unwavering commitment to this project, and to Leo Kraft, who read the entire manuscript with unusual care and offered many insightful suggestions.

To the Student

If you have completed our programed text *Scales, Intervals, Keys, Triads, Rhythm, and Meter,* and are now beginning more advanced work in this book, no additional preparation is necessary, although you may wish to look over the Review of Four-Part Writing Fundamentals on pp. xiii–xx as a warm-up. If you have not completed our more elementary text but are generally familiar with the material in the review mentioned above from other experience, you can prepare for work in this book through careful study of those pages, with special attention to terminology and definitions.

In addition to the Review of Four-Part Writing Fundamentals, we have included several other resources outside the programed text materials themselves. Tests (in standard format) at the end of each part are designed to help you to identify points for needed review before going on to the next part. A set-by-set summary of chord usage and voice leading is provided, for immediate review of sets that you find to be especially difficult, for review after an interval of time away from the book, and for reference purposes at any time, including *during* a working session in the programed parts of the text. The entire range of harmonic progressions studied in this book, except those involving modulation, is represented schematically in a foldout chart located on p. 173. Finally, there is a trouble-shooting guide in the form of a list of possible voice-leading errors, "Can't Find Your Mistake?" located on p. 162.

The program is divided into seven parts, each followed by a test covering the material in that part. Each part contains two or more sets, and each set contains roughly 30–75 frames. In some cases you will be able to do a set comfortably in one sitting; in other cases two or more sittings may be required. Frames are numbered within each set and separated by horizontal lines. Each frame presents information, asks a question, gives a statement to be completed, or directs that a certain operation be carried out. Many frames do two or more of these things. When two or more consecutive frames are separated by a dashed line, the first frame of the group contains instructions that apply to the whole group.

(Students who have completed *Scales, Intervals, Keys, Triads, Rhythm, and Meter* may skip the next four paragraphs.)

To use this book, cover the left-hand side of page 1 with the masking card. Read frame no. 1 and write your answer in the book. Slide the masking card down just far enough to expose the correct answer to frame no. 1, which lies directly to the left of frame no. 1. Check your answer. Next read frame no. 2, write your answer, slide the card down and check it. The great majority of your answers will be correct. When you answer a question incorrectly, reconsider the question and try to find your mistake before going on.

Continue with frame no. 3 and on to the bottom of page 1. *Do not turn the page yet.* Insert the masking card *under* the left-hand side of page 1. It will now cover the answers for page 2 (a right-hand page). Now turn the page and complete page 2. Continue through the book in the same way, doing all right-hand pages in order. When you come to the end of the first half of the programed materials, near the back of the book, turn the book upside down and work back through it to the front. Once again, your work will lie on the right-hand pages only.

In writing your answers to the completion questions, observe these conventions: A single blank line such as this _____ calls for one word; two blanks _____ _____ call for two words, etc. In a dotted blank .... fill in one word, or two words, or any number of words you think will properly complete the statement. Short blanks like this ____ are used when the answer is a letter (**x, y, z**), a numeral or chord symbol (1, 2, 3, I, IV^6, V$^4_3$), the name of a note (C, C#, Cb), the word *yes*, or the word *no*. Each blank is either long or short, exactly as shown above. If your answer is too long for a given blank, simply write your answer near the blank. Many frames require more than one answer, in which case each answer space may be numbered: (1) _____, (2) ...., etc. When blanks calling for a *series* of items are *not* separately numbered, the items may be written in any order.

Close synonyms of the given answer should be considered correct (for example *little* instead of *small*). To save time in writing answers, abbreviations may be improvised (for example *sm* for small) but *it is essential that answers be written, not merely thought*. Looking ahead at the correct answer without writing it is a fatal error. It leads to vague answers, guessing, and consequently to poor learning. Remember: *You will not be judged or scored on your performance* in this book. Your goal is command of the subject matter *after* completing the book, and the practice of looking ahead reduces your chances of achieving it.

The word *close* or *open* above the first note of an exercise refers to the spacing of the first chord only. The spacing of subsequent chords is governed by voice-leading considerations.

For a great many exercises, there are two or more correct bass lines. To avoid the clutter that would result from showing such alternatives, only one correct bass line is given in the solution to each exercise. A bass line is correct if *all* of the following conditions are met:

1. It differs from the given bass line only in the registral (octave) placement of some or all notes.

2. All notes are within the prescribed bass range (see p. xiii).

3. It contains no leaps of a 7th. (In certain special cases, discussed in the text, the descent of a 3rd [as opposed to the ascent of a 6th] is mandatory. Leaps of an octave are permitted.)

4. It does not cross or overlap the tenor. A particular bass note may not be higher than the tenor note in the same chord, nor may it be higher than the tenor note in either the preceding or following chord.

Example:

given solution (with tenor)

correct alternative

incorrect

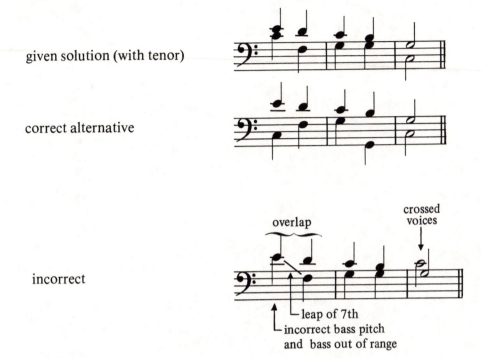

Alternative solutions involving the soprano, alto, or tenor are shown in their entirety or in small notes:

The example above indicates three alternatives for the second chord:

1. All four voices as shown in ordinary notes.

2. SAB as shown in ordinary notes, tenor as shown in small note F.

3. SB as shown in ordinary notes, AT as shown in small notes C and A, respectively.

REVIEW OF FOUR-PART WRITING FUNDAMENTALS

The reader is assumed to be familiar with the content of the following review, based upon the Introduction to Four-part Writing which forms Part 6 of *Scales, Intervals, Keys, Triads, Rhythm, and Meter*. As the review contains precise definitions of important terms and explanations of voice-leading procedures, readers who are not acquainted with *Scales, Intervals, Keys, Triads, Rhythm, and Meter* are strongly urged to peruse the review before working through this book.

Note: Points for review are listed by set number and title, corresponding to the presentation in *Scales, Intervals, Keys, Triads, Rhythm, and Meter*. Following each point is the number of the frame in that set in which consideration of the topic began.

Set 26 / DOUBLING AND SPACING

1. The connection of chords in traditional harmony is best approached through the study of four-part vocal writing.   (*frame 1*)

2. In speaking of combinations of the four voice parts, it is convenient to abbreviate. For example, SA means soprano and alto, and SAT means soprano, alto, and tenor.   (*frame 10*)

3. The ranges of the four voice parts are:

S   A   T   B   (*frame 2*)

4. All members of a chord keep their original names—*root, third,* and *fifth*—regardless of the position or inversion of the chord. In all of the chords below, G is the root, B is the third, and D is the fifth.

(*frame 21 and earlier, beginning in Set 22, frame 4*)

5. As a rule, the root is doubled in root position triads. *(frame 22)*

6. The terms *close* and *open* refer to the spacing among the upper three voices. In *close spacing* (chord **x**) the SAT are as close together as possible with no gaps; in *open spacing* (chord **y**) there is a gap between both SA and AT of one available chord note. *(frame 35)*

7. There are no size limits to the TB interval, except those created by the voice ranges themselves. *(frame 40)*

Set 27 / VOICE LEADING

1. The term *voice leading* is used to refer either to the melodic movement of a single voice or to the combined movement of two or more voices. *(frame 1)*

2. Leaps of a 5th or more are avoided in the AT. *(frame 3)*

3. Motion by two voices in the same direction is called *similar* motion. Motion by two voices in opposite directions is called *contrary* motion. One stationary voice and one moving voice make *oblique* motion. *Parallel* motion is a special kind of similar motion in which two voices maintain an interval of the same general name. In some cases of parallel motion the specific interval name is also maintained. *(frame 22)*

4. *Parallel octaves* (example **s**, SB), *parallel primes* (example **t**, TB) and *parallel perfect 5ths* (example **w**, TB) are avoided because they destroy the impression of four independent voices.

In addition, *consecutive octaves* (example **x**, SB) and *consecutive perfect 5ths* (example **y**, SB) are avoided, as is the movement from a prime to an octave (example **z**, TB) or an octave to a prime.

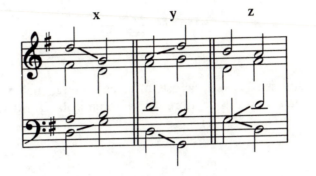

(*frame 33*)

5. For faulty parallel motion to exist, both voices must actually move. In the examples below, the TB *do not* make faulty parallels.

(*frame 41*)

Set 28 / I AND V, COMMON TONE CONNECTION

1. The term *tonic* refers to the function of the I chord; the term *dominant* refers to the function of the V chord. (*frame 1*)

2. I V I is the *fundamental harmonic progression* in Western tonal music. The I chord that opens the progression is referred to as the *opening tonic*; the I chord that closes the progression is referred to as the *closing tonic*. (*frame 4*)

3. When placed above a numeral, the symbol ˆ, called a caret, means "scale degree." Thus, the symbol Î means scale degree 1. The tonic note, no matter what its octave placement, is referred to as scale degree 1. (*frame 10*)

4. The smoothest way to connect two triads having a common tone (such as I and V) is the *common tone-stepwise* connection. The procedure (illustrated below) is:

    1. Keep the common tone in the same voice.
    2. Move the remaining (S, A, or T) voices stepwise.

When this procedure is followed, defects of voice leading, such as faulty parallel motion and AT leaps of a 5th or more, are automatically avoided. *(frame 14)*

Set 29 / I AND V, HARMONIZING A GIVEN MELODY

1. The most common soprano lines in I V I are those using $\hat{1}$ or $\hat{3}$ with I, and $\hat{2}$ or $\hat{7}$ with V.
(frame 5)

2. Many problems in chord connection involve a given soprano pattern which is to be harmonized. Some soprano patterns permit common tone-stepwise connections in the AT, and some do not. AT common tone-stepwise connections are found with the following soprano patterns:

In I V, $\hat{1}$ $\hat{7}$, $\hat{3}$ $\hat{2}$, and $\hat{3}$ $\hat{7}$.
In V I, $\hat{7}$ $\hat{1}$, and $\hat{2}$ $\hat{3}$.

Examples are given below:

(frame 7)

3. In a normal chord connection, the progression V I with a soprano of $\hat{7}$ $\hat{3}$ does not occur. When $\hat{7}$ (the leading tone) is in the soprano voice, it is imperative that the following I chord have $\hat{1}$ in the soprano. *(frame 15)*

4. Soprano patterns that do not allow common tone-stepwise connections are: $\hat{1}$ $\hat{2}$ with I V and $\hat{2}$ $\hat{1}$ with V I. (See example below.)

When writing these connections, remember the following rules:

1. Avoid AT leaps of a 5th or more.
2. Keep voices within their respective ranges.
3. Use correct spacing.

(frame 20)

5. Often in a V I connection with soprano $\hat{2}$ $\hat{1}$, the leading tone (in the alto or tenor) resolves to $\hat{1}$, resulting in a I chord with tripled root, one third, and no fifth (see example below). In all other I V and V I connections both triads have the usual doubling for root position chords: the root is doubled.

(frame 33)

Set 30 / V⁷, CONSTRUCTION

1. V⁷, consisting of $\hat{5}$, $\hat{7}$, $\hat{2}$, and $\hat{4}$, has the same structure in both major and minor keys. All dominant 7th chords are major-minor 7th chords.   *(frame 10)*

2. In four-part writing the fifth of V⁷ is sometimes omitted, in which case the root is doubled. This results in an *incomplete* V⁷. The arrangement with all four members present is the *complete* V⁷.   *(frame 37)*

3. The notes in a complete or incomplete V⁷ chord for four voices may be written close together or with gaps. The general spacing rules that are used for V⁷ and other 7th chords and for triads in inversion are:

1. Voices must stay within their respective ranges.
2. There may be no more than an octave between SA and no more than an octave between AT.   *(frame 42)*

Set 31 / V⁷, RESOLUTION TO I

1. I V⁷ I is another version of the fundamental harmonic progression, I V I. As with V, the function of V⁷ is to lead to a closing tonic. (*frame 5*)

2. In V⁷ I resolutions, the following rules apply:

   1. $\hat{5}$ in the bass always goes to $\hat{1}$.
   2. In the upper voices, $\hat{4}$ always goes to $\hat{3}$; $\hat{2}$ always goes to $\hat{1}$.
   3. $\hat{5}$, if present in an upper voice, remains as a common tone.
   4. The only variable is $\hat{7}$, which must resolve to $\hat{1}$ if it is in the soprano, or which may either resolve to $\hat{1}$ or move down a 3rd if it is in the alto or tenor. (*frame 16*)

3. Based on the rules above, there are three types of V⁷ resolution:

   1. Complete V⁷ to incomplete I

upper $\begin{bmatrix} \hat{4} \to \hat{3} \\ \hat{2} \to \hat{1} \\ \hat{7} \to \hat{1} \end{bmatrix}$
voices

bass $\hat{5} \to \hat{1}$
            V⁷   I

G: V⁷   I

                                           (*frame 16*)

   2. Complete V⁷ to complete I

upper $\begin{bmatrix} \hat{4} \to \hat{3} \\ \hat{2} \to \hat{1} \\ \hat{7}* \to \hat{5} \end{bmatrix}$
voices

bass $\hat{5} \to \hat{1}$
            V⁷   I
*$\hat{7}$ must be in A or T

G: V⁷   I

                                           (*frame 39*)

   3. Incomplete V⁷ to complete I

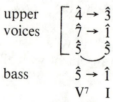

upper $\begin{bmatrix} \hat{4} \to \hat{3} \\ \hat{7} \to \hat{1} \\ \hat{5} \smile \hat{5} \end{bmatrix}$
voices

bass $\hat{5} \to \hat{1}$
            V⁷   I

G: V⁷   I

                                           (*frame 46*)

Set 32 / V⁷, APPROACH FROM I

1. The addition of a passing 7th converts a V chord into a V^7 chord, symbolized, V^{8-7}. The 7th, $\hat{4}$, provides a stepwise passing connection between $\hat{5}$ and $\hat{3}$ (see below).

G: $V^{8\text{-}7}$ I

(*frame 1*)

2. An opening tonic may move directly to V^7. The smoothest connections of I V^7 are marked by either common tone-stepwise movement, resulting in an incomplete V^7 (example **x**), or all stepwise movement, resulting in a complete V^7 (example **y**).

G: I V⁷ I V⁷

(*frame 10*)

3. The connections described in point 2 above "automatically" ensure correct voice leading. If a given soprano will permit neither of those connections, correct voice leading is ensured by observing the following rules:

1. Avoid leaps of a 5th or more in the AT.
2. Keep voices within their respective ranges.
3. Use spacing in the V^7 resulting in no more than an octave between SA or AT.

An example is given below:

G: I V⁷

(*frame 30*)

Detach the masking card from the back cover and place over the left side of page 1.

Set 1 / LEADING TO V

V

1 The fundamental harmonic progression consists of I _____ 1̂. (*Fill in the correct Roman numeral.*)

2 Often the movement in a harmonic progression from the opening tonic to the dominant does not occur directly. Instead, the opening tonic is followed by a chord which prepares the dominant. We will refer to this chord as a *pre-dominant* chord. Chord **x** is a .... chord.

G:

pre-dominant

3 Write the appropriate Roman numeral for each chord in the following example. If a chord is an inversion, write the appropriate Arabic numeral(s) also.

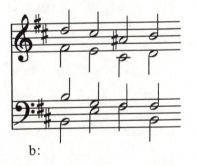

b:

I II⁶ V I

4 We will call a series of chord symbols like those you have written above a *Roman numeral analysis*. Write the Roman numeral analysis of the example below:

F:

I II V I

5 The three most common pre-dominant chords are: IV, II, and II^6. In Part 1 of this book we will study the *basic harmonic progressions* in which these chords occur:

I IV V I
I II V I
I II^6 V I

Basic harmonic progressions are expansions of the fundamental harmonic progression, ...

I V I

---

tonic

6 A basic harmonic progression consists of the movement from an opening __________, through a pre-dominant, to a dominant, and then to a closing tonic.

---

basic
harmonic

7 I IV V I, I II V I, and I II^6 V I are __________ __________ progressions.

First we will consider the connection of each of the pre-dominant chords, IV, II, and II^6, to V, then to V^7, and finally we will consider their approach from I.

---

(1) root
(2) first

8 IV and II are (1) __________ position triads. II^6 is a (2) __________ inversion triad.

---

root

9 In root position triads the __________ is doubled.

---

do not

10 IV and V .... (do *or* do not) have a common tone.

---

(1) SA
(2) SB
(3) AB
any order

11 The smoothest connection of two root position triads that do not have a common tone (such as IV and V) automatically *contains* faulty parallels, and is consequently unusable. No connection of C: IV V could be smoother than that shown, but the (1) ...., the (2) ...., and the (3) .... (*which pairs of voices?*) all produce faulty parallels.

WRONG:

C: IV V

5. Give the analysis of each example below. Bracket and label prolongations, if present.

(1)   (2)

(1) up

(2) down

(3) contrary

(4) does not

12 In the example below, the bass moves

(1) _____ (up *or* down) and the SAT all move

(2) _____ (up *or* down). In other words, the

SAT move in (3) _____ motion to the bass.

The connection (4) .... (does *or* does not)

contain faulty parallels.

C: IV   V

---

contrary

13 In moving from F to D the alto does not move to

the nearest chord tone of V (G), but it does move to

the nearest tone of V *in* _____ *motion to the*

bass.

C: IV   V

---

(1) D

(2) in contrary motion to the bass

14 The tenor does not move to the nearest tone of V.

That would be (1) ____, but it does move to the

nearest tone of V (2) ....

G: IV   V

The questions below will test your mastery of the material in Part 7. Complete the entire test, then check your answers with the correct ones on page 172. For each question that you miss, the corresponding material may be reviewed in the set whose number is given with the correct answer.

1. The pivot chord in diatonic modulation must fulfill two conditions:
    a. It must be a (1) _____ triad which the old and new keys hold in (2) _____.
    b. It must be either (3) _____ tonic or (4) _____ in a basic harmonic progression in the new key.

    If the new key is major, the pivot will be one of the following in the new key:
    (5) I, I⁶, ... (*Give Roman numeral with figured bass as appropriate.*) If the new key is minor, the pivot will be one of the following in the new key: (6) I, I⁶, ...

    The basic harmonic progression in the new key may have the (7) _____ _____ omitted.

2. Name all the keys that are closely related to f♯: (1) ____ ____ ____ ____ ____; to B♭: (2) ____ ____ ____ ____ ____.

3. For each of the following indicated modulations, list all of the suitable pivot chords by giving the Roman numeral of each suitable pivot in both keys. *For the purpose of this question, think just in terms of Roman numerals (not bothering with position or inversion of the chord).*

    (1) old key f♯:
        new key A:

    (2) old key f♯:
        new key b:

    (3) old key B♭:
        new key d:

    (4) old key B♭:
        new key F:

4. Write each of the following four voices:

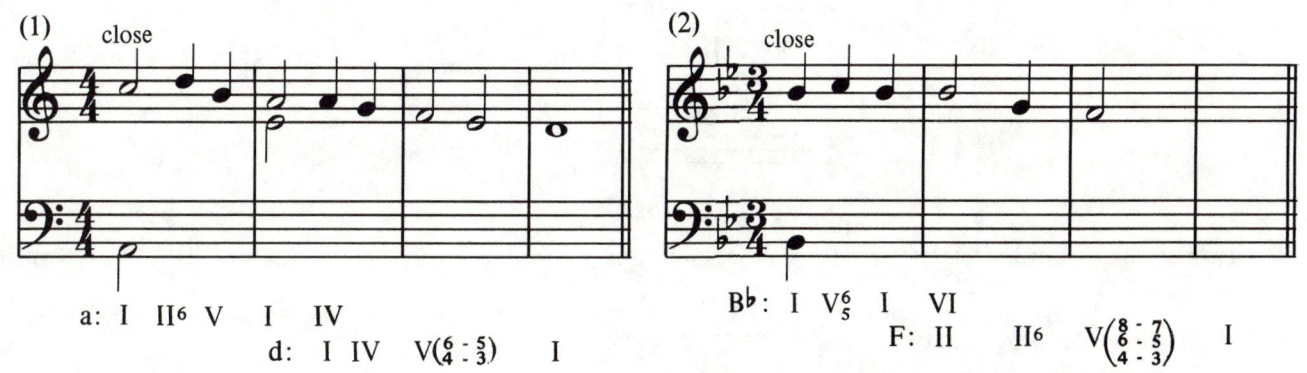

a: I II⁶ V   I   IV
    d: I IV V($^6_4$: $^5_3$)   I

B♭: I V⁶₅ I VI
    F: II   II⁶   V($^{8}_{6}_{4}$: $^{7}_{5}_{3}$)   I

15 When two triads in root position have no common tone, they may be connected by moving the SAT to the nearest chord tones in contrary motion to the bass. We will use the expression *contrary motion-nearest* to represent this manner of connection. The example is a .... connection.

contrary motion-nearest (*You may abbreviate CMN.*)

C: IV   V

16 In the contrary motion-nearest connection two things must occur. The SAT move in contrary motion to the bass, and they move to the nearest chord tones in that direction. Is the example a contrary motion-nearest connection? _____

No. (*The SAT move contrary to the bass, but not to the nearest chord tones in that direction.*)

C: IV   V

17 The smoothest way to connect two root position triads having no common tone, while avoiding faulty parallels, is the contrary motion-nearest connection. There are other correct ways to connect IV V, for example, but no other correct connection is _____ than the contrary motion-nearest connection.

smoother

18 In a contrary motion-nearest connection the
(1) .... (*voices*) move to the (2) ....
in (3) _____ motion to the bass.

(1) SAT (*or* upper)
(2) nearest chord tones
(3) contrary

31 In the example below bracket and label the harmony that is being prolonged:

C: I   VII⁶ I⁶   IV   V⁸⁻⁷   I

I VII⁶ I⁶
I

32 The basic harmonic progression that confirms the new key may contain prolongation of the opening tonic or pre-dominant functions, as studied earlier in this book. In the following modulation, the basic harmonic progression in the new key contains a prolonged opening tonic. Analyze the modulation as usual and bracket the prolongation.

d: I IV V VI

B♭: I VII⁶ I⁶ IV II V⁷ I
        I

33 A note on the example above: Regarded as B♭: I, the pivot chord has an "incorrect" doubled 3rd. However as d: VI (after V), the chord's doubled 3rd is necessary and correct. Unusual doubling and other departures from the norms of voice leading are sometimes necessitated by the dual role of the pivot chord.

34 Analyze the following, bracketing any prolongations:

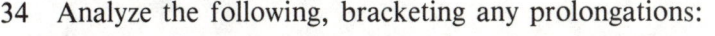

D♭: I V⁶₄ I⁶   IV
         I
    G♭: I IV⁶ I⁶   II⁶ V   I
             I

19 Write the contrary motion-nearest connection for A: IV V. (*Suggested procedure: Spell A:V. The SAT move in which direction? Each voice in the SAT moves to the nearest tone of A:V in that direction.*)

A: IV V

20 Write the following contrary motion-nearest connections of IV V.

b: IV V

21

E♭: IV V

22 Use the indicated spacing for the first chord. (*Reminder: In this exercise and in all similar exercises in this book, instructions for open or close spacing refer only to the first chord of a pattern. The placement of notes in subsequent chords is determined by voice-leading considerations.*)

open

g♯: IV V

(1) 7

(2) 6

28 In this example of modulation, pitches that distinguish the scale of the new key (from that of the old) are first introduced in chord number (1) ____.

Therefore, the pivot is chord number (2) ____. (*Hint: The two keys have the same signatures, but not the same scales.*)

Using the facts discovered above, give the analysis of the example:

c: I⁶ V⁶   I V VI IV

     E♭: II V   I

29 In each of the following examples, find the chord where the pitch(es) distinguishing the scale of the new key are first introduced, and locate the pivot chord. Then analyze the modulation completely.

In the first example below, the cadential $V\binom{6-5}{4-3}$ should be regarded as a *single chord* in the new key. (Remember that the cadential $^6_4$ prolongs dominant harmony through the delaying of dominant chord tones in the upper voices, and should not be considered a separate chord from the dominant chord that it prolongs.)

C: I V⁶   I V I⁶ III VI

     e: IV V$\binom{6-5}{4-3}$ I

30

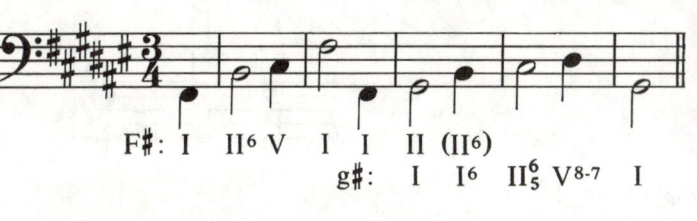

F♯: I II⁶ V I I II (II⁶)

     g♯:   I   I⁶ II⁶₅ V⁸⁻⁷ I

(The pivot chord may be either
F♯: II or F♯: II⁶
g♯: I   g♯: I⁶.)

23

close

f: IV V

---

(1) common tone-stepwise

(2) contrary motion-nearest

24 To review, the smoothest correct connections for root position triads are the (1) .... connection, used for cases where there is a common tone; and the (2) .... connection, used for cases where there is no common tone. These connections automatically avoid faulty parallels.

---

yes

25 Write the smoothest correct connection. (*Is there a common tone? ____*)

B♭: V I

26 Consider the following examples to be chains of individual connections. Connect the first and second chords, and then connect the second and third in the smoothest correct ways. (*Note: In these and all other problems in chord connection, it is a good idea to bear in mind the soprano scale degrees being used.*)

b♭: IV V I

24 The pivot chord (possibly with repetition or change of position) will appear just before the introduction of pitches that distinguish the scale of the new key from that of the old. In the modulation from D to A shown below, the first (and only) appearance of G♯ is in chord number (1) _____. Therefore the pivot chord in this modulation is chord number (2) _____.

(1) 8

(2) 7

D: V IV⁶ V⁶₅ I

25 Give the analysis of the *last two* chords of the example above, in the new key:

A: _____ _____

V^{8-7} I

26 Analyze chord number 7, the pivot chord in both keys:

D: _____

A: _____

D: I^6

A: IV^6

27 Complete the analysis of the example:

D: V IV⁶ V⁶₅ I IV V I⁶

A: IV⁶ V⁸⁻⁷ I

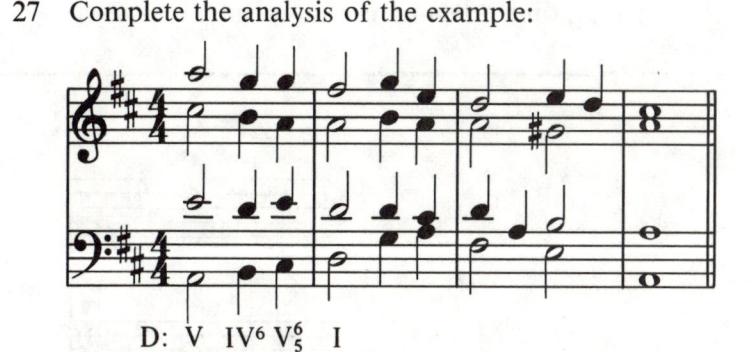

D: V IV⁶ V⁶₅ I

27

A: IV V I

28

F: IV V I

common tone-stepwise connection

29 The smoothest connection of two root position triads that have a common tone, such as I and V, is the ....

(1) do

30 II and V .... (do *or* do not) have a common tone. The smoothest connection of II V, therefore, is (2) ....

(2) common tone-stepwise

31 Write the following common tone-stepwise connections of II V:

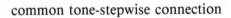

B♭: II V

32   open

G: II V

pre-dominant

19 The above conditions affect the *spelling* of the pivot chord. In locating the pivot chord in the analysis of a modulation, it is also necessary to keep in mind the required *context* for a pivot chord. The pivot chord is either the opening tonic or the _____ in a basic harmonic progression in the new key.

---

basic harmonic progression

20 The pivot chord must be

1. diatonic in both keys, and
2. opening tonic or pre-dominant in a
   .... in the new key.

---

opening tonic

21 If the pivot chord is a pre-dominant in the new key, the _____ _____ may be omitted from the basic harmonic progression in the new key.

22

In the modulation shown above, the old key is D. As signaled by the cadence and the accidental appearing there, the new key is ____.

A

---

(1) G(♮)

(2) G♯

23 The element of difference between the scale of D and the scale of A is: The D scale contains

(1) ____ (*note name*) while the A scale contains

(2) ____.

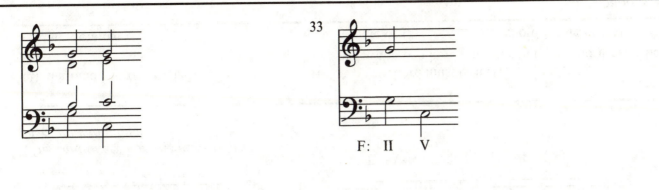

F: II   V

is not

34 The connection below .... (is *or* is not) common tone-stepwise. Sometimes a given soprano does not permit a common tone-stepwise connection between two chords having a common tone. When this is the case, the AT should move to the nearest chord tones that avoid faulty parallels and allow for correct doubling.

B♭: II   V

faulty parallels

35 The specific procedures, common tone-stepwise, for two root position triads having a common tone, and contrary motion-nearest, for two root position triads not having a common tone, automatically avoid faulty parallels. When these *specific* procedures cannot be used, the *general* voice-leading procedure should be followed: Move to the nearest chord tones which avoid _____ _____ and allow for correct doubling. (In following this procedure, you will automatically avoid defects previously considered in *Scales, Intervals, Keys, Triads, Rhythm, and Meter,* such as AT leaps of a 5th or more.)

15 In completing the examples below, check carefully for needed accidentals in *both* keys:

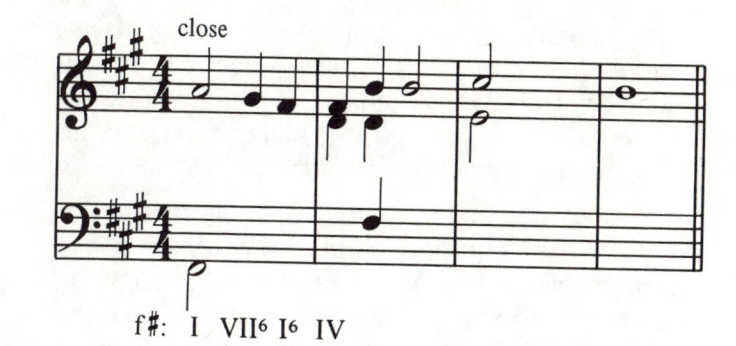

f#: I VII⁶ I⁶ IV

b: I I IV II⁶ V⁸⁻⁷ I

16

b♭: I IV⁶ I⁶ IV V I'

A♭: II II⁶ V$\binom{8-7}{6-5}_{4-3}$ I

17 In the above modulations, the signature was always that of the old key. In the following exercise, the signature is that of the *new* key. In no way does this affect the spelling of chords. It merely dictates where and when accidentals are necessary.

(The cautionary ♮ in the next-to-last measure is optional.)

E♭: V⁶ I V$^4_3$ I⁶ I VI

g: IV V I

(1) diatonic chord (*or* triad)

(2) pre-dominant

18 A pivot chord must be a (1) _____ _____ which the two keys hold in common, and it must be a tonic or (2) _____ chord in the new key.

(1) **z**

(2) There are parallel perfect 5ths in TB and incorrect doubling in V.

36 Which of the solutions to problem **x** is correct?

(1) _____ What is wrong with the incorrect solution?

(2) ....

37 The following are typical soprano patterns for II V which do not allow common tone-stepwise connections. Write the smoothest correct connections following the procedures outlined in frame 35:

38

13 Write the progression for four voices. Note that the two keys have the same signature but their scales differ—watch out for necessary accidentals in the new key.

F: I   VI   V   I   II
d: IV   V($\frac{6}{4}$: $\frac{5}{3}$)   I

---

14 The example below does not contain a key-establishing harmonic progression in the *old* key, as previous examples have, but rather contains a tonic prolongation pattern. In this and similar problems in succeeding frames, you may assume that the old key had been established by means of harmonic progression in a previous phrase.

Complete the four-voice setting, taking care to insert accidentals for the new key as necessary:

A: I   IV   V$_2^4$ I^6
E: IV^6 IV   V$^{8\text{-}7}$ I

(Note: E: IV^6 IV is a prolongation of subdominant harmony. The most common way of indicating a pivot in a case such as this is to consider the *first* chord, IV^6, to be the pivot.)

39 Consider the following examples to be chains of individual connections. First fill in the soprano line according to the given scale degrees. Then add the AT.

D: II   V   I

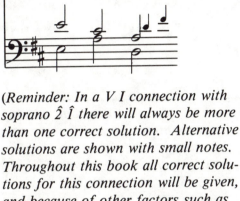

(*Reminder: In a V I connection with soprano 2̂ 1̂ there will always be more than one correct solution. Alternative solutions are shown with small notes. Throughout this book all correct solutions for this connection will be given, and because of other factors such as the desire for a complete I chord, or for an incomplete I chord with resolved leading tone, one solution will not be judged better or smoother than the others.*)

40

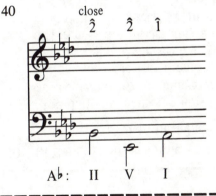

close 2̂   2̂   1̂

A♭:   II   V   I

41

open 2̂   7̂   1̂

B: II   V   I

9 Now continue the example from above as follows: Treat the E♭: II as f: I and fill in the f: I IV V I progression, thereby completing the modulation.

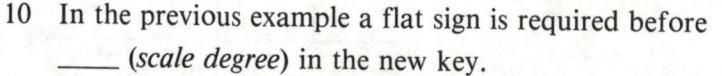

E♭: I   IV   V   I   II
          f: I   IV V I

$\hat{6}$

10 In the previous example a flat sign is required before _____ (*scale degree*) in the new key.

Modulation usually requires the insertion or removal of accidentals (or a change of key signature). Such accidentals reflect differences between the scale of the old key and the scale of the new key. If these differences do not actually appear in the music, no modulation is perceived. In the example below, note the signature, examine the chords following the pivot chord, and insert any accidentals necessitated by the new key.

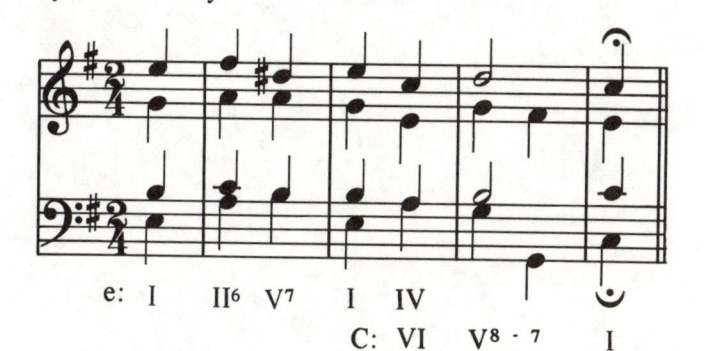

e: I   II⁶ V⁷   I IV
           C: VI V⁸ · ⁷   I

The cautionary ♮ preceding D is optional—remember that accidentals remain in effect only during the measure in which they appear.

11 Find a suitable pivot for the modulation indicated. (*Give Roman numeral and figured bass as appropriate, indicating the specific chord.*)

    old key F: _____

    new key d: _____

F: VI VI⁶ VII⁶ II II⁶
d: I I⁶ II⁶ IV IV⁶
any one of the above pairs

12 Complete the harmonic plan. (*Remember that the pivot chord is part of a basic harmonic progression in the new key, from which the opening tonic may be omitted.*)

V *or* V⁷ *or* V$\binom{6-5}{4-3}$ *or* V$\binom{8-7}{6-5}_{4-3}$

        F: I VI V I II
          d: IV ☐ I

diminished	42 Because of their harsh quality, root position diminished triads are avoided in four-part writing. II in minor, a _____ triad, is, therefore, to be avoided.
pre-dominant	43 The chords, IV, II, and II⁶, when preceding the dominant in basic harmonic progressions, are referred to as _____ chords.
(1) 4, 6, (and) 1 (2) 2, 4, (and) 6	44 IV contains scale degrees (1) ____, ____, and ____. II and II⁶ contain scale degrees (2) ____, ____, and ____.
(1) first (2) two	45 II⁶ is closely related to both II and IV. II⁶ is the (1) _____ inversion of II; II⁶ and IV have (2) _____ (*how many?*) common tones, one of which is the bass note. (*See example below.*)

$$\text{C: IV}\qquad\text{II}^6$$

(1) $\hat{1}$ (2) $\hat{2}$	46 While IV and II⁶ are alike in that they share a bass note and contain $\hat{4}$ and $\hat{6}$, they differ in that IV contains (1) ____ (*scale degree*) and II⁶ contains (2) ____.
$\hat{4}, \hat{6},$ (or) $\hat{1}$	47 In four-voice writing any member of the IV chord may be in the soprano; in other words, IV may have a soprano of ____, ____, or ____ (*scale degrees*). II and II⁶ usually have a soprano of either $\hat{2}$ or $\hat{4}$; they rarely support $\hat{6}$.
(1) IV (2) II, II⁶ (3) IV, II, II⁶ (4) IV	48 Which of the pre-dominant chords under consideration may contain a soprano of $\hat{1}$? (1) .... A soprano of $\hat{2}$ (2) .... A soprano of $\hat{4}$ (3) .... Which commonly has/have a soprano of $\hat{6}$? (4) ....
(1) root (2) third	49 In root position triads the (1) _____ is doubled. In II⁶ the bass, which is the (2) _____ (root, third, *or* fifth) of the chord, is usually doubled.

4 In a basic harmonic progression the dominant may be prolonged by

$$V\left(\begin{smallmatrix}6-\\4-\end{smallmatrix}\ \Box\ \right)$$ (*Fill in the box.*)

$\begin{smallmatrix}5\\3\end{smallmatrix}$

5 When the pivot chord is a pre-dominant in the new key, the opening tonic is omitted from the basic harmonic progression that establishes the new key. Consider the following:

e: I II⁶ V I
D: II V($\begin{smallmatrix}6-5\\4-3\end{smallmatrix}$) I

In this case the progression that establishes the new key (II V($\begin{smallmatrix}6-5\\4-3\end{smallmatrix}$) I) is a basic harmonic progression with the _____ _____ omitted.

opening tonic

6 Find a suitable pivot chord for the modulation indicated:

old key Eb: ____
new key f: ____

Eb: II $\left(or\ \begin{smallmatrix}II⁶\\I⁶\end{smallmatrix}\right)$
 f: I
(*Other answers are incorrect.*)

7 Complete the harmonic plan by placing a symbol for a *triad in root position* in each box:

Eb: I IV V I II
f: □ □ □ □

f: I IV V I

8 In the example below, write Eb: II. Follow the usual voice-leading rules in connecting I to II in Eb. (*Do not complete the remaining chords.*)

Eb: I   IV   V   I   II
      f: I   IV   V   I

50 Although it is also fairly common in major keys to double the root of II⁶, the general rule, which we will follow throughout this book, is to double the _____ of II⁶.

third (*or* bass)

---

51 Complete the following II⁶ chords, doubling the third (the bass) in each case:

B♭ : II⁶

52

c : II⁶

---

53 As the answers to problems in the previous two frames have shown, the spacing in II⁶ may be either close or open. In writing II⁶ (or any other first inversion chord) in close spacing, follow the same procedure as in writing a root position chord in close spacing. Think of the notes to be added; in the case below, ____ and ____. Then write the AT so that the upper voices are as close together as possible. Complete the chord:

B♭ (and) F

A♭ : II⁶

g: IV	63	old key g:
c: I		new key c:
(*c: II and IV contain A♭.*)		

- -

b♭: IV VI I	64	old key b♭:
D♭: II IV VI		new key D♭:

- -

F♯: V VI I III	65	old key F♯:
C♯: I II IV VI		new key C♯:

Set 25 / ESTABLISHMENT OF THE NEW KEY

1 The pivot chord is the first stage of diatonic modulation. The second and final stage is the establishment of the new key by means of harmonic progression. In this stage the pivot chord is taken as the opening tonic or pre-dominant of a basic harmonic progression (I pre-dom. $V^{(7)}$ I) in the new key. The progression is then completed to confirm the new key. For example, in this case

    old key g: IV
    new key c: I

the pivot chord will serve as the opening tonic of a basic harmonic progression in the new key. The complete harmonic plan might be as follows:

    g: I II⁶ V I IV
             c: I IV V I

Here the new key is established by the basic harmonic progression .... (*give Roman numerals*).

I IV V I

2 A basic harmonic progression has the following scheme: (*Fill in the blanks. Do not consider 7th chords.*)

    I—any one of: —$V^{(7)}$ (3) ____
        II (only in maj keys)
            (1) ____
            (2) ____
            IV⁶
        VI (only in maj keys)

(1) II⁶
(2) IV (3) I
(1) and (2) *either order*

3 In a basic harmonic progression, the pre-dominant in a major key may be (1) ____, ____, ____, ____, or ____ (*give Roman numeral with figured bass as appropriate*); the pre-dominant in a minor key may be (2) ____, ____, or ____.

(1) II, II⁶, IV, IV⁶, (or) VI

(2) II⁶, IV, (or) IV⁶

third (*or* bass)

54 Complete the chord below in close spacing.
(*Remember, in a II⁶ the _____ should be doubled.*)

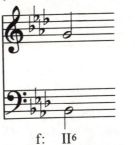

f: II⁶

A♭ (and) C

55 The easiest way to write a II⁶ (or any other first inversion chord) in open spacing is: First, think of the notes to be written; in the example below, ____ and ____. Then, write the AT so that the upper voices are not as close together as possible, at the same time, being certain to avoid having more than an octave between SA or more than an octave between AT. Complete the chord:

E♭: II⁶

(1) **y**

(2) The spacing is incorrect; there is more than an octave between AT.

56 Which of the examples below is correct? (1) ____ What is wrong with the incorrect example?
(2) ....

f♯: II⁶   II⁶

57 Complete the chord below in open spacing:

A: II⁶

57 To find a suitable pivot chord for a particular modulation, examine the tonic and pre-dominant chords in the new key. (These will be I, II, IV, and VI if the key is major, and I, II, and IV if the key is minor.) In each case, determine whether the chord is also a diatonic chord in the old key. Suppose, for example, that we wish to modulate from A to b. We need to examine the triads (1) .... (*give Roman numerals*), in the key of (2) _____.

(1) I, II, IV

(2) b

---

58 Write the indicated chords in b, with the signature for *A* in effect. Insert accidentals as necessary.

b: I   II   IV

---

59 Continuing the above problem, which of the following is/are suitable pivot chords in the modulation from A to b?

b: I II IV   ....
(*Hint: Which of the above is/are also diatonic in A?*)

b: I is suitable.
(*The others contain G♮ and therefore are not diatonic in A.*)

---

60 To determine a suitable pivot for a particular modulation, first think of the (1) _____ and _____ chords in the new key. Then examine each individual chord to see if it is also (2) _____ in the old key. If both the tonic or pre-dominant and the diatonic conditions are met, the chord is a possible pivot.

(1) tonic (and) pre-dominant

(2) diatonic

---

61 For each of the following indicated modulations, list all of the suitable pivot chords by giving the Roman numeral (without figured bass) of each suitable chord in both keys. (*Remember to follow the procedure given above. You may find it helpful to work out your answers on a separate sheet of music manuscript paper.*)

old key C:
new key e:

C: III VI
e: I IV
(*e: II contains F♯—not in the C scale.*)

---

62 old key c♯:
new key E:

c♯: IV VI I
E: II IV VI
(*E: I contains B♮.*)

58 Although there is a common tone between II⁶ and V, the preferred connections for this progression are not common tone-stepwise. In the connection of II⁶ V, as in IV V, the upper voices should descend to the nearest chord tones in contrary motion to the bass. The illustrated connection of II⁶ V is a .... connection.

contrary motion-nearest

B♭: II⁶   V

59 Just as in the connection of IV V, faulty parallels will result in the connection of II⁶ (with doubled bass) to V if the SAT do not move in contrary motion to the bass. In the faulty connection below the (1) .... (*voices*) produce parallel (2) _____ .

(1) AB
(2) octaves

WRONG:

B♭: II⁶   V

(1) SAT (*or* upper)
(2) nearest chord tones
(3) contrary motion

60 In the connection of II⁶ V the (1) ....
(*voices*) move to the (2) .... in
(3) .... to the bass.

61 Write the following contrary motion-nearest connections of II⁶ V:

D: II⁶   V

52 In the problems below, follow these steps:

1. Check the key signature and note carefully the the pitches in the chord.

2. Analyze the chord as a diatonic triad in each of the given keys *if possible*.

3. Tell whether the chord is a suitable pivot for the indicated modulation (circle yes or no).

4. If the chord is *not* a suitable pivot, cite condition 1 or 2 as listed in frame 51.

C: II
f: (not diatonic—contains D♮)
no—condition 1

old key c: ___
new key f: ___

suitable pivot?   yes/no
if not, which condition not present?   1/2

53

A: I
D: V

no—condition 2
(Chord is neither tonic nor predominant in new key.)

old key A: ___
new key D: ___

suitable pivot?   yes/no
if not, which condition not present?   1/2

54

d: I
F: VI

yes

old key d: ___
new key F: ___

suitable pivot?   yes/no
if not, which condition not present?   1/2

55

b♭: (not diatonic)
A♭: VI

no—condition 1

old key b♭: ___
new key A♭: ___

suitable pivot?   yes/no
if not, which condition not present?   1/2

56

f♯: (not diatonic)
A: III

no—Both conditions are violated.

old key f♯: ___
new key A: ___

suitable pivot?   yes/no
if not, which condition not present?   1/2

62 (*Remember to move all upper voices in contrary motion to the bass.*)

e: II⁶ V

63 (*Be sure to use correct doubling.*)

g: II⁶ V

64

F: II⁶ V

65 Consider each of the following examples to be a chain of individual connections. Connect each pair of chords in the smoothest correct way.

c: II⁶ V I

47 There is another restriction on the pivot chord. It must be either a tonic (I or I^6) or pre-dominant chord in the *new key*. (*Remember that in this book we are dealing only with triads—and not 7th chords—as pivots. In this and the next set, all references to pre-dominant chords are to* triads.)

(1) II^6, IV

Pre-dominant chords in major keys are II (1) ____, ____, IV^6, and VI. Pre-dominant chords generally found in minor keys are: II^6, (2) ____, and IV^6. (*Remember, II in minor keys, a diminished triad, does not usually occur in root position. VI does not generally lead directly to V in minor keys because of problematic voice leading.*)

(2) IV

(1) pre-dominant

48 The pivot chord must be tonic or (1) _____ in the new key. In both major and minor keys, the pivot may *not* be III, (2) ____, or ____ (*give Roman numerals without figured bass*), or an inversion of one of these chords, in the new key.

(2) V (or) VII

(1) II, II^6, IV, IV^6, VI

49 Pre-dominant chords in major keys are:
(1) ____, ____, ____, ____, ____
Pre-dominant chords in minor keys are:
(2) ____, ____, ____

(2) II^6, IV, IV^6

50 In the remainder of this set we will be determining the suitability of possible pivots. For the sake of simplicity, we can just think of chord spellings in root position (remembering, of course, that in a musical context, chords in root position and first inversion may be used differently.) If the new key is major, the pivot in the new key must have the Roman numeral I (1) ____, ____, or ____. If the new key is minor, the pivot in the new key must have the Roman numeral (2) ____, II, or ____.

(1) II, IV, (or) VI

(2) I, (II, or) IV

51 In summary, pivot chords must fulfill two conditions. They must be

  1. diatonic in both keys, and
  2. tonic or pre-dominant in the new key.

yes

(none)

Is the chord below a suitable pivot chord for the indicated modulation? ____ (yes *or* no) If not, which of the above conditions does it violate? ....

old key E: V

new key **B**: I

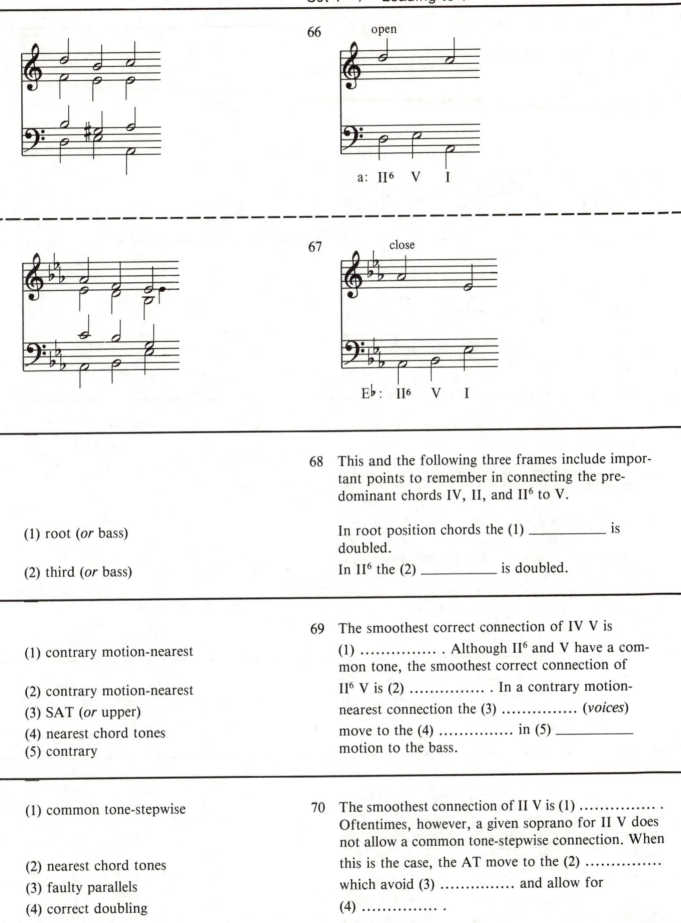

66 open

a: II⁶ V I

67 close

E♭: II⁶ V I

68 This and the following three frames include important points to remember in connecting the predominant chords IV, II, and II⁶ to V.

(1) root (*or* bass)

In root position chords the (1) _____ is doubled.

(2) third (*or* bass)

In II⁶ the (2) _____ is doubled.

69 The smoothest correct connection of IV V is

(1) contrary motion-nearest

(1) .... Although II⁶ and V have a common tone, the smoothest correct connection of

(2) contrary motion-nearest

II⁶ V is (2) .... In a contrary motion-nearest connection the (3) .... (*voices*)

(3) SAT (*or* upper)

move to the (4) .... in (5) _____

(4) nearest chord tones

motion to the bass.

(5) contrary

(1) common tone-stepwise

70 The smoothest connection of II V is (1) .... Oftentimes, however, a given soprano for II V does not allow a common tone-stepwise connection. When

(2) nearest chord tones

this is the case, the AT move to the (2) ....

(3) faulty parallels

which avoid (3) .... and allow for

(4) correct doubling

(4) ....

41 Determine which of the diatonic triads of B♭ (shown below) are diatonic triads in common with d. Show the analysis of those chords in d:

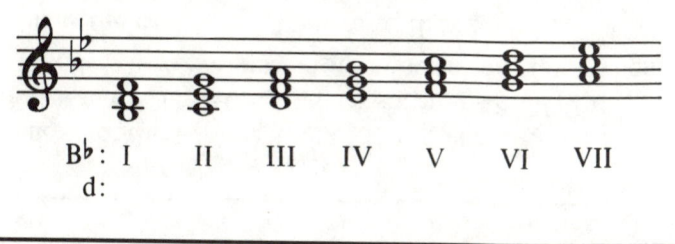

B♭: I   II   III   IV   V   VI   VII
d:

B♭: I   III VI
   d: VI I   IV

42 The three triads in the answer to the previous frame are the (1) _____ triads that B♭ and d hold in (2) _____.

(1) diatonic
(2) common

43 In the following problems, all of the diatonic triads in a particular key are shown and analyzed, with the signature of that key in effect. In each problem, determine which of the triads is/are also diatonic in the second specified key, and show the analysis of those triads in the second key. (*Suggestion: First find the points of difference between the two scales.*)

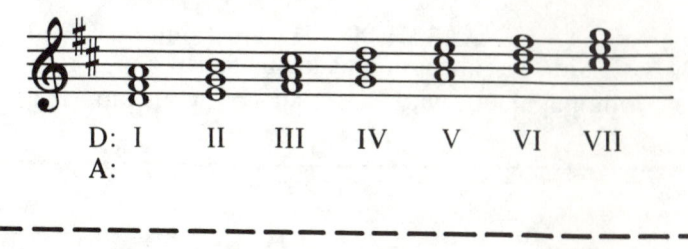

D: I   II   III   IV   V   VI   VII
A:

D: I   III V VI
A: IV VI I   II

44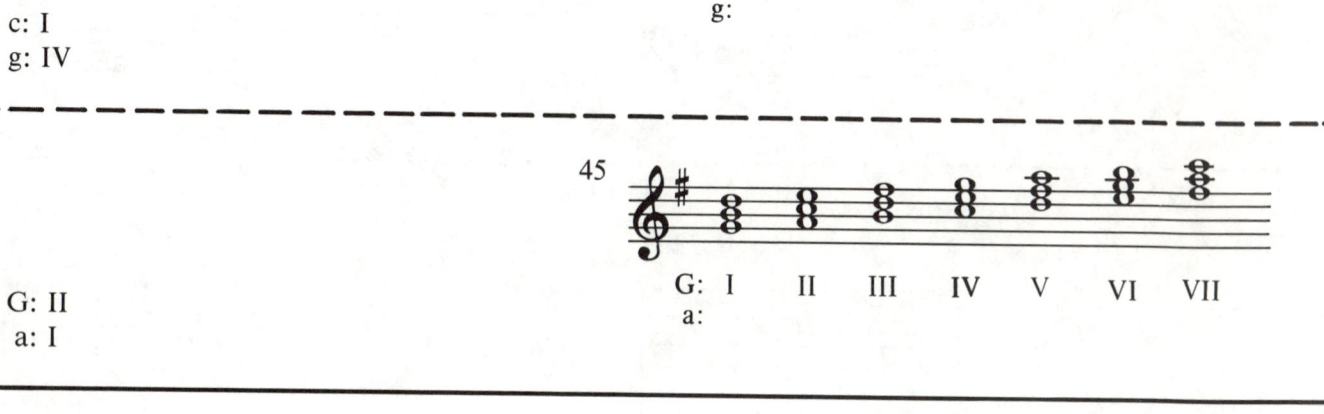

c: I   II   III   IV   V   VI   VII
g:

c: I
g: IV

45

G: I   II   III   IV   V   VI   VII
a:

G: II
a: I

pivot

46 In diatonic modulation, the _____ chord must be a diatonic chord that the two keys hold in common.

(1) $\hat{4}$, $\hat{6}$, (or) $\hat{1}$

(2) $\hat{2}$ (or) $\hat{4}$

71 IV may contain a soprano of (1) ____, ____, or ____ (*scale degrees*). II and II⁶ commonly have a soprano of (2) ____ or ____.

72 Write each of the following progressions in the smoothest correct way:

Ab: IV V I

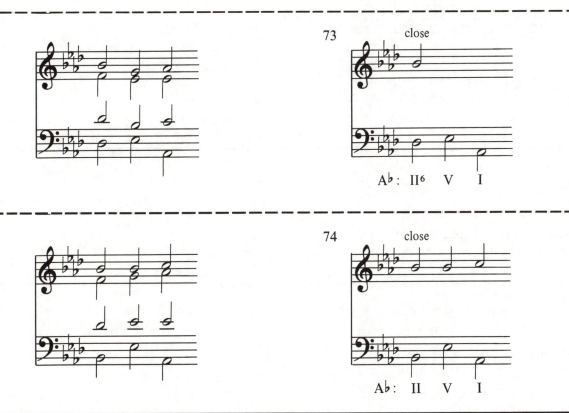

73

Ab: II⁶ V I

74

Ab: II V I

For review and reference purposes, a summary of the material presented in each set is given on pages 151–161.

36 In any diatonic scale the seven pitch names are the letters A through G followed by one of the signs ♮, ♯, ♭, 𝄪, ♭♭, in each case. (If no sign is present, ♮ is understood.) Because of the correspondence of *letters* among the pitch names of all scales, we can pinpoint the differences between two scales by listing the letter names which are associated with different signs. For example, the C major scale and the D major scale each contain two pitch names not present in the other; these are the names with letters "C" and "F." (The C major scale contains C♮ and F♮, whereas the D major scale contains C♯ and F♯.) The C major scale and the F major scale each contain one pitch name not present in the other. The C major scale contains B (1) _____ (♮, ♯, or ♭), while the F major scale contains B (2) _____.

(1) ♮

(2) ♭

37 From the above we can reason that diatonic triads in C which exclude B♮ will also be diatonic triads in (1)_____ (*key name*). Similarly, diatonic triads in F which exclude B♭ will also be diatonic triads in (2) _____.

(1) F

(2) C

38 Shown below are the diatonic triads in C. Using the information from the previous frame, circle the triads that can also be analyzed as diatonic triads in F:

C: I   II   III   IV   V   VI   VII

C: I, II, IV, and VI should be circled.

39 If we compare the B♭ major scale and the D harmonic minor scale, we find that the former contains E♭, while the latter contains E♮. There is another point of difference. The B♭ major scale contains (1) _____, while the D harmonic minor scale contains (2) _____.

(1) C(♮)
(2) C♯

40 Diatonic triads that B♭ and d hold in common must exclude the letter names _____ and _____. (*Name two of A, B, C, D, E, F, G.*)

E (and) C

I V I

1 I V^7 I is another version of the fundamental harmonic progression ....

IV, II, (or) II^6

2 V^7 is often preceded, as is V, by one of the common pre-dominant chords, ____, ____, or ____.

down

3 The seventh of V^7 ($\hat{4}$) is an active tone which has a strong tendency to resolve _____ by step.

(1) 4
(2) all (IV, II, II^6)

4 The seventh of V^7, scale degree (1) ____, is present in which of the following: IV, II, II^6? (2) .... Because it is a strong tendency tone, the seventh of V^7 is not only resolved in a prescribed way, it is also generally approached in a certain way—by common tone from IV, II, or II^6. When the seventh of V^7 is approached by common tone, it is said to be *prepared*.

(1) $\hat{4}$

(2) prepared

5 The smoothest way to move from IV, II, or II^6 to V^7 entails keeping (1) ____ (*scale degree*), as a common tone in the same voice. In this way the seventh of V^7 is (2) _____.

(1) soprano
(2) common tone
(3) prepared

6 The seventh of V^7 is in the (1) _____ (*voice*) below. It is approached by (2) _____ _____; in other words, it is (3) _____.

A: IV   V^7

7 In each case find the seventh of V^7 and write its note of preparation before the chord:

B♭ :   V^7

(1) II, III, and VI

(2) I and IV

30 Minor triads are found as (1) .... (*give Roman numerals*) in major keys, and as (2) .... in minor keys.

5

31 It follows from the above that a *particular* minor triad can occur as a diatonic triad in ____ (*how many*?) keys.

32 Fill in the missing information:

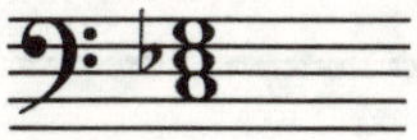

major keys
Bb: II
: III
:

minor keys
c: I
:

Ab(: III)
Eb: VI

g: IV

33 Complete the five possible analyses of the given chord as a diatonic triad. Give key and Roman numeral in each case:

E: I⁶
—: —
—: —
—: —

B: IV^6
A: V^6
a: V^6
g♯: VI^6

(1) VII
(2) II (and) VII

34 The diminished triad occurs as (1) ____ (*Roman numeral*) in major keys and as (2) ____ and ____ in minor keys.

35 Complete the three possible analyses of the given chord as a diatonic triad:

D: VII^6
—: —
—: —

b: II^6
d: VII^6

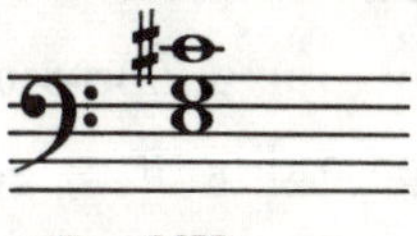

8

g: V⁷

---

(1) prepare

(2) incomplete

9 The smoothest way to connect IV V⁷ is to

(1) _____ the seventh by common tone and to move the other voices stepwise in contrary motion to the bass, as in the example below. This results in

a(n) (2) _____ (complete *or* incomplete) V⁷.

B♭ : IV   V⁷

---

10 Connect IV V⁷.
    1. Prepare the seventh by common tone.
    2. Move the other voices by step in contrary motion to the bass to an incomplete V⁷.

f♯: IV   V⁷

---

11   open

G: IV   V⁷

B♮ (*The E♮ is required by the old key.*)

26 Note that it is not necessary for the key *signature* to change when modulation takes place. If the signature remains the same, in most cases accidentals must be inserted to reflect the scale of the *new* key. In the previous frame, which note has an accidental for this purpose? ____ (*Hint: There is only one such note.*)

27 Now that we have observed some of the features of diatonic modulation, we can proceed to study the idea of the pivot chord more systematically. First it is necessary to review the facts pertaining to structural types of diatonic triads. Complete the table of structural types of diatonic triads in *major* keys by entering the Roman numerals III, IV, V, and VI on the appropriate line below:

(1) (I) IV V

(2) (II) III VI

maj triads: (1) I ....

min triads: (2) II ....

dim triad: VII

28 Do the same for diatonic triads in *minor* keys. (*Reminder: In this book the* harmonic *minor scale is taken as the source of diatonic triads in minor keys.*)

(1) V VI

(2) (I) IV

(3) II VII

(4) III

maj triads: (1) ....

min triads: (2) I ....

dim triads: (3) ....

aug triad: (4) ____

29 The two previous frames show that major triads are found as I, IV, and V in major keys, and V and VI in minor keys. It follows that a *particular* major triad may occur as a diatonic triad in five different keys, corresponding to the five cases listed above. Complete the following list of possible analyses of the G major triad as a diatonic triad, by entering the name of the appropriate key in each box. (*Refer to the two previous frames if necessary.*)

C(: V)

b(: VI)

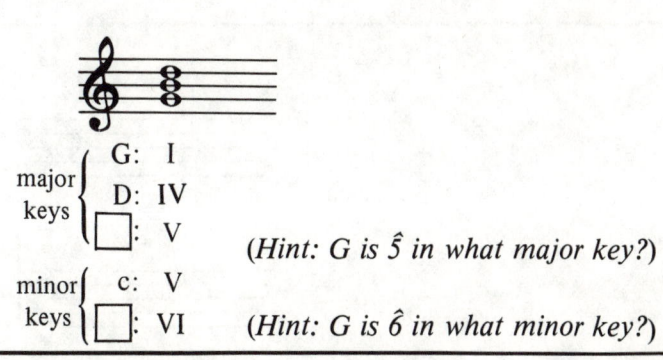

major keys { G: I / D: IV / ☐: V (*Hint: G is $\hat{5}$ in what major key?*)

minor keys { c: V / ☐: VI (*Hint: G is $\hat{6}$ in what minor key?*)

parallel perfect 5ths in SB

12 Identify the error in this example: ....
Using the given IV, rewrite the connection in the smoothest correct way:

C: IV   V⁷   IV   V⁷

---

incorrect doubling (doubled leading tone) in V⁷

13 Identify the error in this example: ....
Rewrite the connection in the smoothest correct way:

F: IV   V⁷   IV.   V⁷

---

(1) TB

(2) minor

14 The connection below is incorrect for two reasons:

1. There are faulty parallels in (1) ....
   (*voices*).
2. There is an augmented 2nd in the alto. The melodic augmented 2nd, found in

   (2) _____ (major *or* minor) keys
   between $\hat{6}$ and $\hat{7}$, is to be avoided in four-part writing.

Both defects in this example are automatically avoided by following the procedure outlined in frame 10. Rewrite the connection in the smoothest correct way:

c: IV   V⁷   IV   V⁷

23 Once the old key is established, modulation can take place. The first stage in diatonic modulation is the *pivot chord*, a diatonic triad which the old and new keys hold in common. (Diatonic *7th* chords work as pivot chords too, but we will not study this usage.) The example contains a modulation from B♭ to F. The pivot chord is marked ↓. Show its analysis in both keys.

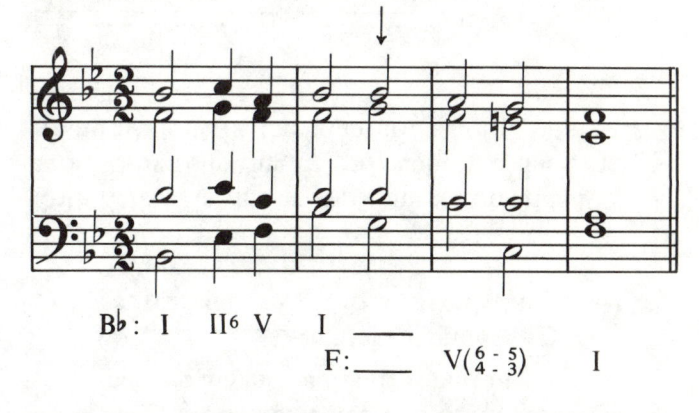

B♭: VI
F: II

Bb: I   II⁶ V   I   ____
F: ____   V($^6_4$ – $^5_3$)   I

24 Following the format of the previous example, complete the analysis of the modulation. First write the name of the new key in the box. (The example ends on the tonic of the new key.) Then fill in the chord symbols, giving the analysis of the pivot chord (marked ↓) in both keys.

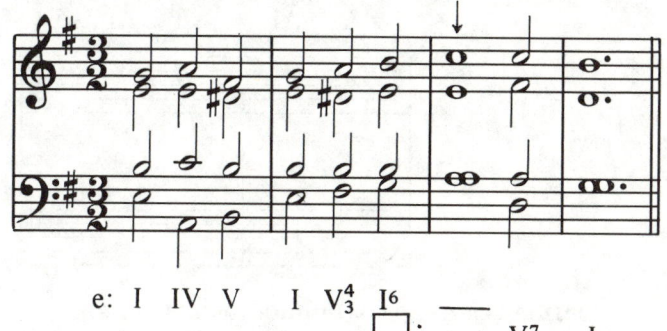

(e:) IV
G: II

e: I   IV   V   I   V$^4_3$ I⁶   ____
☐: ____   V⁷   I

25 Complete the analysis. Fill in the name of the new key (the final chord is its tonic) and place a chord symbol in each blank.

(f:) I VI II⁶₅ V I⁶
      c: IV⁶ IV V⁷ I

f: __ __ __ __ __
☐: __ __ __   I

15 An augmented 2nd can occur in the connection of IV or II⁶ to V or V⁷ in minor keys. (Remember, II, a diminished triad in minor, is rarely used.) By using the contrary motion-nearest connection with IV V and II⁶ V, the augmented 2nd is automatically avoided. This defect is also automatically avoided in IV V⁷ if the seventh of V⁷ is prepared (1) .... and the other voices move by (2) _____ in (3) _____ motion to the bass.

(1) by common tone
(2) step
(3) contrary

16 We now have a complete set of voice-leading rules to follow in moving from a pre-dominant chord to V or V⁷. Prepare the seventh of V⁷ (if present) by common tone. Move other voices to the nearest chord tones which avoid faulty (1) _____, which avoid an (2) .... in minor keys, and which allow for correct (3) _____ .

(1) parallels
(2) aug 2nd
(3) doubling

17 In moving from II or II⁶ to V⁷, _____ the seventh of V⁷, and then follow the other general voice-leading procedures outlined in the previous frame.

prepare

18 In a II⁶ the _____ is doubled.

third (*or* bass)

19 In minor keys II⁶ will always move to an incomplete V⁷, as example **x** illustrates. The connection in example **y** from II⁶ to a complete V⁷ is faulty because of the alto movement of a(n) ....

aug 2nd

16 The above shows that the C major triad is a
_____ triad which C and G hold in common.

diatonic

17 When a chord is analyzed in more than one key, the
symbols are aligned vertically as shown below chord
x. Analyze chord **y** in the two specified keys:

C: I   C:___
G: IV   a:___

C: II
a: IV

18 For C and a, the D minor triad is a diatonic triad
which the two keys hold in _____.

common

19 Analyze each chord in the two specified keys:

E:___
B:___

E: I
B: IV

20

c:___
A♭:___

c: IV
A♭: VI

21

G:___
b:___

G: III
b: I

22 Before modulation can be accomplished, a key must
be already in place or *established* by means of
harmonic progression. We call this key the *old* key
and its successor the *new* key. We cannot modulate
from C (old key) to G (new key) unless ____ (*key
name*) is first established.

C

Study the examples below.

(1) incomplete
(2) complete

20   In major keys II and II^6 may move to either an (1) _____ or a (2) _____ V^7, depending upon a given soprano pattern or upon the desired upper-voice movement.

(1) prepare
(2) nearest chord tones
(3) faulty parallels
(4) an aug 2nd
((3) & (4) *either order*)
(5) correct doubling

21   Complete the following II^6 V^7 connections and II V^7 connections. Remember to (1) _____ the seventh of V^7 and to move the other voices to the (2) .... avoiding (3) ...., avoiding (4) ...., and allowing for (5) ....

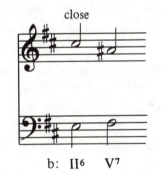

22

(1) same (2) one	7 Closely related keys have signatures that are the (1) _____ or that differ by (2) _____ sharp or flat.
E B g♯ A f♯	8 Name all of the keys that are closely related to c♯: ____ ____ ____ ____ ____
B♭ E♭ c F d	9 A given main key and all of its closely related keys constitute a *family* of closely related keys around the main key. List the family of closely related keys around g: (g) ____ ____ ____ ____ ____
f♯	10 Following is a list of the family closely related keys around A: A f♯ E c♯ D b Since family membership is based on key signature, two keys that have the same signature (relative keys) will generate the same family. Thus, the above is a list of the family of closely related keys around either A or ____.
modulation	11 *Modulation* means change of key by means of harmonic progression. (The way in which this is ef- fected will be studied later.) If the key changes abruptly without harmonic progression, there is no _____.
harmonic progression	12 Change of key by means of _____ _____ is called modulation.
key	13 In this part we will study *diatonic modulation* be- tween closely related keys. As the term implies, diatonic modulation involves the use of diatonic chords to effect change of _____.
harmonic	14 Diatonic triads are derived from the major scale (for major keys) or the _____ minor scale for (minor keys).
IV	15 Diatonic modulation is based on the fact that a pair of keys may have one or more *diatonic triads in common*. For example, the key of C and the key of G both embrace the C major triad as a diatonic triad. As the exam- ple shows, the C major triad might be analyzed as C: I or as G: ____. C: I G: IV

(*Note: G♯ in the alto of V⁷ would produce an aug 2nd.*)

1   In general, pieces of tonal music begin and end in the same key, called the *main key*, and include passages or sections in one or more contrasting keys, called *secondary keys*. In the following scheme the secondary key is G and the _____ key is C.

main

$$C \rightarrow G \rightarrow C$$

2   Often, secondary keys are *closely related* to the main key. Two keys are said to be closely related if their signatures are the same or if they differ by one sharp or one flat. For example, G (one sharp) and D (two sharps) are closely related, but G and A are not because their signatures differ by _____ (how many?) signs.

two

(1) two flats
(2) one flat
(3) are

3   The signature of B♭ is (1) _____ _____ ; the signature of d is (2) _____ _____ . B♭ and d (3) .... (are *or* are not) closely related keys.

closely related keys

4   B and g♯ are _____ _____ _____ , but B and a♭ are not.

5   The following keys are closely related to C:

a	G	e	F	d
(same signature)	(differ by 1♯)		(differ by 1♭)	

Name all of the keys that are closely related to E♭:

c A♭ f B♭ g

____ ____ ____ ____ ____

(Think of the key having the same signature, then the keys having one more flat, then the keys having one less flat.)

6   The following keys are closely related to a:

C G e F d

Note that the closely related key whose tonic lies a perfect 5th above a is e (not E). This illustrates the fact that, given a main key that is *minor*, the dominant *key* is also *minor*, whereas the dominant *chord* is _____ (*what kind of triad?*)

major

(1) incomplete
(2) complete
(3) $\hat{1}$
(4) 3rd

(either order)

(Note: Throughout this book both types of resolution will be considered correct, and both solutions will always be shown. Neither solution will be judged better or smoother because of complicating factors—the wish to have an incomplete I chord with resolved leading tone, or the desire for a complete I chord.)

27 Except when $\hat{7}$ is in the soprano, a complete V⁷ may resolve to either an (1) _____ or a

(2) _____ I. In the former case the leading tone resolves according to its tendency to

(3) ____ (*scale degree*); in the latter case the leading tone moves down a (4) ____ (*general interval*). Resolve the given V⁷ both ways:

G: V⁷   I   V⁷   I

incomplete

28 A complete V⁷ with the leading tone in the soprano must resolve to a(n) _____ (complete *or* incomplete) I. Complete the connection:

G: V⁷   I

(1) complete

(2) common tone

29 An incomplete V⁷ resolves to a(n) (1) _____ (complete *or* incomplete) I. The leading tone and seventh resolve according to their tendencies, and the doubled root of V⁷ is kept as a (2) _____
_____. Complete the connection:

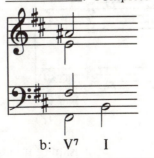

b: V⁷   I

10. Set each figured bass. Provide the Roman numeral analysis.

(1)

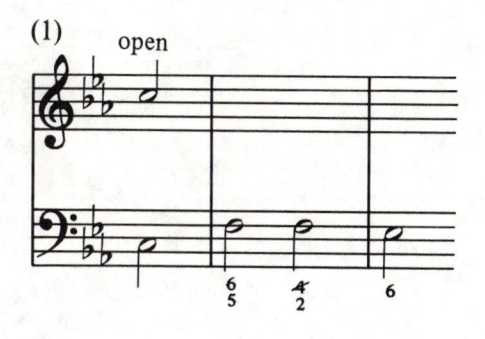

(2)

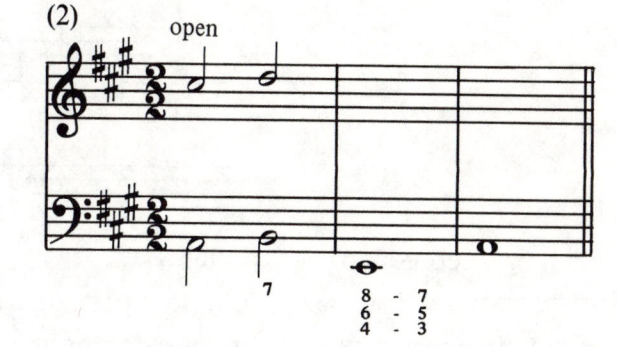

11. Write the following:

(1)

a: I   II$_2^4$ V$_5^6$ I

(2)   close

D: I   II$_5^6$ V($_4^6$ ⁚ $_3^5$)   I

30 Consider the following examples to be chains of individual connections. Connect the chords based on the following procedure:

    1. Complete the bass line.

    2. Prepare and resolve the (1) _____ of V⁷.

    3. Move the remaining upper voice(s) from IV, II, or II⁶, to V⁷, avoiding (2) ...., avoiding (3) ...., and allowing for (4) ....

    4. Resolve V⁷ to I.

(1) seventh
(2) faulty parallels
(3) an aug 2nd
((2) & (3) *in either order*)
(4) correct doubling

f♯: II⁶   V⁷   I

(For the sake of simplicity, only one correct bass line will be shown for the solutions in this book. See Introduction for further details.)

31

close

G: II   V⁷   I

32
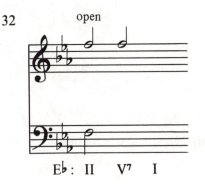

open

E♭: II   V⁷   I

5. Give a Roman numeral illustration of a typical tonic prolongation pattern containing a supertonic 7th chord: I _____ _____ _____

6. Give the *regular* resolution of each chord below. Provide the Roman numeral analysis.

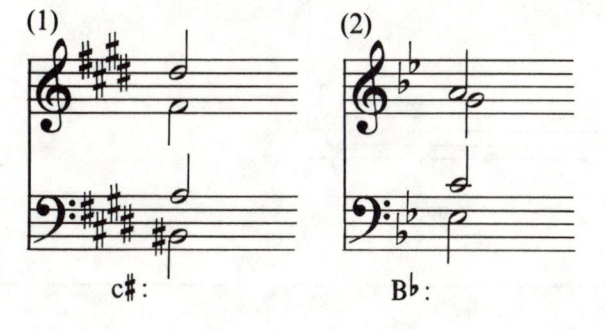

7. One of these chords may be resolved in the exceptional way. Determine which chord that is and resolve it. Give the Roman numeral analysis of the completed resolution.

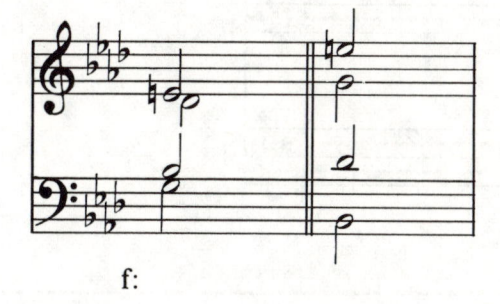

8. Complete the following tonic prolongation patterns. Identify the function (P, N, or IN) of the prolonging chord.

9. Set the following soprano with I II$_5^6$ V I or I II^6 V I, whichever is appropriate:

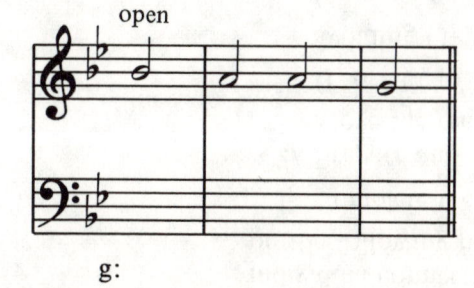

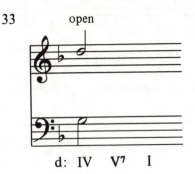

33

d: IV   V⁷   I

(Important note: Bass movement of an ascending 2nd (as in IV V⁷ and II⁶ V⁷) may not be written as a descending 7th.)

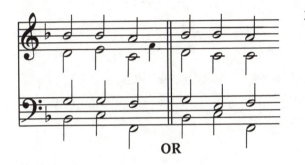

OR

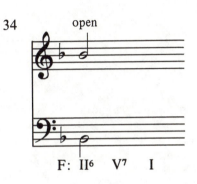

34

open

F: II⁶   V⁷   I

35

open

B: IV   V⁷   I

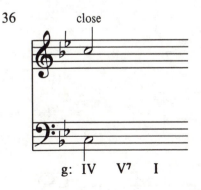

36

close

g: IV   V⁷   I

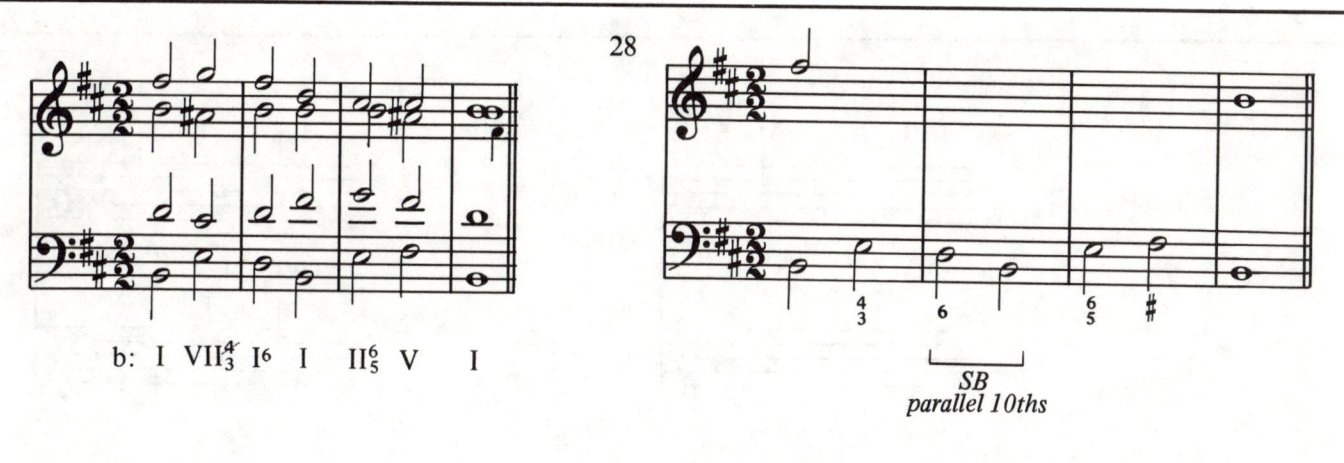

28

b: I VII$^4_3$ I^6 I II$^6_5$ V I

SB
parallel 10ths

TEST COVERING PART 6

The questions below will test your mastery of the material in Part 6. Complete the entire test, then check your answers with the correct ones on page 170. For each question that you miss, the corresponding material may be reviewed in the set whose number is given with the correct answer.

1. Construct the indicated structural types of 7th chords in root position, using D as the root in each case:

     min   maj   dim   dim-min

2. Give the structural type of each of the 7th chords in major and minor keys:

	major keys	*minor keys*
II^7	(1)	(2) ....
VII^7	(3)	(4) ....

3. Write the chord symbols:

   b: (1)   (2)

4. Give a Roman numeral illustration of a typical harmonic progression containing a supertonic 7th chord: I _____ _____ _____

pre-dominant

1 A _____ chord connects an opening tonic to the dominant.

---

2 Through the insertion of a pre-dominant chord, the fundamental harmonic progression, I V I, is expanded. The three expansions of I V I under consideration are:

(1) IV

(1) I _____ V I

(2) II

(2) I _____ V I

(3) II⁶ (*in any order*)

(3) I _____ V I

---

(1) do

3 I and IV (1) .... (do *or* do not) have a common tone. The smoothest connection from an opening tonic to IV, is, therefore, (2) ....

(2) common tone-stepwise

---

4 Write common tone-stepwise connections of I IV:

5

6

I

(*Note: Regular doubling of the root is possible.*)

25

F: I   VII⁷ ____

e: I VII⁷ I II⁶₅ V($^{6-5}_{4-3}$) I

26 Set each figured bass below. (First give the Roman numeral analysis.) Refer to the hints or instructions given for each problem.
Hint: What doubling is necessary in order to prepare the dissonance in the following chord?

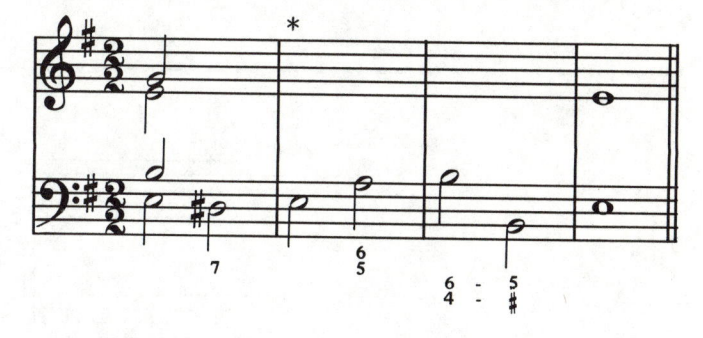

27 *Use regular doubling, being careful to avoid faulty parallels.
**Use complete chord.*

f: I VII⁶₅ I⁶ I II⁷ V⁷ I

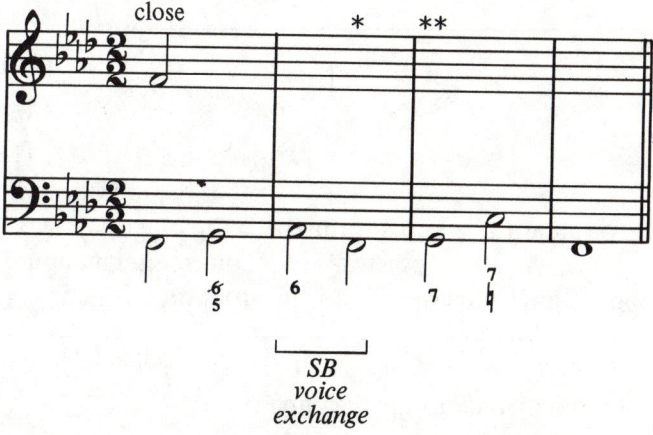

7 Occasionally, as in the example below, a given soprano pattern for I IV will not allow a common tone-stepwise connection. In such a case, follow the voice-leading procedure of moving the AT to the nearest chord tones, avoiding faulty (1) _____ and allowing for correct (2) _____. Complete the connection:

(1) parallels
(2) doubling

A: I   IV

8 Consider the following to be chains of individual connections. Connect in the smoothest correct ways:

close

G: I   IV   V   I

(*Note: If, at any time as you work through this book, you err in completing an example and can't find your mistake, turn to* page 162.)

9

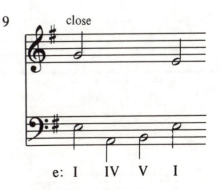

close

e: I   IV   V   I

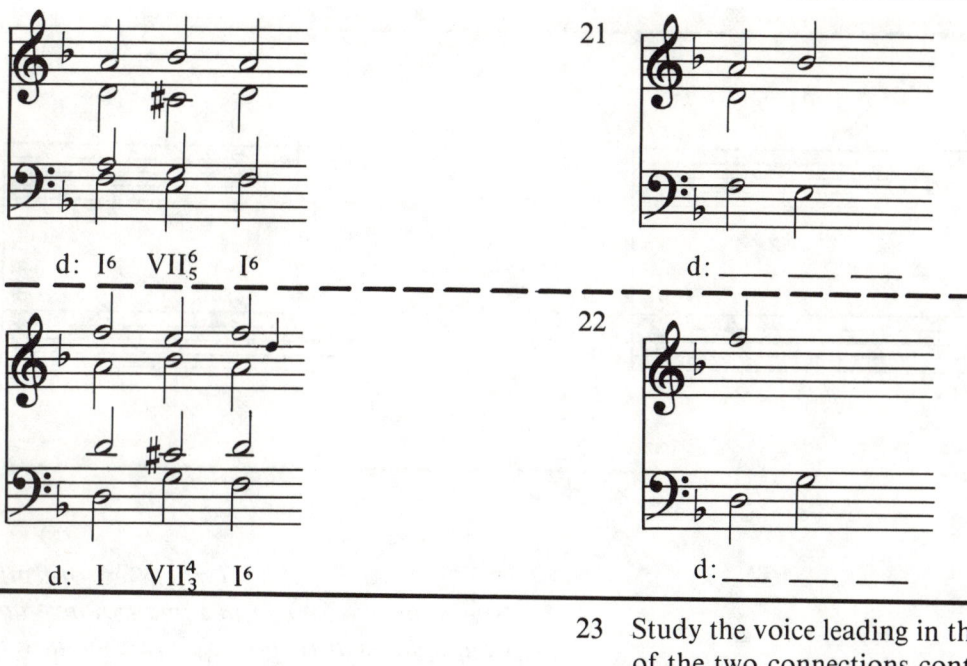

d: I⁶   VII⁶₅   I⁶

21

d: ___ ___ ___

d: I   VII⁴₃   I⁶

22

d: ___ ___ ___

(1) **y**
(2) SA

23 Study the voice leading in the examples below. Which of the two connections contains faulty parallels?

(1) ____ Between which voices? (2) ....

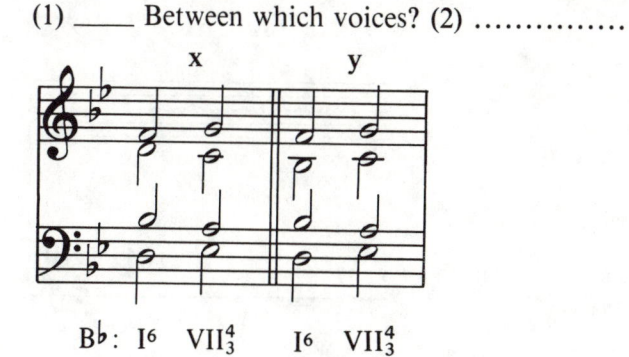

B♭: I⁶   VII⁴₃   I⁶   VII⁴₃

In major keys you must be careful to avoid parallel perfect 5ths in moving from I or I⁶ to VII⁷ or inversion. The normal solution to this problem (**y**) is to double the third in I or I⁶ (**x**). In this way, all the voices move stepwise and the dissonance is introduced smoothly.

24 Complete the following tonic prolongation patterns. Use regular doubling of the root in the opening I or I⁶ if possible. If use of regular doubling would result in faulty parallels, double the third of the opening I or I⁶ instead.

I⁶

F: I⁶   VII⁴₃   ___

10 *(Be sure to prepare and resolve the seventh of V[7].)*

D: I IV V[7] I

(1) do not

(2) contrary motion-nearest
(3) SAT (*or* upper voices)
(4) nearest chord tones
(5) contrary

11 I and II (1) .... (do *or* do not) have a common tone. The smoothest correct connection between two root position triads that do not have a common tone (such as IV V and I II) is a (2) .... connection. In such a connection the (3) .... move to the (4) .... in (5) _____ motion to the bass.

12 Write the contrary motion-nearest connections of I II:

E: I II

13

B♭: I II

Note that the SA of I VII⁷ move in parallel 5ths but not parallel _perfect_ 5ths. This voice leading is correct. The prohibition mentioned in the last sentence of frame 3 is that of a _dim_ 5th to a _perf_ 5th in the _resolution of VII⁷ (or inversion) to I (or I⁶)_. In the resolution above, $\hat{2}$ in the alto (*) must go to $\hat{3}$.

17 Complete the following tonic prolongation patterns, using VII⁷ and its inversions. In these examples stepwise voice leading from I (or I⁶) to VII⁷ (or inversion) is always possible, allowing smooth introduction of the seventh and the other dissonances. Give the Roman numeral analysis where it is not provided.

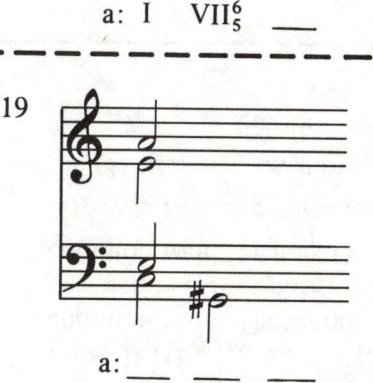

a: I   VII⁷   I

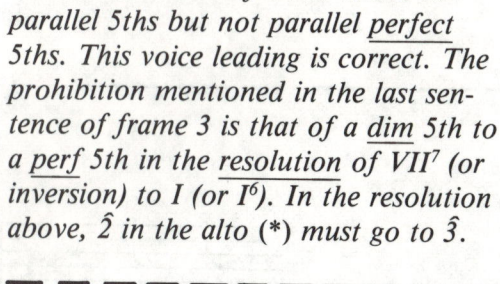

I⁶

18

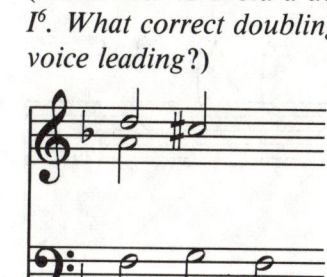

a: I   VII⁶₅   ___

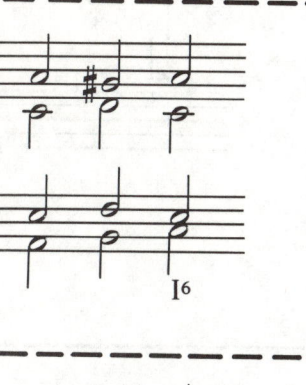

I⁶   VII⁷   I

19

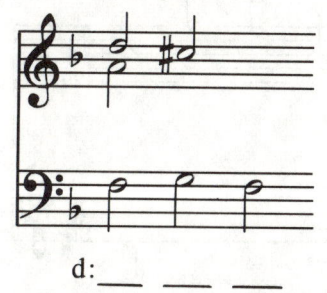

a: ___ ___ ___

20 (Remember to avoid a doubled third in the opening I⁶. What correct doubling will result in all stepwise voice leading?)

d: I⁶   VII⁴₃   I⁶

d: ___ ___ ___

14 Complete the connections below, being certain to follow correct voice-leading procedures:

open

G: I   II   V   I

15 *(Be sure to prepare and resolve the seventh of V⁷.)*

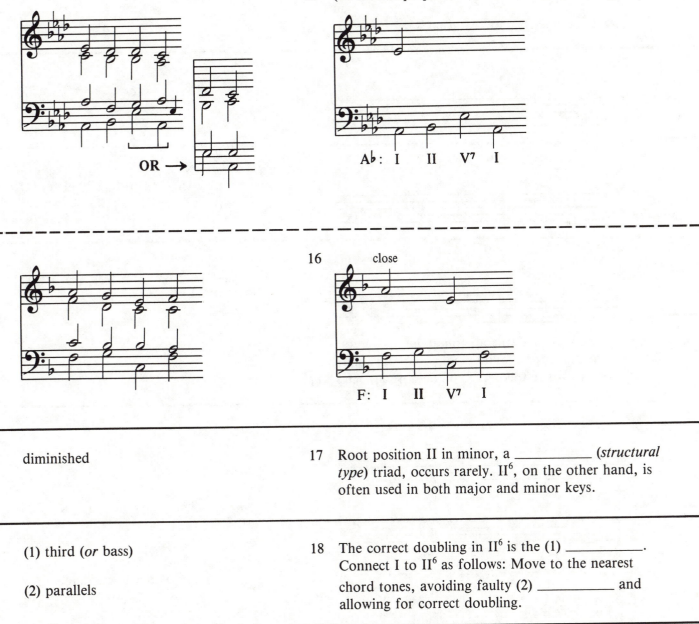

OR →

A♭: I   II   V⁷   I

16 close

F: I   II   V⁷   I

diminished

17 Root position II in minor, a _____ *(structural type)* triad, occurs rarely. II⁶, on the other hand, is often used in both major and minor keys.

(1) third *(or* bass)

(2) parallels

18 The correct doubling in II⁶ is the (1) _____.
Connect I to II⁶ as follows: Move to the nearest chord tones, avoiding faulty (2) _____ and allowing for correct doubling.

(1) $\hat{4}$

(2) neighboring (N)

(3) incomplete-neighboring (IN)

10 VII_3^4, like V_2^4, has (1) _____ (*scale degree*) in the bass. As shown below, it is most frequently used as a

(2) _____ or an (3) _____ chord to I^6.

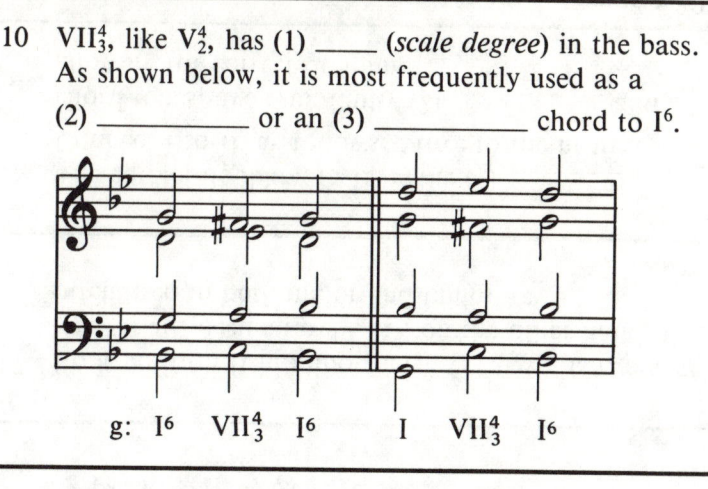

g: I^6 VII_3^4 I^6 I VII_3^4 I^6

11 Give the Roman numeral analysis for each of the following figured bass patterns. Identify the function (P, N, *or* IN) of the prolonging chord.

(1)   (2)

(1) c#: I VII_5^6 I^6 (2) c#: I VII_3^4 I^6
          P   IN

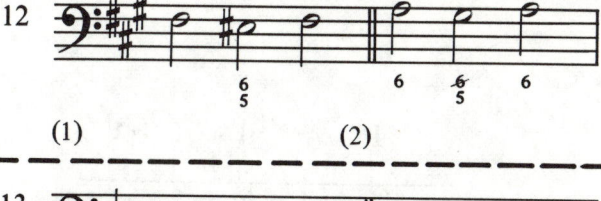

(1)   (2)

(1) f#: I V_5^6 I   (2) f#: I^6 VII_5^6 I^6
          N   N

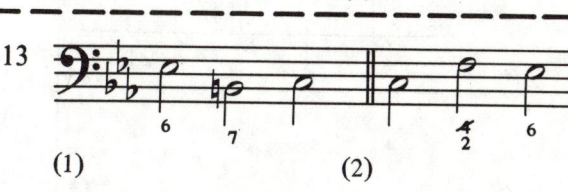

(1)   (2)

(1) c: I^6 VII^7 I   (2) c: I V_2^4 I^6
          IN   IN

14 In summary, typical uses of VII^7 and its inversions are:

VII^7 (like V_5^6)	N, IN to I
VII_5^6 (like V_3^4)	P between I and I^6, N to I^6
VII_3^4 (like V_2^4)	N, IN to I^6
VII_2^4	rarely occurs

(1) I   (2) I^6

15 VII^7 leads to (1) _____. VII_5^6 and VII_3^4 lead to (2) _____.

16 In minor keys the I (or I^6) that *leads* to VII^7 (or inversion) should have regular doubling—that is the

(1) _____ of I should be doubled and the

(2) _____ or _____ of I^6 should be doubled. Remember that the doubling in the I (or I^6) that *follows* VII^7 (or inversion) is a result of voice-leading considerations.

(1) root

(2) root (or) fifth

19 Connect the following. (*Complete the I chord.
    What are the missing notes in II⁶? Move the AT
    according to the procedure outlined above.*)

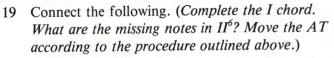

c: I   II⁶

20

D: I   II⁶

2̂ (or) 4̂

21 Remember that with II⁶ (and II) it is better to avoid
    a soprano of 6̂. Instead, a soprano of ____ or ____
    should be used.

22 Complete the following connections. Be aware of
    soprano scale degrees being used.

g: I   II⁶

(*II⁶ should not have E♭ (6̂) in the
soprano.*)

23

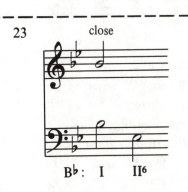

B♭: I   II⁶

(*II⁶ should not have G (6̂) in the
soprano.*)

(1) $\hat{7}$

(2) **x**

(3) **y**

8 The use of VII⁷ and its inversions is very similar to the use of the inversions of V⁷.

VII⁷ and V⁶₅ both have (1) _____ (*scale degree*) in the bass, and they differ in only one note (circled below). It follows that, like V⁶₅, VII⁷ is used as a neighboring chord, as in example (2) _____, or as an incomplete-neighboring chord, as in example (3) _____, in the prolongation of tonic harmony.

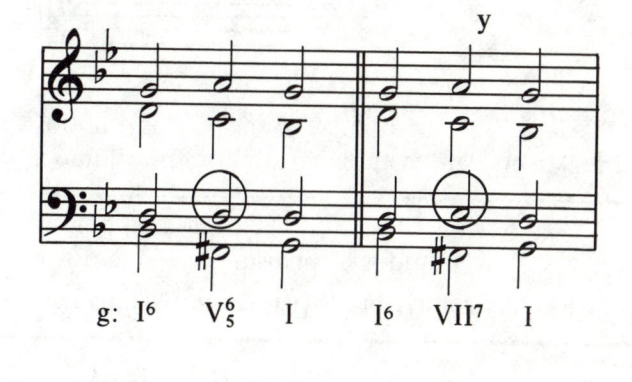

(1) $\hat{2}$

(2) passing (P)

(3) neighboring (N)

9 VII⁶₅ and V⁴₃ both have (1) _____ (*scale degree*) in the bass. As indicated in the example below, VII⁶₅, like V⁴₃, is used primarily as a (2) _____ chord between I and I⁶ and as a (3) _____ chord to I⁶.

24 Complete each of the chord connections below following correct voice-leading procedures. Bear in mind soprano scale degrees being used. (*Remember the smoothest correct connection of II^6 V is* ....)

contrary motion-nearest

f#: I   II^6 V   I

25 (*Be sure to treat the seventh of V^7 correctly.*)

open

E♭: I   II^6 V^7 I

26 *First write the bass line.* (*There is more than one correct solution.*)

close

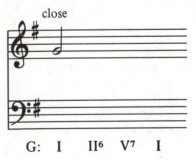

G: I   II^6 V^7 I

OR

27 Frames 27–31 include important points for review. Basic harmonic progressions consist of the movement from an opening tonic, through a _____ chord, to a dominant, and then to a closing tonic.

pre-dominant

x, y

5 Indicate which of the following leading tone 7th chords may be resolved using the exceptional movement of $\hat{2}$ to $\hat{1}$: ....

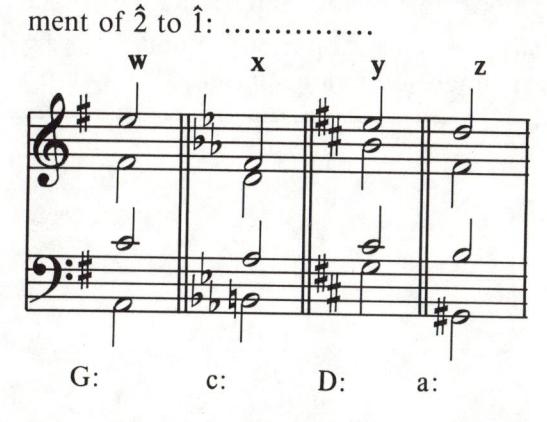

G: c: D: a:

6 The resolution of leading tone 7th chords is as follows:

(1) *Regular resolution*   (2) *Acceptable exception* (if $\hat{2}$ occurs above $\hat{6}$)

(1) $\hat{2}$ $\hat{3}$ (2) $\hat{2}$ $\hat{1}$

    $\hat{4}$ $\hat{3}$ $\hat{4}$ $\hat{3}$

    $\hat{6}$ $\hat{5}$ $\hat{6}$ $\hat{5}$

    $\hat{7}$ $\hat{1}$ $\hat{7}$ $\hat{1}$

(1) *Regular resolution*	(2) *Acceptable exception* (if $\hat{2}$ occurs above $\hat{6}$)
$\hat{2}$ _____	$\hat{2}$ _____
$\hat{4}$ _____	$\hat{4}$ _____
$\hat{6}$ _____	$\hat{6}$ _____
$\hat{7}$ _____	$\hat{7}$ _____

7 Decide which of the following leading tone 7th chords may be resolved using the exceptional movement of $\hat{2}$ to $\hat{1}$ and resolve them, using the exceptional movement. Do not resolve the other chords. Give the Roman numeral analysis of each completed resolution.

F: VII⁷   I

g: b: F:

f#: VII$^{4}_{3}$ I⁶

E: f#:

28 The correct doubling for IV and II is the
(1) _____ .
The correct doubling for II⁶ is the (2) _____ .

(1) root (*or* bass)
(2) third (*or* bass)

29 The smoothest connection of two root position triads having a common tone (such as I IV, V I, and II V) is (1) ....
The smoothest correct connection of two root position triads not having a common tone (such as IV V and I II) is (2) ....
Although II⁶ and V have a common tone, the smoothest correct connection of II⁶ V is
(3) ....

(1) common tone-stepwise

(2) contrary motion-nearest

(3) contrary motion-nearest

30 In connecting a pre-dominant chord to V^7, the seventh of V^7 is prepared by (1) .... In moving to the following I, the seventh of V^7
(2) ....

In connecting the other voices of a pre-dominant to V^7 or when common tone-stepwise and contrary motion-nearest connections are not possible in the connection of two triads, the general voice leading procedure should be followed: Move to the nearest
(3) ...., avoiding faulty (4) _____,
avoiding an (5) .... in minor keys (in the movement from the pre-dominant to the dominant), and allowing for (6) ....

(1) common tone

(2) resolves down by step

(3) chord tones
(4) parallels
(5) aug 2nd

(6) correct doubling

31 IV, which contains (1) ____, ____, and ____ (*scale degrees*), may have any one of its scale degrees in the soprano. II and II⁶ commonly have a soprano of (2) ____ or ____; a soprano of (3) ____ is to be avoided.

(1) $\hat{4}$ $\hat{6}$ $\hat{1}$

(2) $\hat{2}$ $\hat{4}$
(3) $\hat{6}$

32 Write each of these basic harmonic progressions following procedures given in previous frames:

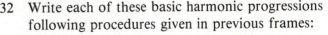

g: I   IV   V   I

2 Label the scale degrees in the following:

REGULAR RESOLUTION: **ACCEPTABLE EXCEPTION:**

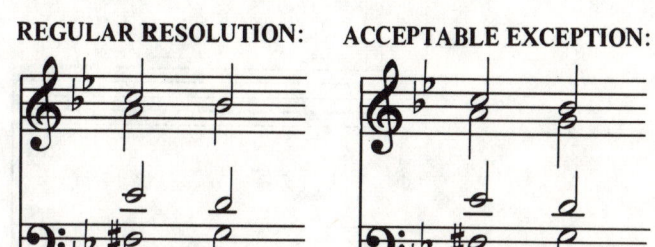

g: VII⁷ I   g: VII⁷ I

(1) 4th

(2) 1̂

(3) root

When, in a leading tone 7th chord, 2̂ occurs above 6̂ forming a (1) _____ (*general interval*), rather than below, forming a 5th, 2̂ may resolve to (2) _____ rather than to 3̂. The resulting I chord will have the (3) _____ doubled.

3 The reason for avoiding the movement from 2̂ to 1̂ when 2̂ is below 6̂ is illustrated in the following example:

incorrect:

B♭: VII⁶₅ I

perfect 5ths

As shown above, in major keys the movement of 2̂ to 1̂ with 2̂ occurring below 6̂ results in parallel _____ _____. Although these faulty parallels do not occur in minor keys, the movement of a dim 5th to a perfect 5th in this context is avoided.

(1) above

(2) 4th

4 The exceptional movement of 2̂ to 1̂ in the resolution of a leading tone 7th chord may be used if 2̂ occurs (1) _____ (*above or* below) 6̂ forming a (2) _____ (*general interval*) or corresponding compound interval.

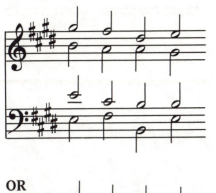

OR

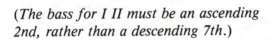

(*The bass for I II must be an ascending 2nd, rather than a descending 7th.*)

33

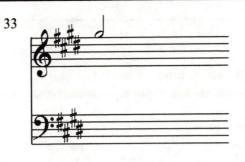

E: I   II   V⁷   I

34   close

F: I   II⁶   V   I

35   open

a: I   IV   V⁷   I

VII$^4_3$ I^6

49
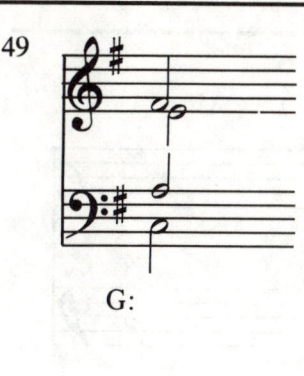

G:

Set 23 / THE LEADING TONE 7TH CHORD (2)

(1) $\hat{5}$

(2) $\hat{3}$

(3) $\hat{3}$

(4) $\hat{1}$

1 The typical resolution of leading tone 7th chords (both dim and dim-min) is:

$\hat{6}$ to (1) ____

$\hat{4}$ to (2) ____

$\hat{2}$ to (3) ____

$\hat{7}$ to (4) ____

There are, however, exceptions to this resolution pattern. A fairly common exception allows for normal doubling of the root in the I chord. $\hat{2}$ may resolve down to $\hat{1}$ if it occurs above $\hat{6}$ forming a 4th (as in example **x**), rather than occurring below it and forming a 5th (as in example **y**). All other scale degrees resolve normally.

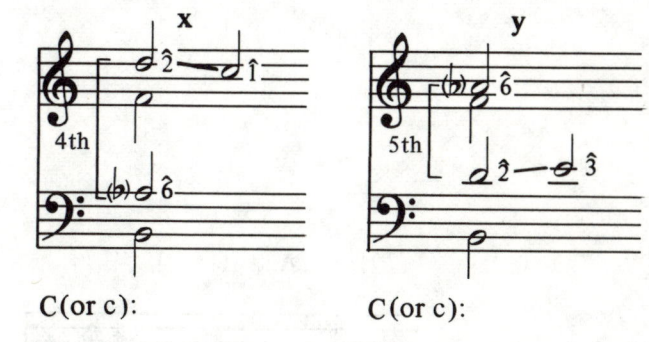

C (or c):   C (or c):

Study these examples and the explanation above before going on to the next frame.

OR

36

B♭: I   II   V   I

37

e: I   II⁶   V⁷   I

38

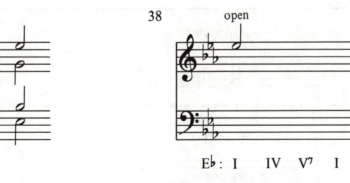

E♭: I   IV   V⁷   I

(1) IV

(2) II, II⁶

(3) IV, II, II⁶

(4) IV

39 Of the pre-dominant chords studied, indicate which may have the following in the soprano:

$\hat{1}$: (1) ....

$\hat{2}$: (2) ....

$\hat{4}$: (3) ....

$\hat{6}$ (commonly): (4) ....

43 Resolve each of these chords:

g: VII⁷   I   G: VII⁷   I

44 Resolve these leading tone dim-min 7th chords:

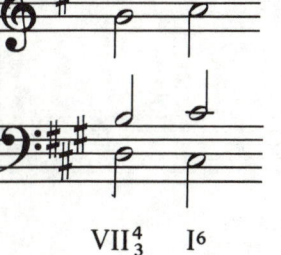

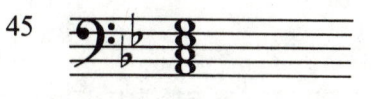

D: VII⁷   I

45

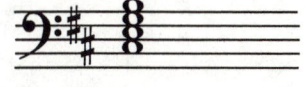

B♭: VII⁷   I

46 Resolve the following chords. Give the Roman numeral analysis.

VII$^4_3$ I⁶

A:

47

VII$^6_5$ I⁶

F:

48

VII⁷   I

E♭:

(1) $\hat{5}$ $\hat{7}$ $\hat{2}$
(2) $\hat{5}$ $\hat{7}$ $\hat{2}$ $\hat{4}$

40 V contains: (1) ____ ____ ____ (*scale degrees*).
V[7] contains: (2) ____ ____ ____ ____.

$\hat{4}$

41 Both V and V[7] can have a soprano of $\hat{2}$ or $\hat{7}$ (or occasionally, $\hat{5}$). Of the two chords, only V[7] can have a soprano of ____.

Note: Since in many cases V and V[7] may be used interchangeably, it is convenient to have a symbol which applies to both chords. The symbol *V(7)* will be used in subsequent frames to refer to *V or V7*.

42 Set each of the following soprano patterns with one of the basic harmonic progressions studied:
    I IV V(7) I
    I II V(7) I
    I II6 V(7) I
First think of the soprano scale degrees and determine the chords to be used. (Refer to frames 39–41, as necessary.)

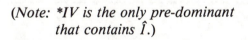

f#: I *IV V(7) I

(*Note: *IV is the only pre-dominant that contains Î.*)

___ :

43 (*Hint: Be particularly careful to avoid faulty parallels.*)

I *II6 V(7) I

(*Note: *II would give parallel octaves between SB; IV does not contain $\hat{2}$.*)

G:

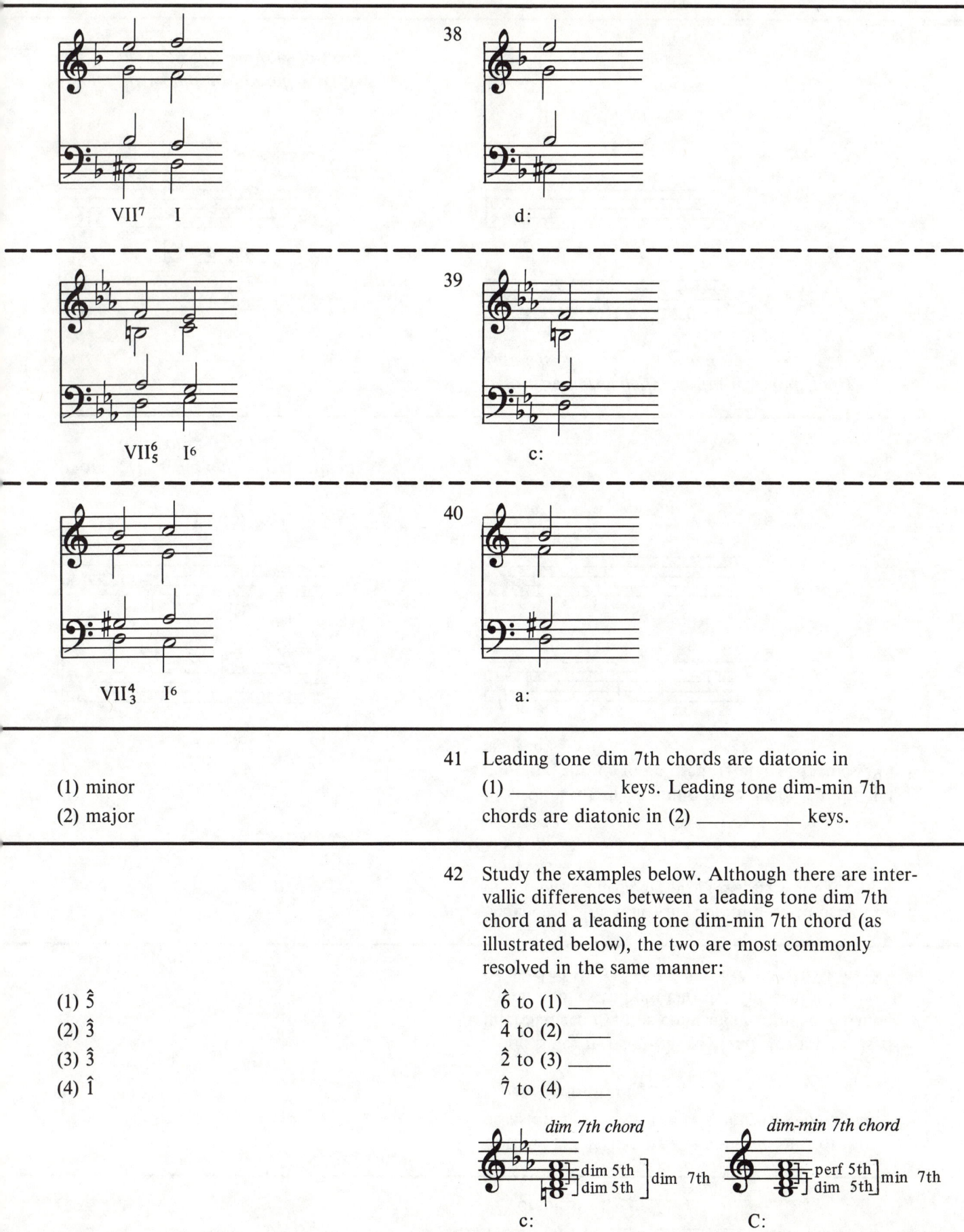

VII⁷ I

38

d:

VII⁶₅ I⁶

39

c:

VII⁴₃ I⁶

40

a:

(1) minor
(2) major

41 Leading tone dim 7th chords are diatonic in
(1) _____ keys. Leading tone dim-min 7th
chords are diatonic in (2) _____ keys.

42 Study the examples below. Although there are inter-
vallic differences between a leading tone dim 7th
chord and a leading tone dim-min 7th chord (as
illustrated below), the two are most commonly
resolved in the same manner:

(1) $\hat{5}$
(2) $\hat{3}$
(3) $\hat{3}$
(4) $\hat{1}$

$\hat{6}$ to (1) ____
$\hat{4}$ to (2) ____
$\hat{2}$ to (3) ____
$\hat{7}$ to (4) ____

dim 7th chord   *dim-min 7th chord*

c: C:

44 Set each of the following soprano patterns two ways, using two different pre-dominant chords. (*Hint: These are difficult problems, and you may find some trial and error necessary. Check each solution carefully for faulty parallels, correct doubling, preparation and resolution of the seventh of V^7, if used, etc.*)

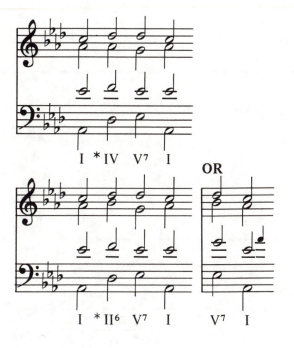

I *IV V^7 I

OR

I *II^6 V^7 I V^7 I

(*Note: *II will not work with the given soprano; a contrary motion-nearest connection between I and II is not possible.*)

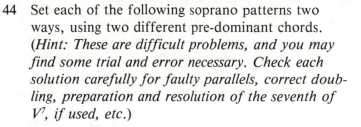

A♭:

A♭:

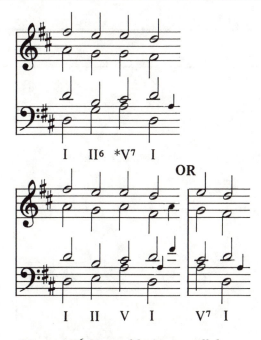

I II^6 *V^7 I

OR

I II V I V^7 I

(*Note: *II^6 V would give parallel octaves between AB.*)

45

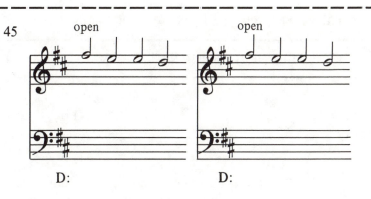

open   open

D: D:

I^6

32

b: VII_3^4 ____

---

33 The resolution pattern for dim 7th chords (no matter what the inversion or position) is:

(1) $\hat{5}$ $\hat{6}$ to (1) ____

(2) $\hat{3}$ $\hat{4}$ to (2) ____

(3) $\hat{3}$ $\hat{2}$ to (3) ____

(4) $\hat{1}$ $\hat{7}$ to (4) ____

---

(1) I   (2) I^6

34 VII^7 leads to (1) ____ . VII_5^6 and VII_3^4 lead to (2) ____ .

---

35 Resolve the leading tone dim 7th chords below. Give the Roman numeral analysis.

VII_5^6 I^6

g:

VII^7 I

36

e:

37

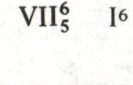

VII_3^4 I^6

c♯:

figured

46 In addition to problems in setting a given soprano, another common problem in chord connection is that of setting a given bass. Often a given bass line is figured; that is, it is accompanied by _____ bass symbols, as illustrated in the example below. Such a pattern is referred to as a *figured bass*.

47 Arabic numerals given with a bass line mean the same thing that they do when they accompany a Roman numeral:

(1) first

The figure "6" refers to a (1) _____ inversion triad.
The figure "7" refers to a root position

(2) 7th

(2) _____ chord.

When no figure is present, a root position triad is assumed.

48 A figured bass always indicates precisely what chords are to be used, and it is, therefore, a simple matter to give the Roman numeral analysis of a figured bass. In the example below the first chord

(1) root

indicated is in (1) _____ position/inversion,

(2) B♭

having a bass of (2) ____ (*note name*). In the key of B♭, it is a I chord. The second chord indicated is in

(3) first

(3) _____ inversion, with a bass of

(4) E♭

(4) ____ (*note name*); in other words, a II⁶ chord. Complete the Roman numeral analysis:

(5) I II⁶ V⁷ I

(5) B♭ : I   II⁶

49 Give the Roman numeral analysis of each of the following figured bass patterns:

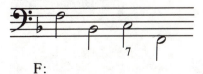

F:

I IV V⁷ I

28 (*Note the aug 2nd in the SA of VII⁶₅. This is perfectly acceptable. It is only the* <u>melodic</u> *aug 2nd which is to be avoided*.)

I⁶

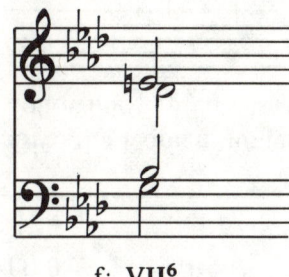

f: VII⁶₅ ____

(1) VII⁴₃

(2) 3̂

(3) I⁶

29 The chord below is (1) ____ (*chord symbol*). Because of the bass resolution of 4̂ to (2) ____, the chord of resolution will be (3) ____. Complete the resolution:

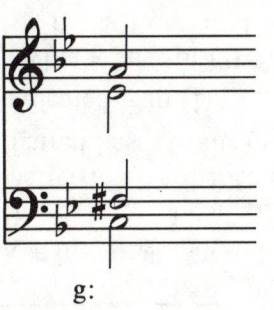

g:

30 Resolve these VII⁴₃ chords:

d: VII⁴₃ I⁶

I⁶

31

c: VII⁴₃ ____

I II⁶ V I

50

$$\text{D:}$$

---

leading

51 Just as key signatures apply to notes unless an alteration is indicated by means of an accidental, key signatures apply to a figured bass unless otherwise indicated. In minor keys the _____ tone is indicated by means of an accidental. In minor keys the figured bass for chords containing the leading tone is modified to indicate an accidental.

3rd

52 The only chords in the basic harmonic progressions being studied that contain the leading tone are V and V⁷. In these root position dominant chords the leading tone is a _____ (*what general interval?*) above the bass.

B♮

53 The alteration of the 3rd above the bass of a triad is always indicated by an accidental standing alone under the bass note as shown in the examples below:

$$\text{x} \qquad\qquad \text{y}$$

$$\text{g:} \qquad\qquad \text{c:}$$

In example **x**, the accidental indicates that the 3rd above the bass, F, is to be altered to F♯. In example **y**, the accidental indicates that the 3rd above the bass, B♭, is to be altered to _____.

3rd

54 An accidental standing alone under a bass note refers to the alteration of the _____ (*general interval*) above the bass.

24

g: VII⁷   I

---

(2) $\hat{1}$

(3) $\hat{3}$

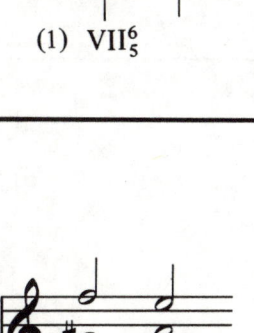

(1) VII$^6_5$

25 Give the Roman numeral analysis of the chord below. The leading tone, though not in the bass, must still resolve to (2) _____ (*scale degree*). Because of the bass resolution of $\hat{2}$ to (3) _____, the chord of resolution will be I⁶. Write the resolution:

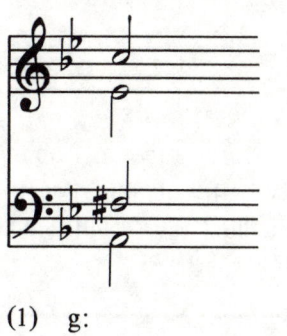

(1)   g:

26 Resolve these VII$^6_5$ chords. (*You will probably find it helpful to label scale degrees in these and all similar problems in this set.*)

a: VII$^6_5$ I⁶

I⁶

27

e: VII$^6_5$ ___

55 A given figured bass for a dominant 7th chord in a minor key can be understood according to the same principles followed in interpreting a figured bass for a dominant triad in a minor key. Compare examples **x** and **y** below. In each case the sharp sign indicates that the (1) _____ (*general interval*) above the bass, G, is to be altered to (2) _____. The difference between the two examples is that the figure "7" for example **y** indicates a root position (3) _____ chord, whereas the absence of numerals in example **x** indicates a root position (4) _____.

(1) 3rd

(2) G♯

(3) 7th

(4) triad

56 Give the Roman numeral analysis of each of the following figured bass patterns:

I II⁶ V I

57

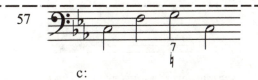

I IV V⁷ I

58 Set each figured bass below for four voices following this procedure:

1. Give the Roman numeral analysis.
2. Complete the first chord using the indicated spacing.
3. Connect each pair of chords in the smoothest correct way. (*Note: A figured bass in no way gives the arrangement or placement of notes in the upper voices. Follow voice leading and doubling rules as usual.*)

I   IV   V⁷   I

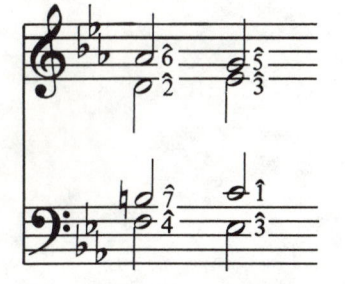

20 This same resolution pattern is used when a dim 7th chord is written for SATB in root position or in inversion. Label scale degrees in the examples below:

c: VII⁷   I   c: VII₃⁴   I⁶

It is generally easier to identify the scale degrees and resolve each of them according to its tendency rather than to think of the resolution of intervals (which can get rather complicated with inversions and SATB spacing).

21 Resolve the following root position leading tone dim 7th chords. Label scale degrees.

b: VII⁷   I

22

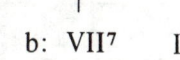

d: VII⁷   I

23

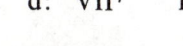

f♯: VII⁷   I

e:

TEST COVERING PART 1

The questions below will test your mastery of the material in Part 1. Complete the entire test, then check your answers with the correct ones on page 163. For each question that you miss, the corresponding material may be reviewed in the set whose number is given with the correct answer.

1. Complete the list of the most common pre-dominant chords and provide the information requested in the table:

chord	chord member doubled	common soprano scale degrees	found in maj and/or min keys?
(1) IV	_____	....	*maj and min*
(2) ____^{6}	_____	....	....
(3) ____	_____	....	....

2. A basic harmonic progression consists of:

opening tonic — (1) _____ — (2) _____ — closing tonic

3. For each of the following chord pairs the smoothest correct connection is either common tone-stepwise (CTS) or contrary motion-nearest (CMN). Fill in each blank (using the sample as a guide):

sample: V I CTS   IV V (1) ____   II^6 V (4) ____

II V (2) ____   I II (5) ____

I IV (3) ____

4. In the connection of a pre-dominant to V^7, the seventh of V^7, (1) ____ (*scale degree*), is (2) _____ by .... In the connection of the other voices, the procedure to follow is: Move to the nearest (3) ...., avoiding faulty (4) _____, avoiding an (5) .... in minor keys, and allowing for (6) ....

15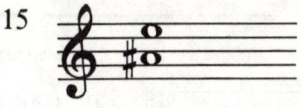

---

(1) third
(2) fifth

16 With both dim 5ths in a dim 7th chord resolved correctly, the following I chord will have one root, a doubled (1) _____, and one (2) _____. (*See example below.*)

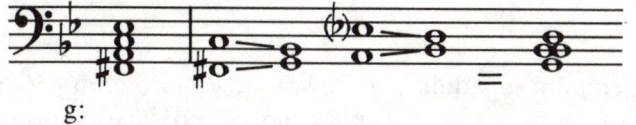

g:

Up to this point we have avoided doubling the third in a tonic chord. There are times, however, when voice-leading considerations and the resolution of dissonance must take precedence over doubling considerations. This is the case with the resolution of leading tone 7th chords.

---

17 A dim 7th chord with all dissonances resolved leads to a tonic as outlined below:

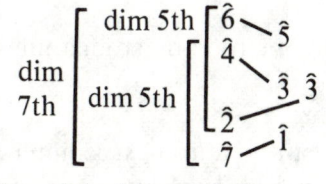

Complete this resolution:

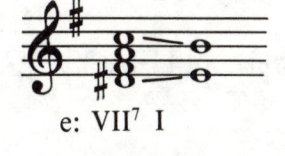

e: VII⁷ I

---

18 Resolve this dim 7th chord. (*First resolve the dim 7th, then complete the resolution of each dim 5th.*)

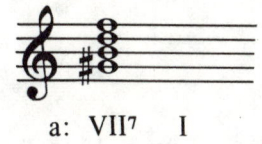

a: VII⁷   I

---

(1) $\hat{5}$
(2) $\hat{3}$
(3) $\hat{3}$
(4) $\hat{1}$

19 In the resolution of a leading tone dim 7th chord,

$\hat{6}$ resolves to (1) ____;

$\hat{4}$ resolves to (2) ____;

$\hat{2}$ resolves to (3) ____;

$\hat{7}$ resolves to (4) ____.

5. Write each of the following as indicated:

(1) close

D: I   IV   V⁷   I

(2) open

c: I   II⁶   V   I

(3) open

A♭: I   II   V⁷   I
                 complete

6. Set each soprano, using one of the basic harmonic progressions studied, and providing Roman numeral analysis:

(1) close

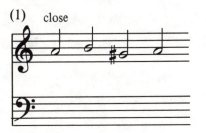

(2) open

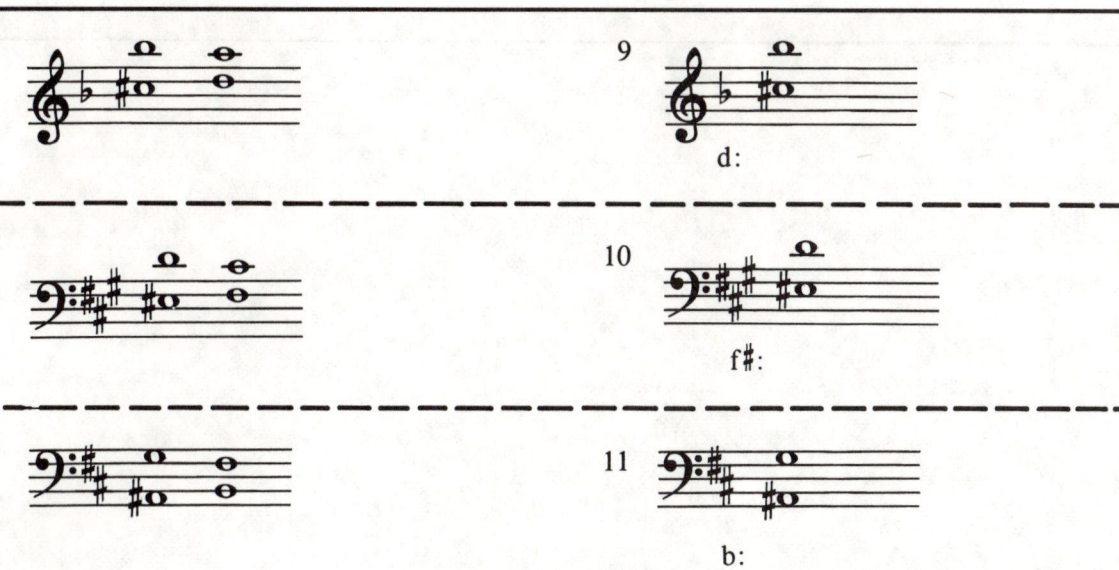

9

d:

10

f#:

11

b:

12 The interval of a dim 7th is not the only dissonant interval in the dim 7th chord. Label the bracketed intervals below:

(1) dim
(2) dim

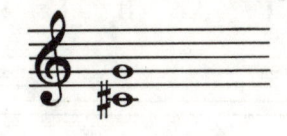

(1) ____ 5th
(2) ____ 5th] dim 7th

c: VII⁷

13 Although we have not previously been concerned with the resolution of the dim 5th (or aug 4th), the resolution of this interval *is* important in the highly dissonant leading tone 7th chord. Generally, in the resolution of a dim 7th chord, a dim 5th resolves inward by step-motions to a 3rd. Conversely, its inversion, an aug 4th, resolves outward by step-motions to a 6th. (*See examples below.*)

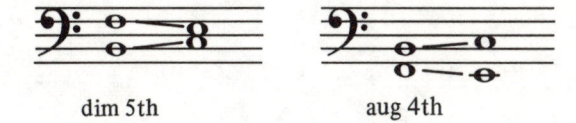

dim 5th   aug 4th

Resolve the following without using ♯s and ♭s:

14

1 Basic harmonic progressions move from an opening (1) _____, through a pre-dominant, to a dominant, and then to a (2) _____ _____.

(1) tonic
(2) closing tonic

---

2 Often the opening tonic in a basic harmonic progression is extended over time, or *prolonged*. This process of extending or prolonging is called *prolongation*. A basic harmonic progression often begins with a _____ of the opening tonic.

prolongation

---

3 Tonic harmony may be prolonged through simple repetition or by repetition with change of soprano. In the example below, the tonic is _____ through repetition with change of soprano.

prolonged

G: I   I

---

4 A common way of prolonging tonic harmony is through the use of I⁶. In this example the movement from I to I⁶ is a _____ of tonic harmony.

prolongation

G: I   I⁶

---

5 In I I⁶, as in four-voice writing in general, the most important voices are the outer voices, namely, the ....

SB

2 There are two types of leading tone 7th chords:

(1) minor

    1. dim 7th chords (the more common of the two types), which are diatonic in (1) _____ keys;

(2) major

    2. dim-min 7th chords, which are diatonic in (2) _____ keys.

---

3 Although the leading tone triad in root position is not commonly used, the leading tone 7th chord in root position is. Write the diatonic leading tone 7th chords in the following keys:

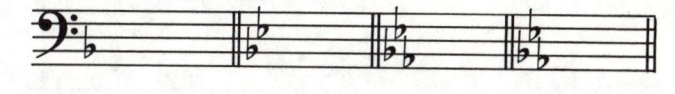

    F: VII⁷   g: VII⁷   E♭: VII⁷   c: VII⁷

---

4 The leading tone 7th chord is typically found as a complete chord, consisting of scale degrees:

$\hat{7}$ $\hat{2}$ $\hat{4}$ $\hat{6}$

____ ____ ____ ____.

---

5 Since the most common function of the leading tone 7th chord is prolongation of tonic harmony, it follows that the resolution of the leading tone 7th chord is to the _____ chord.

tonic (*or* I)

---

6 In our study of the resolution of leading tone 7th chords, we will first deal with the dim 7th chord, found in (1) _____ keys, and then with the dim-min 7th chord, diatonic in (2) _____ keys.

(1) minor
(2) major

---

7 The interval between the root and seventh in a dim 7th chord is a (1) _____ _____. In its resolution to I, the leading tone, $\hat{7}$, leads to (2) ____ (*scale degree*). The seventh, $\hat{6}$, resolves down by step to (3) ____.

(1) dim 7th
(2) $\hat{1}$

(3) $\hat{5}$

    a: VII⁷   I

---

8 Think of each of the following dim 7ths as the root and seventh of a dim 7th chord. Resolve each. Remember, $\hat{7}$ resolves to (1) ____; $\hat{6}$ resolves to (2) ____.

(1) $\hat{1}$
(2) $\hat{5}$

    c:

parallel

6 There are two very common SB patterns in I I⁶, one of which is illustrated below. In this example the SB move in _____ 10ths.

parallel 10ths

7 The SB in this pattern move in _____ _____.

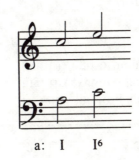

parallel 10ths

8 Sometimes the specific interval between SB is an octave more than a 10th, a 17th. Still the term for the SB pattern is parallel 10ths. The term for the SB movement in this pattern is _____ _____.

37 As illustrated in the previous frame, supertonic harmony may be prolonged by the movement of II⁷ to II⁶₅ (or II⁶₅ to II⁷) in the same way that it is prolonged by II II⁶ (or II⁶ II).

As shown above, a typical SB pattern in II⁷ II⁶₅, as in II II⁶, is _____ _____.

voice exchange

38 As with II and II⁶, II⁷ and II⁶₅ may be connected with a passing ⁶₃ chord. Complete the Roman numeral analysis below:

(1) d: ⌞I__ I⁶⌟ ⌞II⁷__ II⁶₅⌟ V(⁶ᐟ⁵ ₄ᐟ₃) I
         I   II⁷

(1) I⁶

II⁷ and II⁶₅ are connected by means of a

(2) _____ ⁶₃ chord.

(2) passing

39 Provide the Roman numeral analysis of the following. Bracket and label prolongation of tonic harmony (with I) and prolongation of supertonic 7th harmony (with II⁷).

B: ⌞I IV⁶ I⁶⌟ ⌞II⁷ I⁶ II⁶₅⌟ V⁸⁻⁷ | VI |
        I   II⁷

⌞II⁶₅ I⁶ II⁷⌟ | V(⁸⁻⁷ ₆⁻⁵ ₄⁻₃) | I ‖
      II⁷

Set 22 / THE LEADING TONE 7TH CHORD (1)

$\hat{7}$

1 The 7th chord built on the leading tone, ____ (*scale degree*), is termed the *leading tone 7th chord*. The most common function of the leading tone 7th chord is prolongation of tonic harmony.

9 The other very common SB pattern in I I⁶ is illustrated in example **x**. The term for this is *voice exchange*. The SB exchange notes, staying within their respective ranges, of course, in moving from I to I⁶. The term for the SB pattern in example **y** is

_____ .

voice exchange

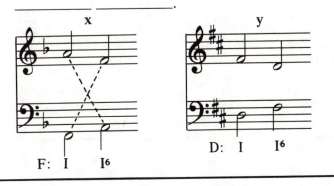

F: I   I⁶

D: I   I⁶

10 Label the SB patterns in the following examples:

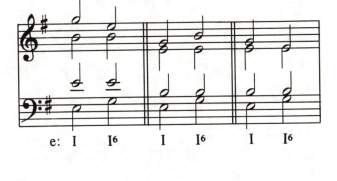

e: I   I⁶   I   I⁶   I   I⁶

(1) voice exchange
(2) parallel 10ths
(3) voice exchange

(1) .... (2) .... (3) ....

11 Add the soprano voice to this bass voice, forming a parallel 10th pattern:

F: I   I⁶

12 Illustrate voice exchange by adding a soprano voice to this bass:

F: I   I⁶

(Soprano may be written an octave higher.)

$$\text{I} \quad \text{IV} \quad \text{V} \quad \text{I}$$

$$\text{I} \quad \text{II}_3^4 \quad \text{V}^7 \quad \text{I}$$

$$\text{I} \quad \text{II}_5^6 \quad \text{V} \quad \text{I}$$

$$\text{I} \quad \text{II}_5^6 \quad \text{V}_2^4 \quad \text{I}^6$$

35 Choosing from the following chord successions, set this soprano four ways:

$$\text{I} \quad \text{II}^6 \quad \text{V} \quad \text{I}$$
$$\text{I} \quad \text{IV} \quad \text{V} \quad \text{I}$$
$$\text{I} \quad \text{II}_3^4 \quad \text{V}^7 \quad \text{I}$$
$$\text{I} \quad \text{II}_2^4 \quad \text{V}_5^6 \quad \text{I}$$
$$\text{I} \quad \text{II}_5^6 \quad \text{V} \quad \text{I}$$
$$\text{I} \quad \text{II}_5^6 \quad \text{V}_2^4 \quad \text{I}^6$$

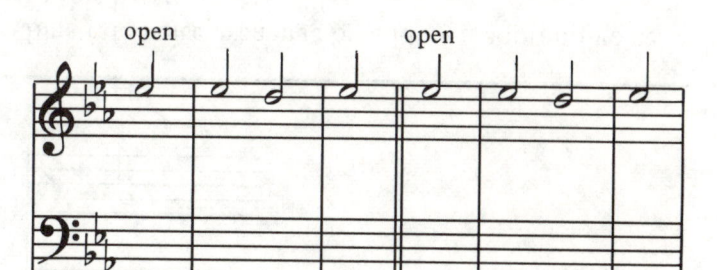

E♭ :

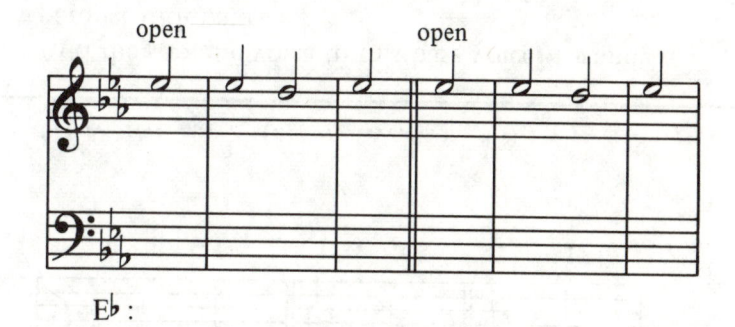

E♭ :

36 Give the Roman numeral analysis of the following progression:

d: I I⁶ | II⁷ II$_5^6$ | V($_{4-3}^{6-5}$) | I ‖

fifth

13 While there is the rule that the root of I should be doubled in four-voice writing, there is no similar hard-and-fast rule for doubling in I⁶. However, in I⁶ it is generally better *not* to double the third (the bass) of the chord. As shown in the example below, it is better to double either the root of I⁶, as in example **x**, or the _____ (*chord member*) of I⁶, as in example **y**.

(1) root

(2) fifth

14 In I I⁶, the best voice leading results from keeping the AT notes stationary, while the SB engage in either voice exchange or parallel 10th movement. In the former case (see example **x**), this results in a doubled (1) _____ (*chord member*) of I⁶, in the latter case (see example **y**), this results in a doubled (2) _____ of I⁶.

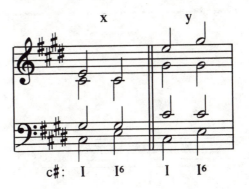

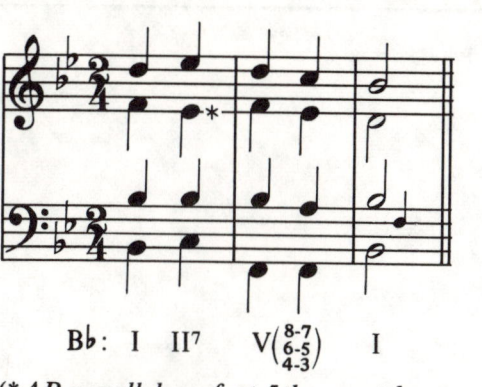

Bb: I II⁷ V$\binom{8\text{-}7}{6\text{-}5}{}_{4\text{-}3}$ I

(*AB parallel perfect 5ths must be avoided.*)

32

open

$\begin{matrix} & 8 & - & 7 \\ 7 & 6 & - & 5 \\ & 4 & - & 3 \end{matrix}$

---

33 *Bracket and label the prolongation of opening tonic.*

b: I II$_2^4$ V$_5^6$ I II⁶ V$\binom{6\text{-}5}{4\text{-}3}$ I

I

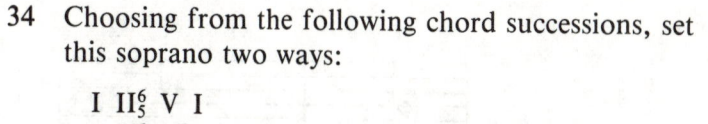

close

$\begin{matrix}4 \\ 2\end{matrix}$ $\begin{matrix}6\\5\end{matrix}$ 6 $\begin{matrix}6 & - & 5\\4 & - & \#\end{matrix}$

---

34 Choosing from the following chord successions, set this soprano two ways:

I II$_5^6$ V I
I II$_5^6$ V$_2^4$ I⁶
I II⁷ V⁷ I
I II⁷ V I
I II$_2^4$ V$_5^6$ I

I   II⁷ V⁷   I

I II$_2^4$ V$_5^6$ I

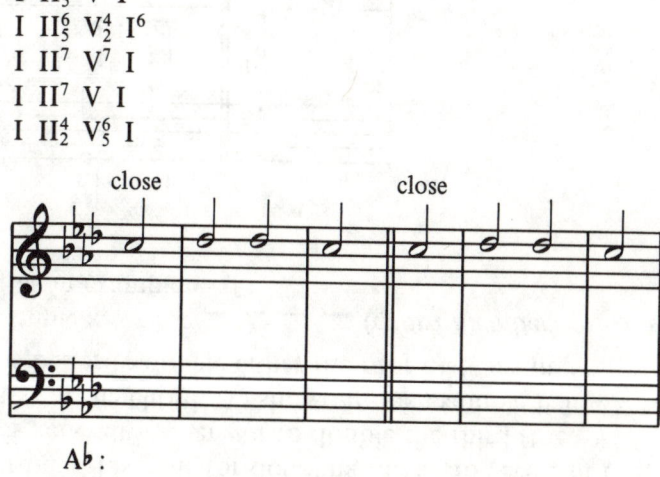

close   close

Ab:

15 Although there are other possible inner voice lead-ings in I I⁶ with SB voice exchange or parallel 10ths, none is as smooth as keeping the .... (voices) stationary.

Throughout this book we will be concerned with smoothness of voice leading, and unless otherwise indicated, all exercises are to be completed in the smoothest correct way.

Complete the connections below:

AT

F: I   I⁶

16

A♭: I   I⁶

---

(1) parallel 10ths (and)
    voice exchange

(2) root

(3) AT

17 Two very common SB patterns in I I⁶ are

(1) _____ _____ and _____ _____. In these tonic prolongation patterns, the correct doubling for I is, as usual, the

(2) _____. The best doubling for I⁶ (the root or fifth) will automatically occur as a result of keep-ing the (3) .... (*voices*) stationary in com-pleting the connection.

---

parallel 10ths

18 Label the given SB pattern and then complete each of the following connections in the smoothest way:

close

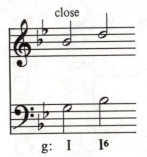

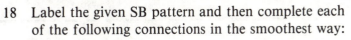

g: I   I⁶

F: I   II$_5^6$ V$_2^4$ I^6

27

$\begin{smallmatrix}6\\5\end{smallmatrix}$ $\begin{smallmatrix}4\\2\end{smallmatrix}$ 6

F: I   II$_2^4$ V$_5^6$ I

28   close

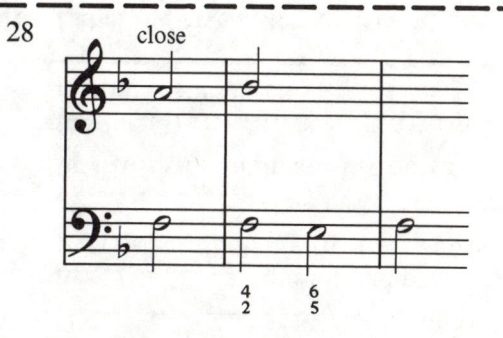

$\begin{smallmatrix}4\\2\end{smallmatrix}$ $\begin{smallmatrix}6\\5\end{smallmatrix}$

c#: I^6 II$_5^6$ V$\left(\begin{smallmatrix}6-5\\4-3\end{smallmatrix}\right)$ I

29

6   $\begin{smallmatrix}6\\5\end{smallmatrix}$ $\begin{smallmatrix}6\\4\end{smallmatrix}$ - $\begin{smallmatrix}5\\\#\end{smallmatrix}$

c#: I   II^7 V^7 I

30   open

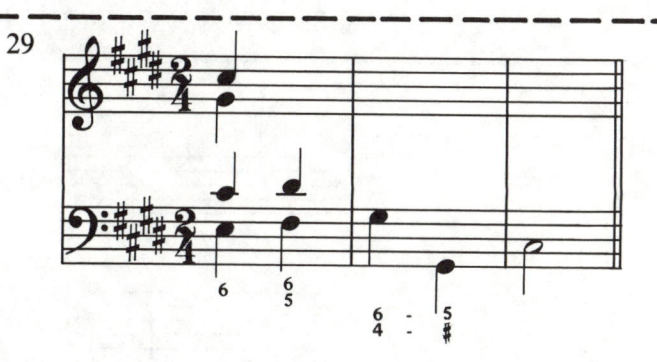

7

complete $\begin{smallmatrix}7\\\#\end{smallmatrix}$

B♭: I   II$_3^4$ V^7 I

31   open

$\begin{smallmatrix}4\\3\end{smallmatrix}$ 7

voice exchange

19   open

....

g: I   I⁶

20   For the following connections, add the indicated soprano; then write the AT:

voice exchange
open

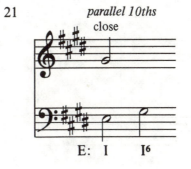

a: I   I⁶

21   *parallel 10ths*
close

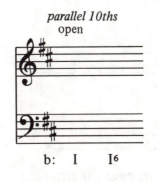

E: I   I⁶

22   *parallel 10ths*
open

b: I   I⁶

23 Complete the following:

e: I   II$_2^4$ V$_5^6$ I

24 (*Be sure to prepare and resolve the seventh of* V$_5^6$.)

 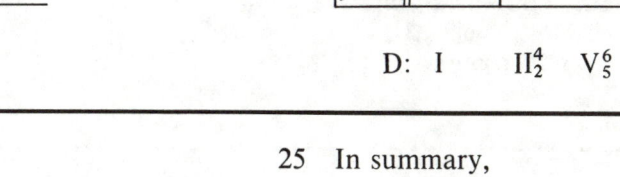

D: I   II$_2^4$ V$_5^6$ I

25 In summary,

1. Supertonic 7th chords may occur in these harmonic progressions:

I II$_5^6$ V I   I VI II$_5^6$ V I
I II^7 V$^{(7)}$ I
I II$_3^4$ V$^{(7)}$ I

(V$^{(7)}$ in the above may, of course, be prolonged by a cadential $_4^6$.)

2. Common usages of supertonic 7th chords in tonic prolongation patterns are:

I II$_5^6$ V$_2^4$ I^6
I II$_2^4$ V$_5^6$ I

26 Set each figured bass below. First give the Roman numeral analysis.

 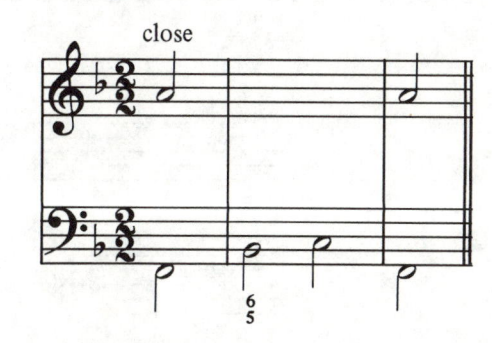

F: I   II$_5^6$ V   I

(*SAT may be written an octave higher.*)

23

voice exchange
close

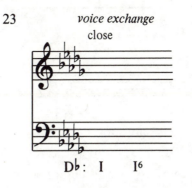

D♭: I   I⁶

---

(1) parallel 10ths
(2) voice exchange
(*either order*)

24 Although movement from I to I⁶ is more common in the prolongation of tonic harmony, the reverse, I⁶ to I, also occurs. As with I I⁶, the most common SB patterns in I⁶ I are (1) .... and (2) ....

---

25 Complete the indicated connections:

voice exchange

G: I⁶   I

26 parallel 10ths

G: I⁶   I

---

(1) opening tonic
(2) pre-dominant
(3) dominant
(4) closing tonic

27 Basic harmonic progressions lead from an (1) _____ _____, through a (2) _____, to a (3) _____, and then to a (4) _____ _____.

---

prolongation

28 I I⁶ is a _____ of opening tonic harmony.

---

19 Give the Roman numeral analysis of the example below:

(1)   F: _____

II_3^4 is the least common supertonic 7th chord. Its most characteristic usage is in the harmonic progression illustrated above. Note that, as usual, the dissonances are prepared by (2) .... and resolved (3) ....

(1) I II_3^4 V^7 I

(2) common tone

(3) down by step

---

20 Complete the following progression:

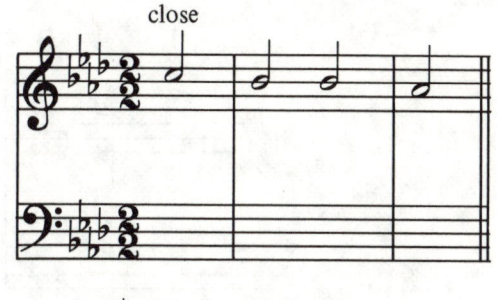

$A^\flat$: I II_3^4 V^7 I

---

21 II_5^6, II^7, and II_3^4 commonly occur in harmonic progressions, leading from (1) .... to (2) ....

(1) an opening tonic (*or* I)

(2) a root position dominant (*or* V)

---

22 II_2^4, on the other hand, never precedes a root position dominant. II_2^4, which has the (1) _____ (*chord member*) in the bass, is frequently used within the context of I II_2^4 V_5^6 I to prolong opening tonic harmony. Write the bass line for this chord succession. Note the preparation by (2) .... and the resolution (3) .... of the dissonant Î in II_2^4.

(1) seventh

(2) common tone

(3) down by step

$B^\flat$: I II_2^4 V_5^6 I

29 The concluding exercises of this set involve writing basic harmonic progressions beginning with a prolongation of tonic. Before writing these progressions, it is necessary to review a few points.

In root position chords (such as I, II, IV, V), the

(1) root (*or* bass)

(1) _____ is doubled.

(2) third (*or* bass)

In II⁶, the (2) _____ is doubled.

---

30 The smoothest connection of two root position triads having a common tone (such as I IV, V I, and II V) is (1) .... The smoothest correct connection of two root position triads not having a common tone (such as IV V and I II) is (2) .... Although II⁶ and V have a common tone, the smoothest correct connections of II⁶ V are (3) ....

(1) common tone-stepwise

(2) contrary motion-nearest

(3) contrary motion-nearest

---

31 When, in the connection of triads in a basic harmonic progression, common tone-stepwise and contrary motion-nearest connections are not possible, follow the general voice-leading procedure: Move to the nearest (1) ...., avoiding faulty (2) _____, avoiding an augmented 2nd in minor keys, and allowing for correct doubling.

(1) chord tones

(2) parallels

---

32 In connecting a pre-dominant chord to V⁷, the seventh of V⁷ is prepared by (1) ...., and other voices move according to the procedure outlined in the previous frame. In moving to the following I, the seventh of V⁷ (2) ....

(1) common tone

(2) resolves down by step

---

33 IV may have any one of its scale degrees, (1) ____, ____, or ____, in the soprano. II and II⁶, on the other hand, commonly have a soprano of (2) ____ or ____, while avoiding a soprano of (3) ____.

(1) $\hat{4}$, $\hat{6}$, (or) $\hat{1}$

(2) $\hat{2}$ (or) $\hat{4}$

(3) $\hat{6}$

---

34 Write each of the following basic harmonic progressions in the smoothest correct way. (*Refer to the review in frames 29–33, as necessary.*)

a: I   IV   V   I

cadential $^6_4$

15 In the example below, II$^6_5$ moves to a .... rather than moving directly to V. Often II$^6_5$ and II^7 lead to a cadential $^6_4$, sustaining the dissonant $\hat{1}$ in the same voice and delaying its resolution. (*See example.*)

16 When the dominant is preceded by a cadential $^6_4$, smooth introduction of the seventh of V^7 is assured. Therefore, both II$^6_5$ and II^7 may lead equally well to V^7 through the cadential $^6_4$.
Complete these connections:

G: I   II$^6_5$ V $\left(\begin{smallmatrix}8\\6\\4\end{smallmatrix} : \begin{smallmatrix}7\\5\\3\end{smallmatrix}\right)$ I

17

g: I   II^7 V $\left(\begin{smallmatrix}8\\6\\4\end{smallmatrix} : \begin{smallmatrix}7\\5\\3\end{smallmatrix}\right)$ I

(1) fifth

(2) root (or) third

(3) complete

18 Although II^7 may be a complete chord or an incomplete chord with (1) _____ omitted and (2) _____ or _____ doubled, the inversions of II^7 (II$^6_5$, II$^4_3$, and II$^4_2$) are (3) _____ (complete *or* incomplete) chords.

35 close

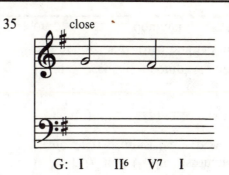

G: I II⁶ V⁷ I

36 close

D: I IV V⁷ I

37 open

e: I II⁶ V⁷ I

(*Note: AT movement in I II⁶ is parallel 5ths, but not parallel perfect 5ths.*)

11 Complete the following progressions, taking care to prepare and resolve all dissonances:

f#: I   II⁷ V⁷   I
     complete

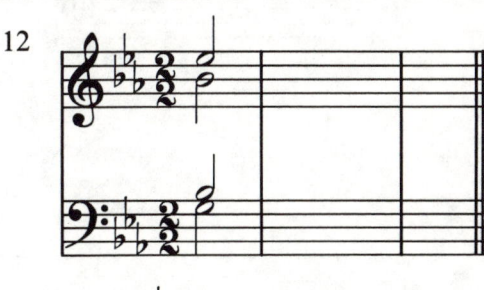

12

E♭: I⁶   II⁷ V⁷   I
     complete

13   open
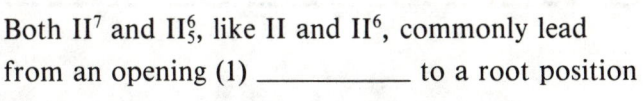

D: I   II⁷ **V⁷**   I
    dbl. root

14 To review:

Both II⁷ and II⁶₅, like II and II⁶, commonly lead
from an opening (1) _____ to a root position
(2) _____.

In both II⁷ and II⁶₅ the dissonant seventh, (3) ____
(*scale degree*), must be prepared and resolved.

II⁶₅ is a(n) (4) _____ (complete *or* incomplete)
chord.

II⁷ may occur as a complete chord or as an incomplete chord with fifth omitted and (5) _____
or _____ doubled.

(1) tonic

(2) dominant

(3) Î

(4) complete

(5) root
    (or) third

38 The bass movement following a tonic prolongation of I I⁶ is usually up to IV or II⁶ rather than down to II. In moving from a prolonged tonic of I I⁶ to either IV or II⁶, use, as always, the smoothest correct voice leading: Move to the *nearest* chord tones that avoid faulty parallels and that allow for correct doubling.

Consider problem **x** below. What are the notes to be added in the AT of the IV chord? (1) ____ ____

(1) E G♯

B: I   I⁶   IV

Which solution (**y** or **z**) gives the smoother voice leading? (2) ____

(2) **z**
(*In solution z the A moves by step and the T leaps a 3rd. That is smoother than solution y in which the A also moves by step but the T leaps a 4th.*)

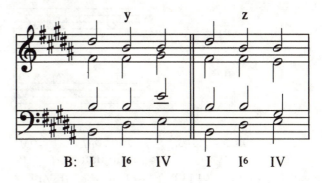

B: I   I⁶   IV   I   I⁶   IV

39 What are the notes to be added in the AT of the II⁶ chord in the problem below? ____ ____ Complete the AT in the smoothest way:

C E♭

g: I   I⁶   II⁶

(1) V

(2) V⁷

8   Unlike II⁶₅, which generally leads to (1) _____ and not to (2) _____, II⁷ leads well to both V and V⁷. Complete this connection. First resolve the seventh of II⁷.

e: II⁷   V

9   Complete the following connections. Remember to resolve the seventh of II⁷ and to prepare the seventh of V⁷ by common tone.
(*Note that the root of II⁷ is to be doubled*.)

A: II⁷   V⁷
     dbl. root

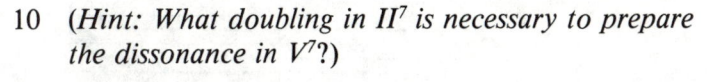

10   (*Hint: What doubling in II⁷ is necessary to prepare the dissonance in V⁷?*)

g: II⁷   V⁷

40 Complete each of the following connections in the smoothest correct way:

A: I I⁶ IV

41

A: I I⁶ IV

(Note: The parallel 5ths in AT of I⁶ II⁶ are not parallel __perfect__ 5ths.)

42

A wild image

f: I I⁶ II⁶

43

f: I I⁶ II⁶

5 Although II⁶₅ (and the other inversions of II⁷) are typically complete chords, II⁷ in major keys frequently occurs as an incomplete chord with (1) _____ omitted and (2) _____ or _____ doubled.

(1) fifth
(2) root (or) third

6 Unlike the root position II triad, which is generally avoided in minor keys, II⁷ is used in both major and minor keys. In minor keys, parallel *perfect* 5ths are not a danger in I II⁷ connections. Nevertheless, II⁷ may occur as an incomplete chord in minor, though the complete chord is more common.

Write this connection two ways: first with a complete II⁷ and then within an incomplete II⁷ (fifth omitted) with third doubled.

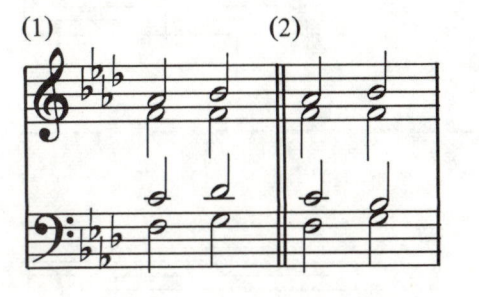

f: I   II⁷   I   II⁷

7 In moving from I⁶ to II⁷ use whatever doubling in II⁷ (complete, incomplete with doubled root, incomplete with doubled third) gives the *smoothest correct* voice leading. Complete these connections:

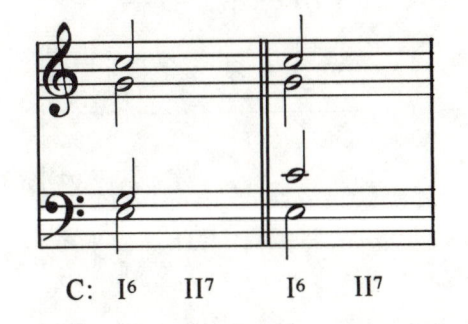

C: I⁶   II⁷   I⁶   II⁷

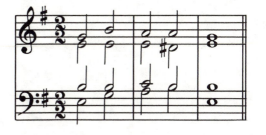

44 Complete the following progressions as indicated, using the smoothest correct voice leading in all cases:

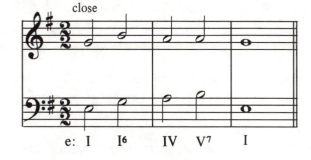

e: I   I⁶   IV   V⁷   I

45 Use SB voice exchange for I I⁶. (*Hint: Remember what scale degree is to be avoided in the soprano of II⁶.*)

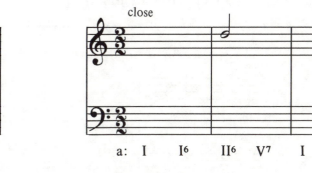

D: I   I⁶   II⁶   V   I

46 Use SB parallel 10ths for I I⁶. (*First write the bass.*)

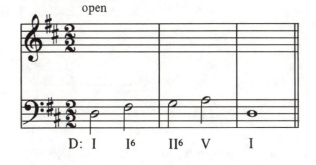

a: I   I⁶   II⁶   V⁷   I

47 Use SB voice exchange for I I⁶.

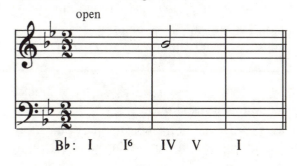

B♭: I   I⁶   IV   V   I

harmonic

1 While II$_5^6$ typically occurs in both harmonic progressions and tonic prolongation patterns, II^7 typically occurs in _____ progressions only, as, for example, I II^7 V^7 I.

TB

2 It is very easy to write faulty parallels in leading from I to II^7 in major keys. In this example there are faulty parallel perfect 5ths between .... (*voices*).

F: I   II^7

common tone

3 In order to avoid faulty parallels, yet still have smooth voice leading, II^7 in major keys often occurs as an incomplete chord with the fifth omitted and either the root or the third doubled.
Complete this I II^7 connection, omitting the fifth and doubling the *third* of II^7. Remember to prepare the seventh by _____ _____.

F: I   II^7

4 Complete this I II^7 connection, omitting the fifth and doubling the *root* of II^7:

F: I   II^7

OR

48 Set the following figured bass for four voices. Use one of the typical SB patterns in prolonging the opening tonic. (*First give the key and Roman numeral analysis*.)

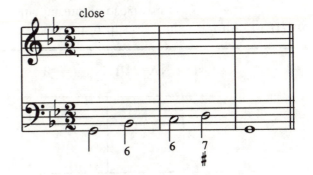

Set 5 / VII AND V⁶ (1)

1 Tonic harmony may be prolonged by reiteration of the I chord or by direct movement from I to I⁶ (or I⁶ to I). Oftentimes, instead of directly following one another, tonic chords are linked by non-tonic chords. These non-tonic chords serve to further prolong tonic harmony.

Both of the patterns below are examples of tonic prolongation. In example **x** (1) _____ moves directly to (2) _____. In example **y** I and I⁶ are linked by a (3) _____ (tonic *or* non-tonic) chord.

(1) I

(2) I⁶

(3) non-tonic

prolongation

45 Study the examples below.

I V_2^4 I^6 (example **x**) is a _____ of tonic harmony. The insertion of II$_5^6$ into this chord succession (example **y**) serves to further prolong tonic.

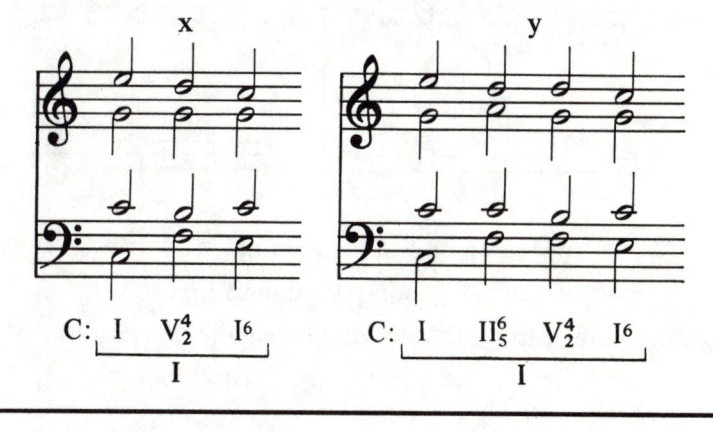

(1) soprano

(2) bass

46 In the following example the seventh of II$_5^6$ is prepared and resolved in the (1) _____ (*voice*). The seventh of the V_2^4 is prepared and resolved in the (2) _____ (*voice*). Write the inner voices:

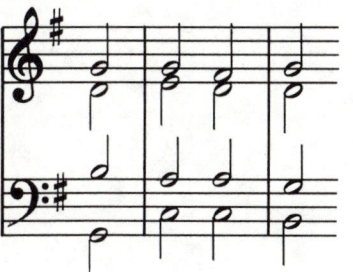

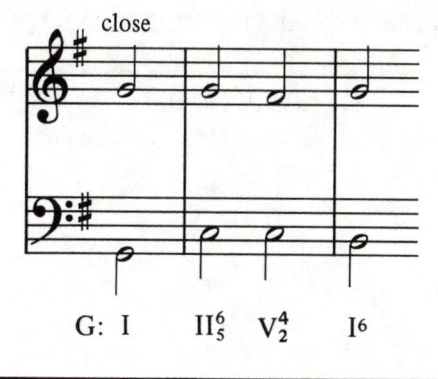

47 Complete this tonic prolongation pattern:

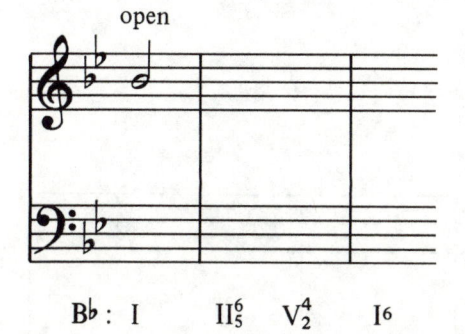

48 As studied in this set, important uses of II$_5^6$ are in the harmonic progressions

(1) (I) II$_5^6$ V I

(2) (I VI) II$_5^6$ V I

(3) I II$_5^6$ V_2^4 I^6

(1) I ....

(2) I VI ....

and in the tonic prolongation pattern (3) ....

1, 3, (and) 5

2   To understand how a non-tonic chord can prolong tonic harmony it is first necessary to understand the concepts of *active* and *stable* tones within a key. In prolongation of tonic harmony, the stable tones are the notes of the tonic triad, scale degrees ____, ____, and ____. All other tones are active—they lead to stable tones.

---

(1) 1, 3, (and) 5
(2) active

3   The stable tones, in the prolongation of tonic harmony, are scale degrees (1) ____, ____, and ____. All other tones are (2) _____ tones.

---

passing tone

4   Active tones are categorized according to their relationships to stable tones. An active tone which passes between two stable tones is labeled a *passing tone*. In the example below, $\hat{2}$, an active tone, passes between $\hat{1}$ and $\hat{3}$, two stable tones. $\hat{2}$ is, in this case, a _____ _____.

G:

---

passing tone

5   In the example below, $\hat{4}$ is a _____ _____ leading from $\hat{5}$ to $\hat{3}$.

B♭:

---

passing chord

6   A chord whose *bass* note has passing function is referred to as a *passing chord*. The chord between I and I⁶ in each of these examples is a _____ _____.

f♯: I   I⁶   f♯: I   I⁶

41 (*Hint: Be careful to avoid faulty parallels in* I^6 II^6_5.)

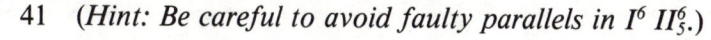

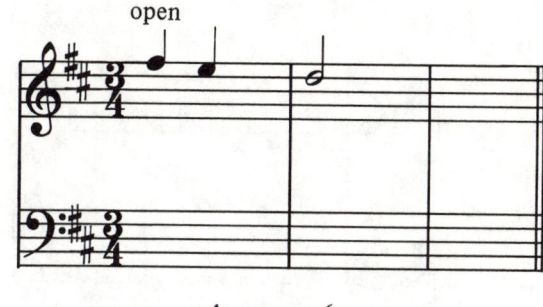

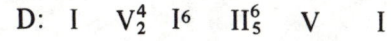

D: I V^4_2 I^6 II^6_5 V   I

42 Oftentimes II^6_5 is used instead of II^6 in the descending 3rd bass progression as given below. Complete the following. (*Remember to prepare the seventh by common tone.*)

A: I   VI II^6_5 V   I

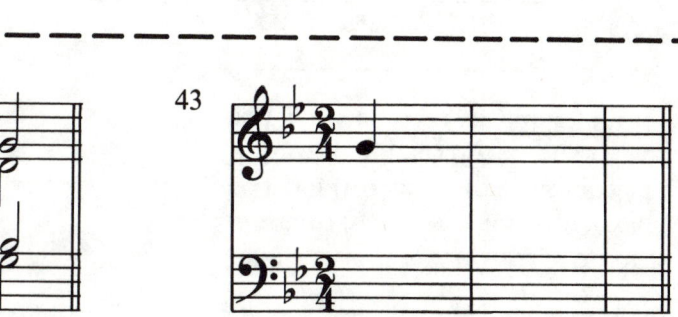

43

g: I   VI II^6_5 V   I

44 In the uses of II^6_5 studied thus far,

   I II^6_5 V I,

   I VI II^6_5 V I,

II^6_5 has been part of a harmonic progression; it has preceded a .... II^6_5 may also precede an inverted dominant; it may occur as part of a tonic prolongation pattern.

root position dominant (*or* V)

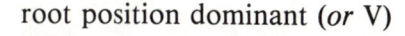

(1) passing chord

(2) VII⁶

7 The chord between I⁶ and I in this example is a
(1) _____ _____. Give the Roman
numeral analysis of this chord: (2) ....

D: I   I⁶

8 Write the Roman numeral analysis of the pattern
below:

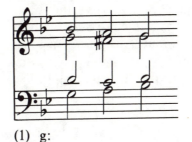

(1) g:

(1) I   VII⁶   I⁶

(2) passing chord

The second chord is part of the prolongation of
tonic harmony; it is a (2) _____ _____ .
It consists of active tones which lead from the stable
tones of I to the stable tones of I⁶.

9 An active tone which moves by step from a stable
tone and then back to the same stable tone is termed
a *neighboring tone*. Neighboring tones may occur
either above or below stable tones. In example **x**, $\hat{7}$
is a neighboring tone. In example **y**, $\hat{2}$ is a

neighboring tone

_____ _____ .

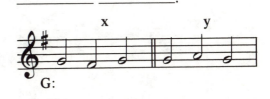

G:

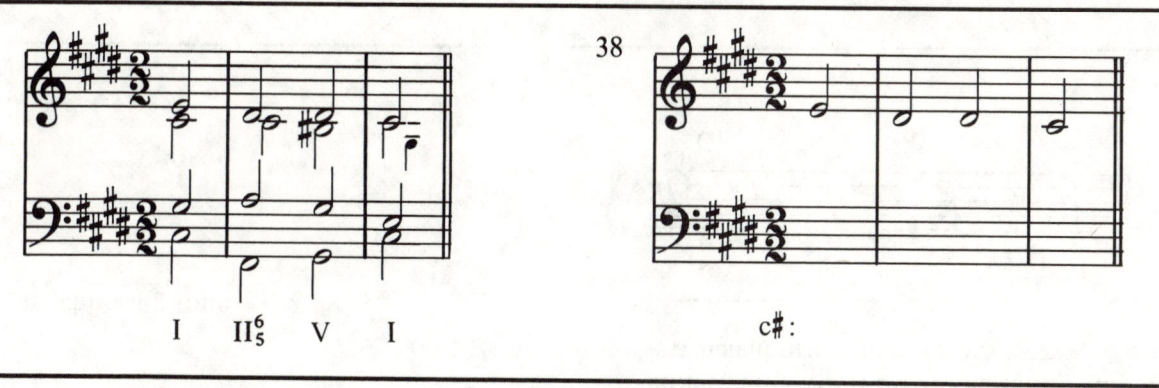

I   II$_5^6$ V   I

38

c#:

---

z

39 II$_5^6$ often follows a I^6 (or a prolonged tonic). Be careful with the voice leading in I^6 II$_3^6$; in major keys it is easy to write faulty parallels. Which of the connections below contains faulty parallels? ____

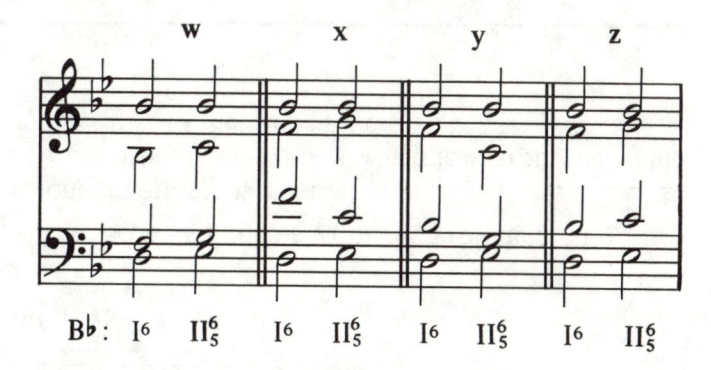

w   x   y   z

B♭: I^6 II$_5^6$ I^6 II$_5^6$ I^6 II$_5^6$ I^6 II$_5^6$

Carefully study the correct solutions shown above. In example **w** the faulty parallels of example **z** are avoided by inverting the AT to have parallel 4ths rather than parallel perfect 5ths.

In example **x** the faulty parallels are avoided by doubling the fifth of the I^6.

In example **y** the faulty parallels are avoided through the AT movement by leap from the perfect 5th to a 4th.

---

40 Complete the following progressions. (*Use SB voice exchange in I I^6.*)

close

F: I   I^6 II$_5^6$ V   I

10 A chord having a bass note which functions as a neighboring tone is referred to as a *neighboring chord*. The second chord in the example below is a _____ _____.

neighboring chord

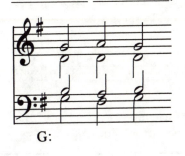

G:

11 Give the Roman numeral analysis of the pattern below:

(1) F:

(1) I   V⁶   I

(2) neighboring chord

The second chord is a (2) _____ _____.

12 Write the Roman numeral analysis of each of the following patterns:

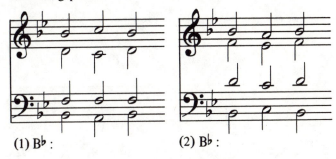

(1) B♭ :   (2) B♭ :

(1) I V⁶ I
(2) I VII⁶ I

(3) neighboring

In each case the second chord functions as a

(3) _____ chord in the prolongation of tonic harmony.

33 Write these I II⁶₅ V I connections. (*Hint: It is often a good idea to complete the voice having the dissonance before completing the other voices.*)

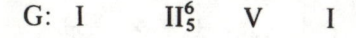

G: I   II⁶₅   V   I

34

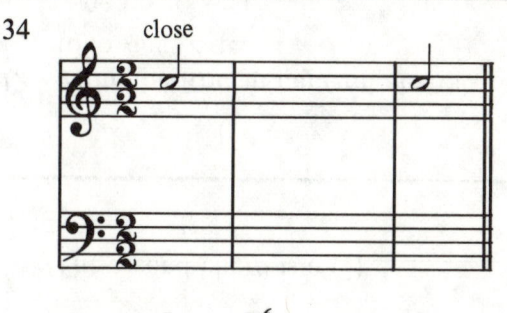

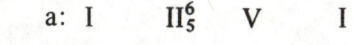

a: I   II⁶₅   V   I

35

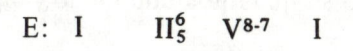

E: I   II⁶₅   V⁸⁻⁷   I

(1) (2̂) 2̂

(2) (2̂) 7̂

36 A common soprano in II⁶₅ V is (1) 2̂ ____. A common soprano in II⁶ V is (2) 2̂ ____.

37 Set the following sopranos. Choose I II⁶₅ V I or I II⁶ V I as appropriate in each case.

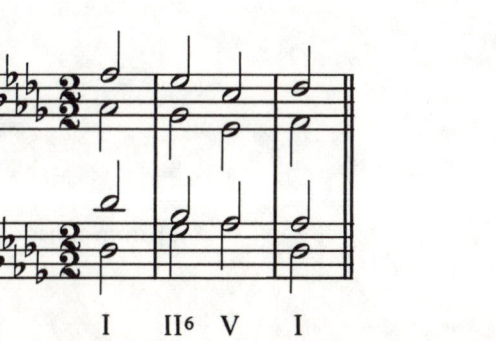

I   II⁶   V   I

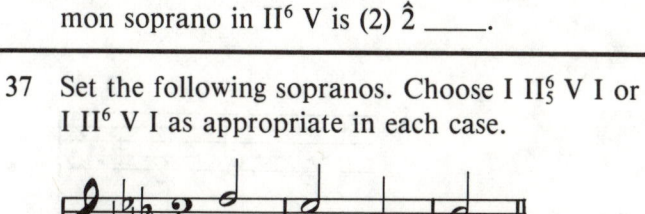

D♭:

13 An *incomplete-neighboring tone* is an active tone
having a stepwise neighboring relationship to either
the stable tone that precedes it or the stable tone
that follows it, but not both. Examples of incomplete-
neighboring tones are given below:

In example **x** there is a stepwise neighboring relationship between $\hat{4}$ and $\hat{3}$. In example **y** there is a
stepwise neighboring relationship between _____ and
_____ (*scale degrees*). Each of these patterns is termed
incomplete-neighbor because the active tone relates
as a neighbor to only one of the stable tones.

$\hat{7}$ (and) $\hat{1}$

14 Label each of the following patterns as P (passing),
N (neighboring), or IN (incomplete-neighboring):

(1) N
(2) IN
(3) IN

(4) P
(5) N

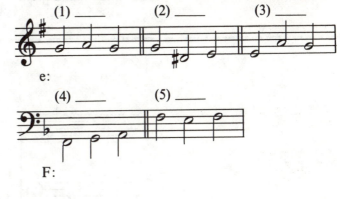

15 The bass note in the second chord of the pattern
below functions as an incomplete-neighboring tone
within the prevailing tonic harmony. This chord is,
therefore, termed an _____ _____
chord.

incomplete-neighboring

common tone

29 The approach to II$_5^6$ from I is given below. The seventh is prepared by .... and all other upper voice leading is stepwise.

c: I   II$_5^6$

30 Complete these I II$_5^6$ connections. Be sure to prepare the seventh:

open

G: I   II$_5^6$

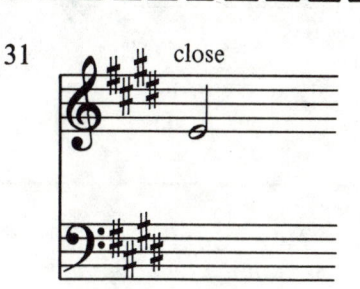

close

31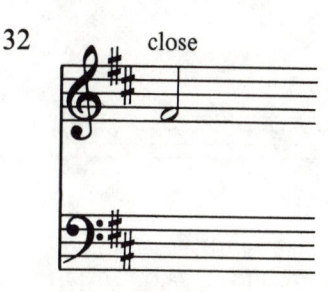

E: I   II$_5^6$

32 close

b: I   II$_5^6$

16 Give the Roman numeral analysis of this pattern:

(1) I⁶ V⁶ I

(1) E♭ :

(2) incomplete-neighboring chord

The second chord is a(n) (2) ....

17 The following are tonic prolongation patterns with passing, neighboring, or incomplete-neighboring chords. Give the Roman numeral analysis of each pattern, and label the second chord with P, N, or IN according to the function of the bass:

C: I VII⁶ I⁶
    P

18

g: I⁶ V⁶ I
    IN

19

D: I⁶ VII⁶ I
    P

25

II_5^6 II^6

d: ___ V ___ V

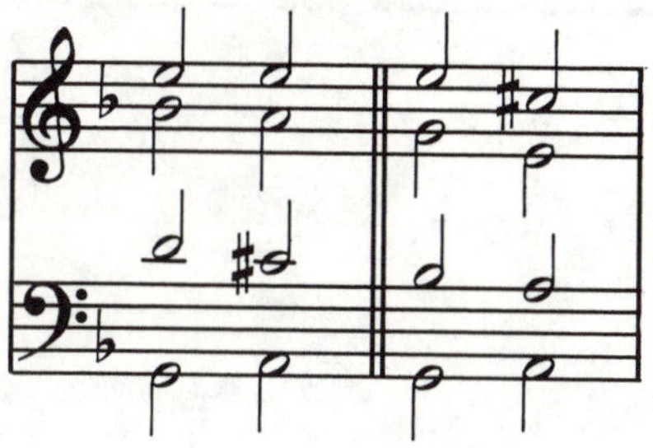

---

(1) $\hat{2}$ (or) $\hat{4}$

(2) $\hat{2}$, $\hat{6}$, (or) $\hat{1}$

(3) ($\hat{2}$) $\hat{7}$

(4) ($\hat{2}$) $\hat{2}$

26 Although they have obvious similarities, II^6 and II_5^6 differ in that:

    1. II^6 commonly supports (1) _____ or _____ (*scale degrees*) in the soprano. II_5^6 may support a soprano of (2) _____, _____, or _____.

    2. A typical soprano in II^6 V is (3) $\hat{2}$ _____. A typical soprano in II_5^6 V is (4) $\hat{2}$ _____.

---

(1) $\hat{2}$ $\hat{6}$ $\hat{1}$

(2) $\hat{4}$

27 There is another way in which II_5^6 differs from II^6. Unlike II^6, which often leads to either V or V^7, II_5^6 usually leads to V and not V^7.

II_5^6 is typically found as a complete chord, having $\hat{4}$ in the bass and (1) _____ _____ _____ in the upper voices. As illustrated in the example below, in a II_5^6 V^7 connection there is no way to prepare the seventh of V^7 since there is no (2) _____ (*scale degree*) in the upper voices of II_5^6.

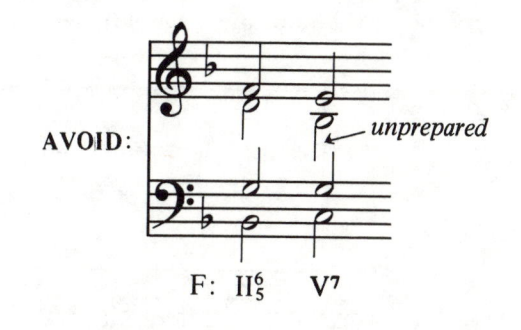

AVOID: ← *unprepared*

F: II_5^6 V^7

---

(1) complete

(2) V

28 II_5^6 is a(n) (1) _____ (complete *or* incomplete) chord which leads to (2) _____ rather than V^7.

20

a: I V⁶ I
   N

---

21 The most common usage of VII⁶ is that of a passing chord between I and I⁶ or I⁶ and I. Give the Roman numeral analysis of the patterns below:

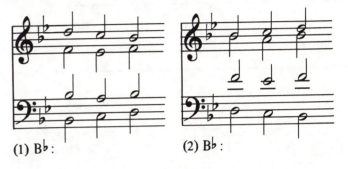

(1) B♭:   (2) B♭:

(1) I VII⁶ I⁶
(2) I⁶ VII⁶ I
(3) passing

In both cases VII⁶ is a (3) _____ chord in the prolongation of tonic harmony.

---

22 The term for the relationship between SB in this example is _____ _____ .

voice exchange

G: I   I⁶

---

23 A common usage of VII⁶ is illustrated below in example **x**. The voice exchange in the SB of I I⁶ is connected by passing tones in the SB of VII⁶. Complete the outer voices in example **y**, connecting the voice exchange with passing tones:

(1) nearest chord tones
(2) contrary

(3) TB

21 In a II⁶ V connection the upper voices should move to the (1) .... in (2) _____ motion to the bass, as in example **x**, giving a soprano of $\hat{2}$ $\hat{7}$. If a soprano of $\hat{2}$ $\hat{2}$ is attempted, as in example **y**, faulty parallels result, in this case between the (3) .... (*voices*).

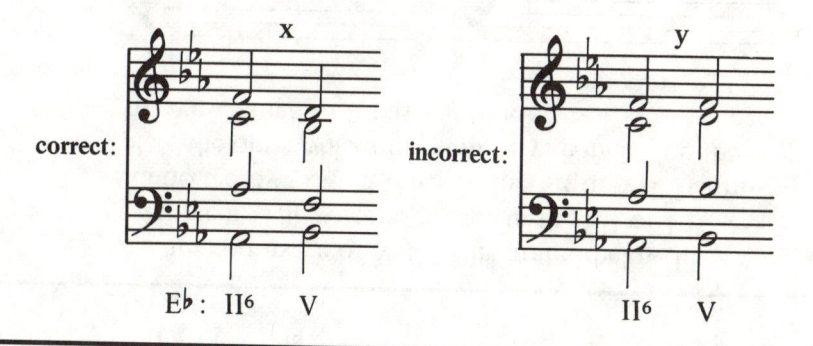

(1) **z**

(2) **y**

22 By contrast, in II⁶₅ V, a soprano of $\hat{2}$ $\hat{2}$ (example **x**) permits good voice leading, whereas a soprano of $\hat{2}$ $\hat{7}$ is problematic. In example (1) ____, the doubling in the V chord is faulty (a doubled leading tone). In example (2) ____, the seventh of II⁶₅ does not resolve down by step (and parallel perfect 5ths between TB result).

(1) ($\hat{2}$) $\hat{2}$
(2) ($\hat{2}$) $\hat{7}$

23 A common soprano for II⁶₅ V is (1) $\hat{2}$ ____. A common soprano for II⁶ V is (2) $\hat{2}$ ____.

24 Complete each connection below:

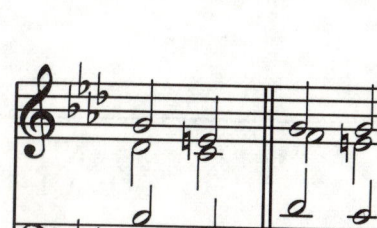

(1) passing

(2) prolongation

24 VII⁶ is most commonly used as a (1) _____ chord in the (2) _____ of tonic harmony.

25 Write the outer voices of this pattern using voice exchange connected with passing tones:

b: I   VII⁶   I⁶

26 The chord member that is almost always doubled in a VII⁶ is the third (the bass). When the SB voice exchange in I I⁶ is connected by VII⁶ as in example **x**, the doubling of the third occurs automatically. Complete the VII⁶ chord in example **y**. (*Remember that VII⁶ contains the leading tone, which in minor keys must be notated by means of an accidental.*)

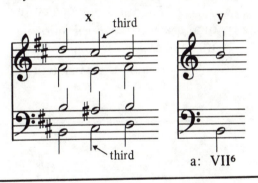

a: VII⁶

27 Complete the VII⁶ chords below:

g: VII⁶

28

E♭: VII⁶

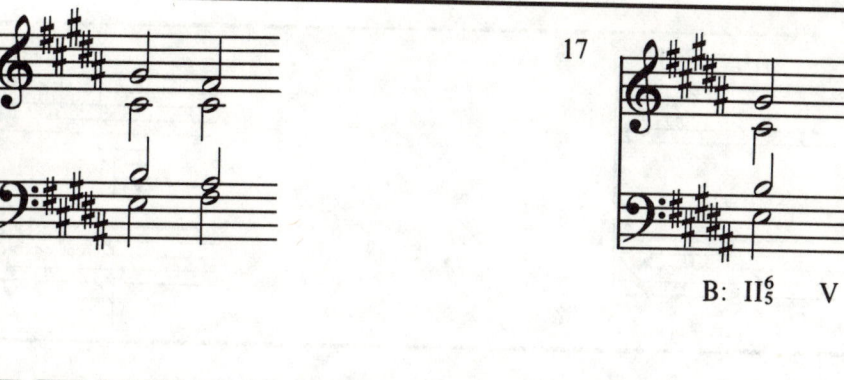

17

B: II$^6_5$ V

18

A♭: II$^6_5$ V

(1) $\hat{2}$, $\hat{6}$, (or) $\hat{1}$

(2) $\hat{2}$ (or) $\hat{4}$

(3) $\hat{2}$

19   II$^6_5$ may have a soprano of (1) ____, ____, or ____. II^6 generally has a soprano of (2) ____ or ____. The only scale degree which both II$^6_5$ and II^6 support in the soprano is (3) ____.

(1) ($\hat{2}$) $\hat{7}$

(2) ($\hat{2}$) $\hat{2}$

20   Note the differences, in the examples below, between II^6 and II$^6_5$ (each having $\hat{2}$ in the soprano) in their resolution to V. II^6 V has a soprano of (1) $\hat{2}$ ____; II$^6_5$ V has a soprano of (2) $\hat{2}$ ____. The reasons for this difference will be made clear in the following frames.

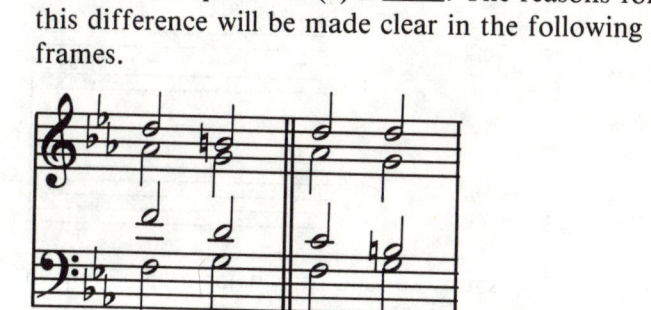

c: II^6 V   II$^6_5$ V

29

d: VII⁶

î, ĝ, (and) ŝ

30 VII⁶ contains the active tones $\hat{7}$, $\hat{2}$, and $\hat{4}$, which lead to the stable tones in I⁶ (or I), namely, ____, ____, and ____. (*See example, if necessary*.)

F: VII⁶ I⁶

---

dim 5th

31 A dissonance is formed in VII⁶ by the active tones $\hat{7}$ and $\hat{4}$—either an augmented 4th, as in example **x**, or its inversion, a ...., as in example **y**.

F: VII⁶   F: VII⁶

(1) pre-dominant

12 Although there are differing characteristic usages for II⁷, II₅⁶, II₃⁴, and II₂⁴, they all have two things in common:

1. They all function as (1) _____ chords, leading from I to V.
2. They all have the same preparation and resolution pattern. The seventh is prepared by

(2) common tone
(3) down by step

(2) .... in the preceding chord (usually I) and is resolved (3) .... in the following dominant harmony.

dominant (*or* V)

13 As do II and II⁶, II⁷ and II₅⁶ commonly occur in harmonic progressions leading to root position _____ chords. Just as II⁶ is more commonly used than II, II₅⁶ is more commonly used than II⁷.

(1) $\hat{2}$ (or) $\hat{4}$

14 II⁶ typically has a soprano of (1) ____ or ____ (*scale degrees*), but rarely supports a soprano of $\hat{6}$. II₅⁶ may support any of its scale degrees, other than $\hat{4}$ (its bass note), in the soprano; that is, II₅⁶ may have a soprano of (2) ____, ____, or ____.

(2) $\hat{2}$, $\hat{6}$, (or) $\hat{1}$

15 Typical II₅⁶ V connections are given below. Study each and label soprano scale degrees. Note that in all cases the voice leading is common tone-stepwise with the seventh, of course, resolving (1) ....

(1) down by step

(2) $\hat{1}$ $\hat{7}$ (3) $\hat{2}$ $\hat{2}$ (4) $\hat{6}$ $\hat{5}$

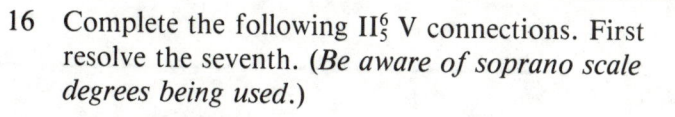

D: II₅⁶ V   II₅⁶ V   II₅⁶ V

16 Complete the following II₅⁶ V connections. First resolve the seventh. (*Be aware of soprano scale degrees being used.*)

f♯: II₅⁶ V

32 Because the dissonant interval created by $\hat{7}$ and $\hat{4}$ occurs between upper voices and not between the bass and an upper voice, we will not be concerned with its resolution at present. (The resolution of this dissonance will be discussed in detail in Set 22.) The procedure we will follow in moving from VII⁶ to I⁶ (or I) is to use the smoothest possible voice leading and correct doubling; this will result in all stepwise movement.

Complete the connection below, using all stepwise movement and correct doubling in I⁶. Observe that following this procedure results in the resolution of $\hat{7}$ to $\hat{1}$.

C: I   VII⁶   I⁶

(Note that although there are parallel 5ths between AT, they are not parallel <u>*perfect*</u> *5ths. The 5th between AT in* <u>*VII⁶*</u> *is diminished.)*

---

33 In connecting I VII⁶ I⁶ use the smoothest possible voice leading. As shown in the example in the previous frame, the resulting movement will be all

(1) _____. Remember to double the

(2) _____ of I, as usual, and to use the doubling in I⁶ that gives the best voice leading—in these cases, a doubled root. (Do not forget, a doubled

(3) _____ in I⁶ is to be avoided.) The best doubling for a VII⁶ is the (4) _____, which automatically occurs when VII⁶ connects the SB voice exchange in I I⁶ with passing tones.

(1) stepwise
(2) root (*or* bass)

(3) third (*or* bass)
(4) third (*or* bass)

---

34 Complete the connections below:

close

g: I   VII⁶   I⁶

(1) Î

(2) common tone

(3) down by step

(4) 7̂

II⁶₅

8 Circle the seventh of the supertonic 7th chord in the example below. The seventh, (1) _____ (*scale degree*), is prepared by (2) _____ _____ in the I chord. The seventh resolves (3) .... (*how?*) to (4) _____ (*scale degree*) in the V chord.

G: I   II⁶₅   V   I

(1) by common tone

(2) down by step

9 The dissonant seventh in supertonic 7th chords is prepared (1) .... in the preceding chord (usually I) and resolved (2) .... in the following V.

10 Complete the soprano line for this progression, preparing and resolving the dissonance in the II⁶₅:

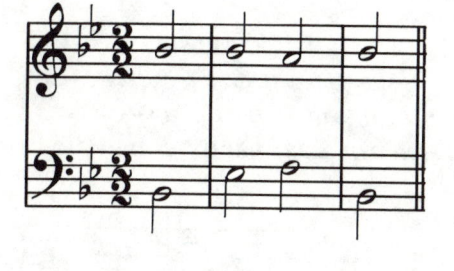

B♭ : I   II⁶₅   V   I

11 Complete the soprano line for this progression, preparing and resolving the dissonance in the II⁷:

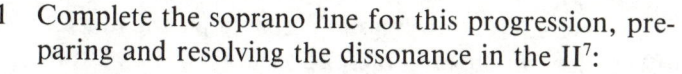

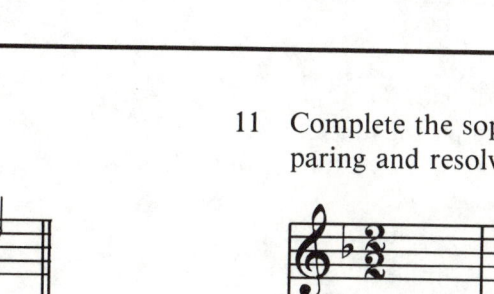

d: I   II⁷   V⁷   I

35

D: I⁶ VII⁶ I

36 Write the following tonic prolongation patterns, using SB voice exchange:

close

f#: I VII⁶ I⁶

37

E♭: I⁶ VII⁶ I

38 VII⁶ with a passing bass between I and I⁶ is also used with other soprano patterns. Complete the following, using the smoothest correct voice leading. Remember that the correct doubling in a VII⁶ is the

(1) _____ and that the doubling to be *avoided*

in a I⁶ is the (2) _____.

(1) third (*or* bass)
(2) third (*or* bass)

open

F: I VII⁶ I⁶

supertonic	1 II and its inversions are supertonic triads; II^7 and its inversions are _____ 7th chords.

dominant	2 The supertonic triads, II and II^6, and the supertonic 7th chords, II^7, II^6_5, II^4_3, and II^4_2, all have a common function. They are pre-dominant chords; that is, they precede the _____ (*chord*).
	
	 There are two types of dominant chords:
	
	     1. those that are in root position and occur in harmonic progressions;
	     2. those that are in inversion and occur in tonic prolongation patterns.
	
	 Pre-dominant chords may precede both types of dominant chords.

min	3 Write the supertonic 7th chord in G major: The structural type of supertonic 7th chords in major keys is ....
dim-min	4 Write the supertonic 7th chord in g minor: The structural type of supertonic 7th chords in minor keys is ....
$\hat{2}$ $\hat{4}$ $\hat{6}$ $\hat{1}$	5 Supertonic 7th chords consist of scale degrees: ____ ____ ____ ____
$\hat{1}$	6 The dissonant note, the seventh in a supertonic 7th chord, is ____ (*scale degree*).
(1) pre-dominant (2) resolved	7 Supertonic 7th chords, like supertonic triads, function as (1) _____ chords, but the presence of the chord seventh gives them a stronger ''pull'' to dominant harmony. As in the case of V^7, the seventh of II^7 must be prepared and (2) _____ .

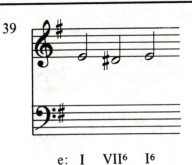

e: I VII⁶ I⁶

---

(1) passing

(2) tonic

40 Although VII⁶ most often functions as a

(1) _____ chord in the prolongation of

(2) _____ harmony, it is also used as a neighboring chord to both I and I⁶. Complete the connections below, using the smoothest correct voice leading:

close

D: I   VII⁶   I

41

D: I⁶   VII⁶   I⁶

---

42 In summary, VII⁶ is most often used as a passing chord between I and I⁶ or I⁶ and I. When voice exchange between the SB is used, the following patterns result:

$$\hat{3} \quad \hat{2} \quad \hat{1} \qquad \hat{1} \quad \hat{2} \quad \hat{3}$$
$$\text{I} \quad \text{VII}^6 \quad \text{I}^6 \qquad \text{I}^6 \quad \text{VII}^6 \quad \text{I}$$

Another common soprano pattern for both I VII⁶ I⁶ and I⁶ VII⁶ I is $\hat{1} \hat{7} \hat{1}$.

VII⁶ is sometimes used as a neighboring chord to either I or I⁶, a common soprano pattern being $\hat{1} \hat{7} \hat{1}$.

52

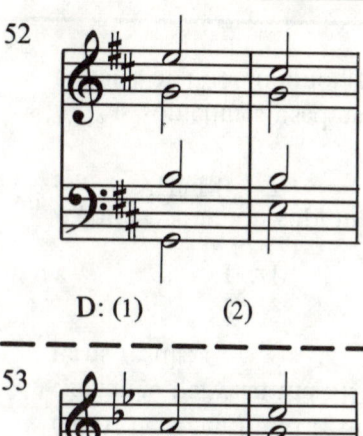

(1) II⁶

(2) VII₅⁶

D: (1)   (2)

53

(1) VII⁷

(2) II₃⁴

g: (1)   (2)

54 Using the given soprano notes, write the following for four voices. Each should be a complete 7th chord. (*Remember to follow the spacing rule of no more than an octave between SA and no more than an octave between AT.*)

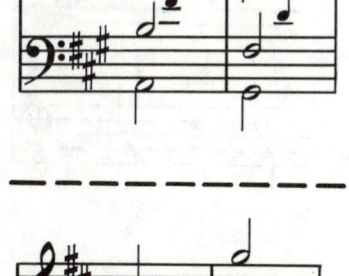

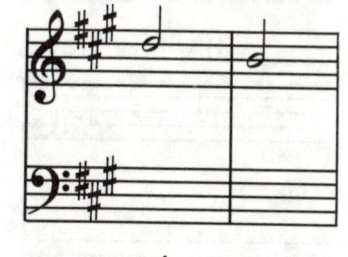

A: II₂⁴   VII⁷

55

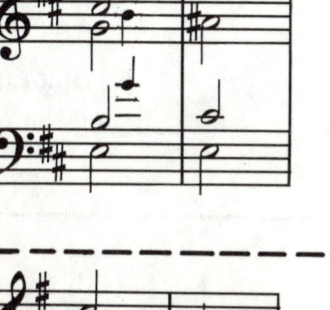

b: II₅⁶   VII₃⁴

56

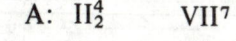

e: VII₅⁶   II₃⁴

(1) I⁶ VII⁶ I

(2) I VII⁶ I⁶ *or*

    I⁶ VII⁶ I *or*

    I VII⁶ I *or*

    I⁶ VII⁶ I⁶

(3) I VII⁶ I⁶

43 Give the chord symbols to show how each of these soprano patterns might be set in prolonging an opening tonic. (*If there is more than one correct answer for a problem, give any one.*)

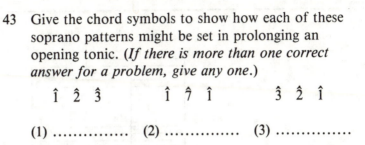

(1) ....   (2) ....   (3) ....

44 Complete the following tonic prolongation patterns as instructed, using VII⁶ as the second chord. Give the Roman numeral analysis of each. Label the VII⁶ P or N according to the function of the *bass*. (*Suggestion: Refer to the summary above as necessary, bearing in mind the soprano scale degrees in each problem.*)

Use SB voice exchange.

I   VII⁶   I⁶
     P

A:

I⁶   VII⁶   I⁶
     N

45

c:

I   VII⁶   I⁶
    P

46 close

g:

46

a: VII$^6_5$
dim

—: —
....

47

g: II$^4_3$
dim-min

—: —
....

48 Write the following chords without key signature:

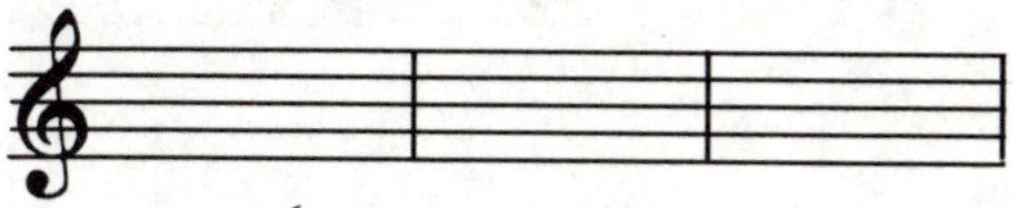

E: II$^6_5$ VII$^4_3$ VI$^6_5$

49

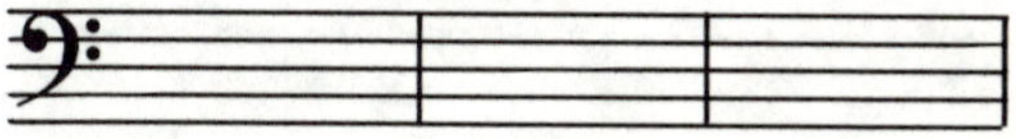

g: VII$^6_5$ II$^4_2$ IV$^4_3$

50 Write the chord symbols for the following:

(1) III^7
(2) II$^4_2$

E♭ : (1)   (2)

51

(1) IV$^6_5$
(2) VII$^4_3$

f♯: (1)   (2)

I⁶ VII⁶ I
P

47

Use SB voice exchange.

B♭ :

F: I VII⁶ I
N

48 close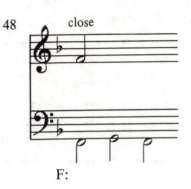

F:

Set 6 / VII⁶ AND V⁶ (2)

1 Write the Roman numeral analysis of the example below:

C:

I I⁶ V V⁶ I

Just as I⁶ prolongs I, V⁶ may be used to prolong V.

(1) VII$_3^4$
(2) II$_5^6$

39

    (1)   E: VII ___   (2)   f: II ___

40 Write the chord symbols for the following and identify the structural type of the chord. In this and the next three frames assume the major key corresponding to the key signature.

    ___: ___

A: II$_3^4$
  min

....

41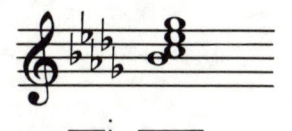

    ___: ___

D: I$_2^4$
  maj

....

42

    ___: ___

F: VII$_5^6$
  dim-min

....

43

    ___: ___

E♭: III$_3^4$
  min

....

44 In this and the next three frames assume the minor key corresponding to the key signature.

    ___: ___

b♭: II$_2^4$
  dim-min

....

45

    ___: ___

c: IV$_5^6$
  min

....

(1) voice exchange

(2) parallel 10ths

2 As with I I⁶ (and I⁶ I), typical SB patterns in V V⁶ (and V⁶ V), as illustrated in the examples below are (1) _____ _____ and (2) _____ _____.

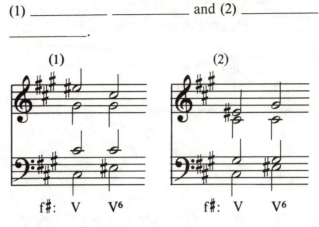

(1) neighboring

(2) prolongation

3 Although V⁶ may be used to prolong V, its most common usage is that of a neighboring chord to I. In the example below, V⁶ is a (1) _____ chord in the (2) _____ of tonic harmony.

4 Give the Roman numeral analysis of the pattern below:

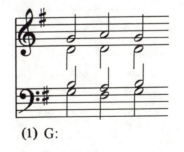

(1) G:

(1) I V⁶ I

(2) neighboring chord

The second chord is a (2) _____ _____.

dim-min

dim-min

dim

min

min

32 Write these 7th chords with key signature. Identify the structural type of each:

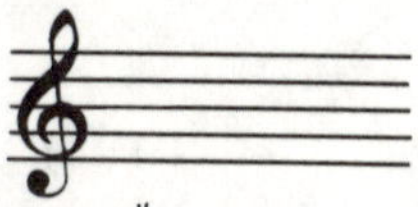

f#: II⁷

....

33

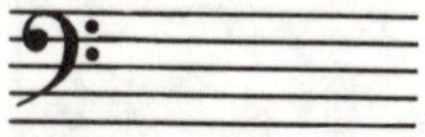

D: VII⁷

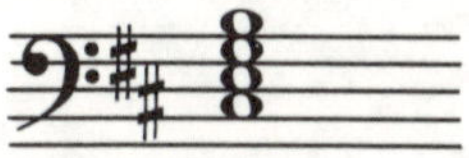

....

34

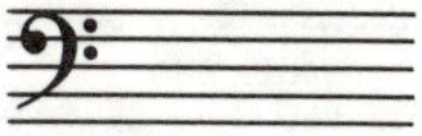

g#: VII⁷

....

35

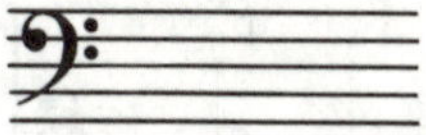

b: IV⁷

....

36

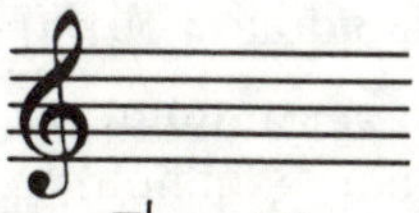

E♭: II⁷

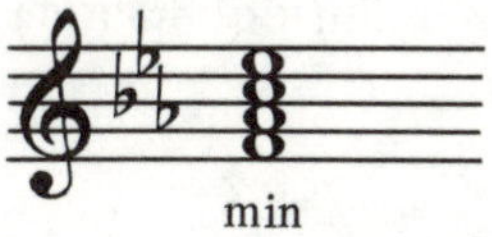

....

37 The figured bass symbols that are combined with Roman numerals to indicate inversions of 7th chords are as follows:

first inversion $\frac{6}{5}$

(1) $\frac{4}{3}$

second inversion (1) ____

(2) $\frac{4}{2}$

third inversion (2) ____

38 Complete the analysis of the chords below by adding the appropriate figured bass symbols:

(1) II$\frac{4}{2}$
(2) IV$\frac{6}{5}$

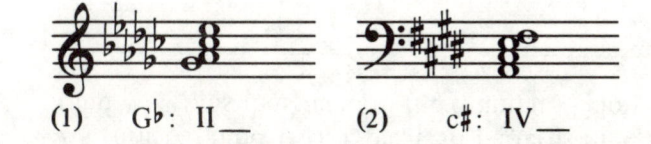

(1)   G♭: II__   (2)   c#: IV__

5 In a V^6 (as in a I^6) either the root or fifth may be doubled, depending upon which gives the smoothest voice leading. In a V^6, the bass, which is the leading tone, must never be doubled. Complete the AT, giving two possible doublings for the V^6 below:

either order

F: V⁶   V⁶

6 Soprano patterns typically found with I V^6 I are used in the problems in the following frames. Your task is to complete the inner voices, using the smoothest correct voice leading. Remember to double either the _____ or the _____ of V^6. In a particular problem choose whichever doubling of V^6 allows for the smoothest correct voice leading. (*Hint: In these problems all common tone-stepwise movement is possible.*)

root (or the) fifth

b: I   V⁶   I

7

A♭: I   V⁶   I

26 In both major and minor keys, the 7th chords, in addition to V⁷, that occur most frequently are II⁷ and VII⁷. (Typical uses of these chords will be covered in detail in the following sets.) Of the remaining diatonic 7th chords, IV⁷ is relatively common. Give the structural type of each of these diatonic 7th chords in the minor keys. (*Refer to the example in the previous frame, if necessary.*)

(1) dim-min

(2) min

(3) dim

II⁷ (1) ....

IV⁷ (2) ....

VII⁷ (3) ....

27 Given minor key and Roman numeral, write the following diatonic 7th chords with key signatures. Identify the structural type of each. (*Remember to notate the leading tone by means of an accidental in chords containing 7̂.*)

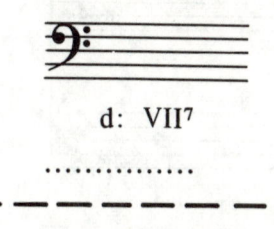

d: VII⁷

....

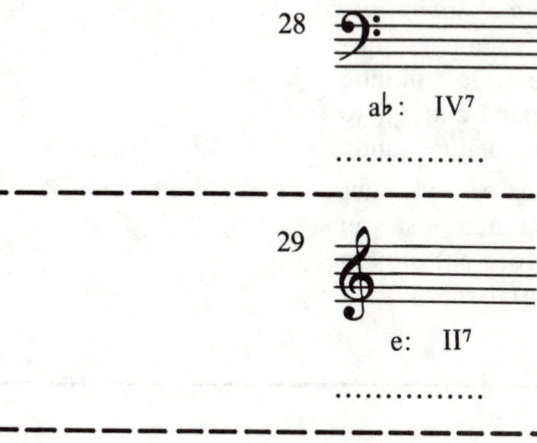

28

a♭: IV⁷

....

29

e: II⁷

....

30

c: VII⁷

....

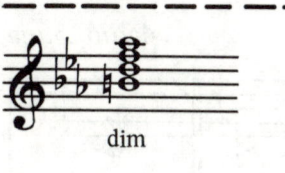

31 Give the structural type of each of the following 7th chords in major and minor keys:

(1) min   (2) dim-min

(3) maj   (4) min

(5) dim-min (6) dim

	major keys	minor keys
II⁷	(1)	(2) ....
IV⁷	(3)	(4) ....
VII⁷	(5)	(6) ....

8

close

c: I   V⁶   I

9

open

E: I   V⁶   I

10   Write the Roman numeral analysis of the pattern
below:

(1) G:

(1) I⁶ V⁶ I

The second chord is a(n) (2) _____ _____
chord in the prolongation of tonic harmony.

(2) incomplete-neighboring

11   It is almost always the case that the leap to an
incomplete-neighbor will be from the direction
opposite to the direction of its resolution, as indicated in example **x** below. Write the correct bass for
example **y**:

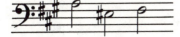

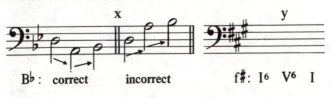

B♭: correct   incorrect   f♯: I⁶ V⁶ I

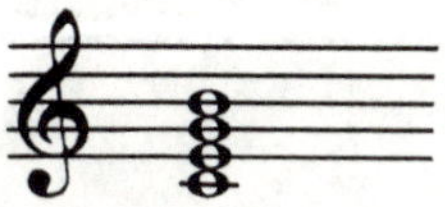

maj

20  G: IV⁷

....

dim-min

21 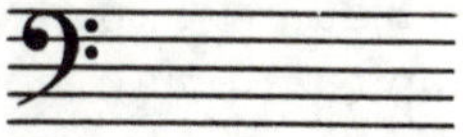 E: VII⁷

....

min

22 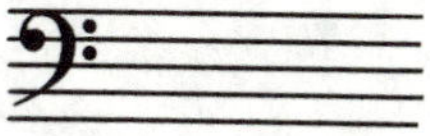 D♭: III⁷

....

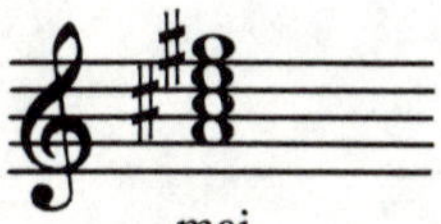

maj

23 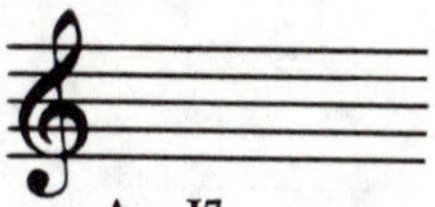 A: I⁷

....

(1) I⁷ IV⁷

(2) V⁷

(3) II⁷ III⁷ VI⁷

(4) VII⁷

24 List the diatonic 7th chords in the major keys according to structural type:

maj   (1) ....

maj-min (2) ....

min   (3) ....

dim-min (4) ....

(1) harmonic

(2) G minor

25 In minor keys, diatonic 7th chords, like diatonic triads, are derived from the (1) _____ minor scale.

Below are diatonic 7th chords in the key of

(2) ....

I⁷   II⁷   III⁷   IV⁷   V⁷   VI⁷   VII⁷

12 Complete each of the following incomplete-neighboring patterns in the smoothest correct way. (*Hint: It is not possible to have all common tone-stepwise voice leading in the AT of these problems. Connect I⁶ to V⁶ in the smoothest correct way, and then V⁶ and I, being sure to use correct doubling and spacing in I.*)

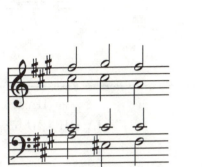

f♯: I⁶ V⁶ I

13

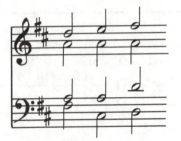

D: I⁶ V⁶ I

14

B♭: I⁶ V⁶ I

(1) bass

(2) I

15 The reverse of I⁶ V⁶ I, I V⁶ I⁶, does not normally occur. The leading tone, which is in the

(1) _____ (*voice*) of V⁶, must resolve to Î when it is in an outer voice. Therefore, V⁶ will always be followed by (2) ____.

16 The following tonic prolongation patterns have been studied thus far:

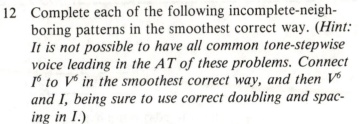

I I⁶   I⁶ I
I VII⁶ I⁶   I⁶ VII⁶ I   I VII⁶ I   I⁶ VII⁶ I⁶
I V⁶ I   I⁶ V⁶ I

prolong

These patterns may be used to _____ the opening tonic in a basic harmonic progression.

14 Construct the indicated structural types of 7th chords, using C as the root in each case:

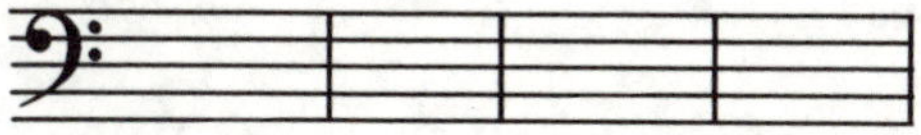

dim   maj   dim-min   min

15 Construct the indicated structural types of 7th chords, using F♯ as the root:

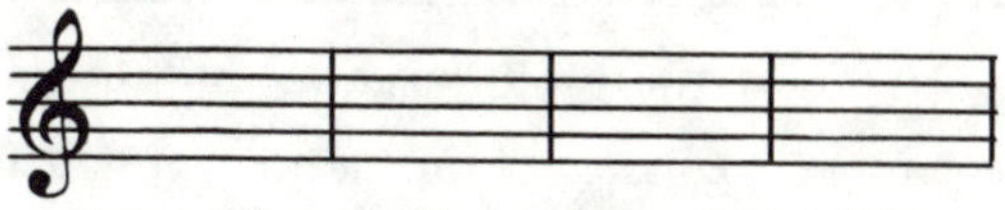

maj   min   dim -min   dim

I⁷   II⁷   III⁷   IV⁷
maj min   min   maj

V⁷   VI⁷   VII⁷
maj-min min   dim-min

16 Below are the diatonic 7th chords in the key of D major. Label the structural type of each:

D: I⁷   II⁷   III⁷   IV⁷   V⁷   VI⁷   VII⁷

....

17 Write the diatonic 7th chords in the key of B♭ major without using a key signature. Label the structural type of each:

B♭: I⁷   II⁷   III⁷   IV⁷   V⁷   VI⁷   VII⁷
    maj   min   min   maj   maj-min min dim-min

B♭ : I⁷   II⁷   III⁷   IV⁷   V⁷   VI⁷   VII⁷

....

18 In major keys the structural types of diatonic 7th chords are as follows:

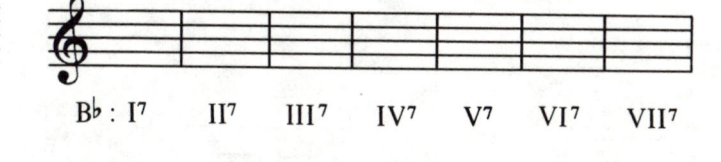

maj   I⁷   IV⁷
maj-min (1) ____
min   (2) II⁷   ____ ____
dim-min (3) ____

(1) V⁷
(2) (II⁷) III⁷ VI⁷
(3) VII⁷

19 Given major key and Roman numeral, write the following 7th chords without key signatures. Identify the structural type of each:

F: II⁷

....

min

17 The following are the doubling rules for the tonic prolongation patterns listed above:

(1) root (*or* bass)

(2) third (*or* bass)

(3) root (or the) fifth

I — Double the (1) _____.

VII⁶ — Double the (2) _____.

I⁶ and V⁶ — Double the (3) _____ or the
_____, whichever gives the smoothest correct voice leading. Do not double the third (the bass note).

---

(1) voice exchange (and) parallel 10ths

18 In I I⁶ (and I⁶ I) typical SB patterns are

(1) _____ _____ and _____
_____.

In I VII⁶ I⁶ (and I⁶ VII⁶ I) the common SB pattern is

(2) voice exchange

(2) _____ _____.

---

(1) P

(2) N

(3) N ⎱ *either*
(4) IN ⎰ *order*

19 VII⁶ most frequently occurs as a(n) (1) ____ (P, N, or IN) chord in prolonging tonic, though it may also function as a(n) (2) ____ chord.

In the prolongation of tonic harmony, V⁶ may function as either a(n) (3) ____ chord or a(n) (4) ____ chord.

---

(1) tonic

(2) tonic

20 Basic harmonic progressions consist of the movement from an opening (1) _____, which is often prolonged, to a pre-dominant, followed by a root position dominant, and then to a closing

(2) _____.

---

(1) prolongation

(2) closing

21 The function of VII⁶ and V⁶ is very different from the function of V and V⁷. VII⁶ and V⁶ are used as P, N, or IN chords in the (1) _____ of opening tonic harmony. The function of root position V and V⁷ is to lead to the (2) _____ tonic in a harmonic progression.

---

22 Give the Roman numeral analysis of the following:

B♭: I VII⁶ I⁶ IV V I

min

6   This is a .... 7th chord.

dim

7 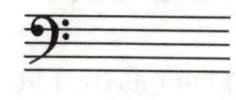   This is a .... 7th chord.

8   Label the structural types of the following 7th chords, using contractions where possible. Remember first to identify the structural type of triad, then the structural type of 7th.

(1) min
(2) dim
(3) maj-min
(4) dim-min

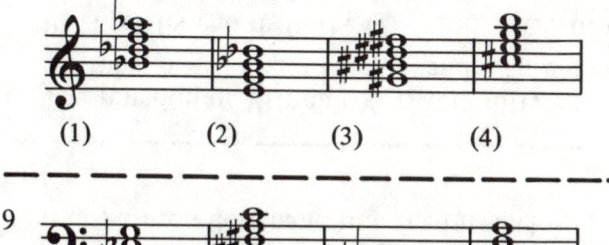

  (1)   (2)   (3)   (4)

(1) maj
(2) dim
(3) min
(4) dim-min

9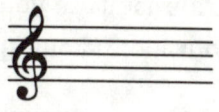

  (1)   (2)   (3)   (4)

10   Write a dim-min 7th chord having a root of F♯:

11   Write a maj 7th chord having a root of D♭:

12   Write a min 7th chord having a root of G:

13   Write the 7th chords as indicated, using the given note as root:

     min   dim-min maj   dim

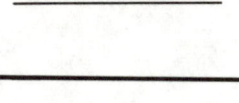

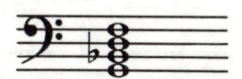

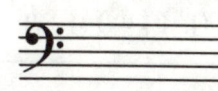

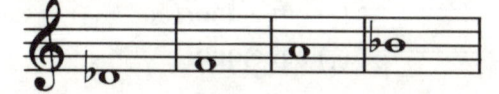

23 The bracket and Roman numeral under the first three chord symbols below indicate that they are a

(1) prolongation

(1) _____ of tonic harmony.

$$\underbrace{\text{I } \text{VII}^6 \text{ I}^6}_{\text{I}} \text{ IV V I}$$

Indicate in similar fashion the tonic prolongation in the following:

$$\text{I}^6 \text{ V}^6 \text{ I II } \text{V}^7 \text{ I}$$

(2)

(2) $\underbrace{\text{I}^6 \text{ V}^6 \text{ I}}_{\text{I}}$

24 Write the Roman numeral analysis of the following. Bracket and label the prolongation of opening tonic as in the previous frame.

f♯: $\underbrace{\text{I } \text{V}^6 \text{ I}}_{\text{I}} \text{ II}^6 \text{ V I}$

25 (*Note that the F♯ accidental, which occurs in measures 1 and 2 in the same octave, is repeated. Accidentals remain in effect only during the measure in which they appear.*)

g: $\underbrace{\text{I } \text{VII}^6 \text{ I}^6}_{\text{I}} \text{ IV } \text{V}^7 \text{ I}$

1 As there are different structural types of triads, there are different structural types of 7th chords. There are two parts to the full name used in describing the structural type of a 7th chord. The first part of the name refers to the type of triad formed by the root, third, and fifth. The second part refers to the kind of 7th between the root and seventh.

The structural type of a V^7 is major-minor. In this name, *major* refers to the structural type of the

(1) triad

(2) 7th

(1) _____ formed by the root, third, and fifth; *minor* refers to the kind of (2) ____ formed by the root and seventh. (*See example below, if necessary.*)

2 The 7th chord below is composed of a

(1) dim

(2) min

(3) dim-min

(1) _____ triad and a (2) _____ 7th. The structural type is (3) _____-_____.

3 This 7th chord is composed of a (1) _____ triad and a (2) _____ 7th. The structural type is (3) _____-_____.

(1) min

(2) min

(3) min-min

4 When both the triad and the 7th have the same label, as in the case of *min-min* or *maj-maj* or *dim-dim*, the name for the structural type of the 7th chord is usually contracted to min 7th, maj 7th, or dim 7th. From now on we will use only the short forms of these names. The term *min 7th chord* refers to a 7th chord composed of a (1) _____ triad and a (2) _____ 7th.

(1) min

(2) min

5 This 7th chord is composed of a (1) _____ triad and a (2) _____ 7th. The label for the structural type is (3) .... 7th chord.

(1) maj

(2) maj

(3) maj

26 The following problems involve writing harmonic progressions in which the opening tonic is

_____ before leading to the pre-dominant, then to the dominant, and finally to the closing tonic. (Before you begin these problems, you may wish to review material previously covered by referring to the *Summary of Chord Usage and Voice Leading*, beginning on page 151.)

Based upon the chord vocabulary and voice leading procedures studied thus far, complete each progression. First determine the chords to be used and give the Roman numeral analysis; then write the missing voices. Bracket and label the prolongation of opening tonic.

prolonged

I V⁶ I II⁶ V⁽⁷⁾ I
I

G:

---

27 Use SB voice exchange.

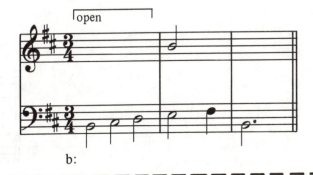

I VII⁶ I⁶ IV V⁽⁷⁾ I
I

open

b:

---

28 Use SB voice exchange.

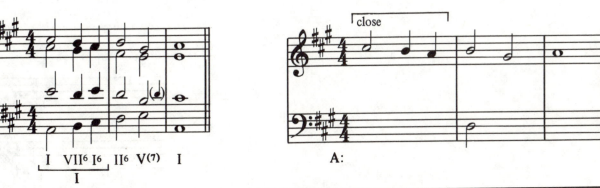

I VII⁶ I⁶ II⁶ V⁽⁷⁾ I
I

close

A:

5.

c#: I   I⁶   I⁶₄

. . . .

6. *Give the Roman numeral analysis.*

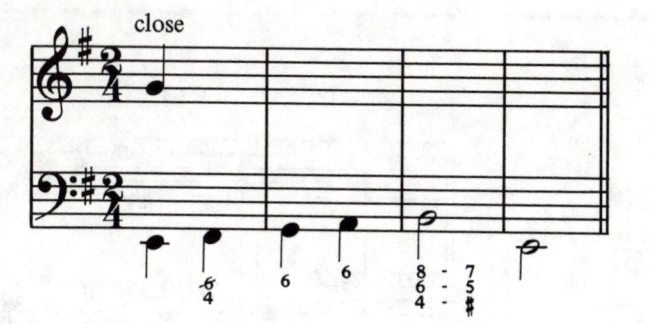

. . . .

29 Give the Roman numeral analysis of the following figured bass:

(1)

In this example the ♯ (under the bass note in the second measure) refers to the (2) _____ tone, which, in minor keys, must be indicated, in both the figured bass and on the staff, by means of an accidental.

(1) g: I I⁶ II⁶ V I

(2) leading

---

30 In each of the examples below the ♮ indicates the alteration of the (1) ____ (*general interval*) above the bass from B♭ to (2) ____.

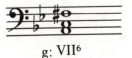

(1) 3rd
(2) B♮

---

31 Given a figured bass in a minor key, any chord containing the leading tone above the bass will have this accidental indicated in the figures. In a VII⁶ the leading tone is the ____ (*general interval*) above the bass. (*See example below, if necessary.*) Thus, the figured bass for a VII⁶ in a minor key must show that the 6th above the bass is altered.

g: VII⁶

6th

---

32 The alteration of the 6th above the bass is indicated by a modification of the figure 6. For example, ♯6 (example **x**) means that the 6th above the bass is modified by a sharp; that is, D is altered to (1) ____. ♮6 (example **y**) means that the 6th above the bass is modified by a (2) _____; that is, (3) ____ is altered to (4) ____.

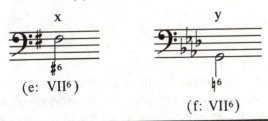

(e: VII⁶)   (f: VII⁶)

(1) D♯
(2) natural
(3) E♭
(4) E♮

The questions below will test your mastery of the material in Part 5. Complete the entire test, then check your answers with the correct ones on page 169. For each question that you miss, the corresponding material may be reviewed in the set whose number is given with the correct answer.

1. Name the harmony prolonged by each chord succession:

I I_4^6 I^6 (1) _____

I V_4^6 I^6 (2) _____

V$\binom{6-5}{4-3}$ (3) _____

I IV_4^6 I   (4) _____

Complete the following problems for four voices. Identify the types of all $^6_4$ chords.

2.

A♭:   I   IV   V($^6_4$: $^5_3$)   I

. . . .

3. *Use a neighboring soprano.*

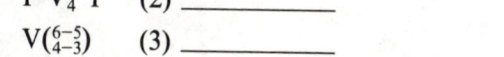

f: I   IV$_4^6$ I

. . . .

4.

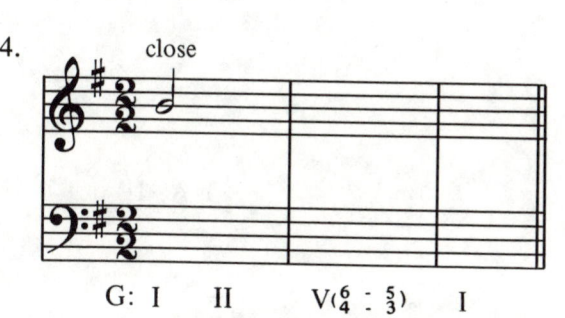

G: I   II   V($^6_4$: $^5_3$)   I

. . . .

33 In both of the examples in the previous frame, the 6th above the bass was *raised*. Another way that these basses might be figured is shown below:

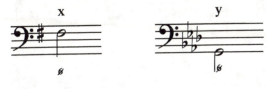

A slash through the 6 (ϕ) means that the 6th above the bass is to be _____.

raised

---

(1) 6th
(2) raised

34 In each example below the (1) _____ above the bass is to be (2) _____. Give the Roman numeral analysis of each:

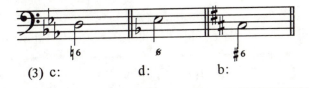

(3) c: VII⁶   d: VII⁶   b: VII⁶

(3) c: d: b:

---

35 Give the Roman numeral analysis of the figured bass below:

f: I VII⁶ I⁶ IV V⁷ I

_____:

OR

36 Set this figured bass for four voices. Use a typical SB pattern in prolonging the opening tonic.

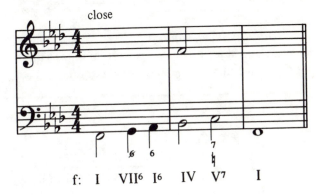

f: I   VII⁶   I⁶   IV   V⁷   I

36 Write the following connection. (*Be sure to use the smoothest correct voice leading and correct doubling in all chords.*)

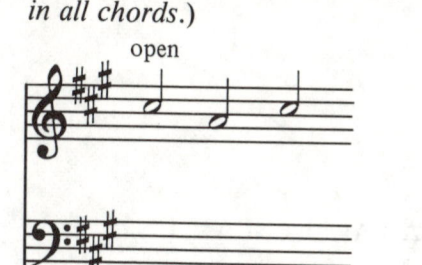

f#:   I   I$^6_4$ I^6

37 Set the figured bass below. First provide the Roman numeral analysis. Bracket and label the tonic prolongation.   *Use the typical soprano.*

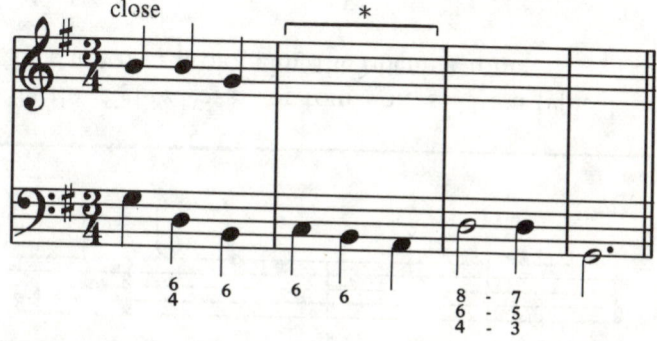

G: I I$^6_4$ I^6 II^6 I^6 II V$\binom{8\text{-}7}{6\text{-}5}_{4\text{-}3}$ I

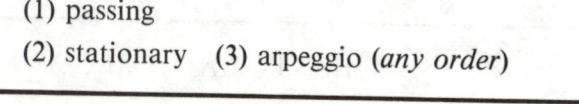

I

(1) passing

(2) stationary   (3) arpeggio (*any order*)

38 In summary, the types of $^6_4$ chord that are typically used to prolong tonic are the (1) _____ $^6_4$, the (2) _____ $^6_4$, and the (3) _____ $^6_4$.

39 Fill in the chord symbols, illustrating a typical usage of each $^6_4$. Label the $^6_4$ according to type.

(1) I IV$^6_4$ I   (2) stationary

(3) I I$^6_4$ I^6 (*or* I^6 I$^6_4$ I)   (4) arpeggio

(5) I V$^6_4$ I^6 (*or* I^6 V$^6_4$ I)   (6) passing

(1) ____ IV$^6_4$ ____   (2) _____ (*type*)

(3) ____ I$^6_4$ ____   (4) _____

(5) ____ V$^6_4$ ____   (6) _____

40 Give the Roman numeral analysis of the following and identify the type of each $^6_4$ chord:

F: I I$^6_4$ I^6 I | V$^6_5$ I V$^6_4$ I^6 |
      (1)   (2)
  IV II V$\binom{6-5}{4-3}$ | I IV$^6_4$ | I ‖
         (3)   (4)

(1) arpeggio $^6_4$ (2) passing $^6_4$
(3) cadential $^6_4$ (4) stationary $^6_4$

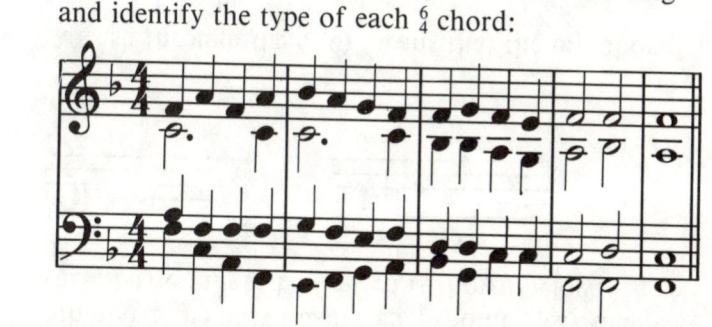

1   Figured bass symbols have two somewhat different uses:

    1. They are used in combination with Roman numerals in labeling chords, that is, as part of a Roman numeral analysis.

    2. They may occur with a bass line, showing the specific chords to be used in setting a figured bass.

We will begin this set by covering the figured bass symbols that apply to inversions of 7th chords. (Ways in which the figured bass symbols are altered, when they are part of a figured bass to be set, to indicate the leading tone in minor will be dealt with in the next set.)

Figured bass symbols are used to indicate inversions of 7th chords. As with triads, the numbers refer to intervals above the _____ (*voice*).

bass

---

2   A 7th chord in first inversion, like a triad in first inversion, has the _____ (*chord member*) in the bass. The complete figured bass for a 7th chord in first inversion is $\frac{6}{5}$, abbreviated $\frac{6}{5}$.

third

---

3   A 7th chord in second inversion, like a triad in second inversion has the _____ (*chord member*) in the bass. The complete figured bass for a 7th chord in second inversion is $\frac{6}{4}$, abbreviated $\frac{4}{3}$.

fifth

---

4   The abbreviated figured bass for a first inversion 7th chord is (1) ____, for a second inversion 7th chord is (2) ____.

(1) $\frac{6}{5}$
(2) $\frac{4}{3}$

---

5   A 7th chord in third inversion has the _____ (*chord member*) in the bass. The complete figured bass is $\frac{6}{4}$, abbreviated $\frac{4}{2}$.

seventh

(1) V$^6_4$

(2) IV$^6_4$

30 The passing $^6_4$ that prolongs tonic harmony is (1) _____ (*chord symbol*). The stationary $^6_4$ that prolongs tonic harmony is (2) _____.

---

active

31 Both the passing and the stationary $^6_4$ chords contain _____ tones which lead away from and back to the stable tones of tonic.

---

32 The final type of $^6_4$ chord that we will deal with is different in that it contains no active tones.

Just as I^6 can prolong tonic harmony by repeating chord tones in a different position, so can I$^6_4$. Give the Roman numeral analysis of the example below:

B♭: I I^6 I$^6_4$ | IV II^6 | V$^{8-7}$ | I ‖

---

bass

33 Notice, in the previous frame, that the bass of I I^6 I$^6_4$ outlines the I chord. A broken chord such as this is called an *arpeggio*, and the bass is said to be arpeggiated. The I$^6_4$ is, therefore, referred to as an *arpeggio* $^6_4$, because of the arpeggiated _____. It is composed entirely of the stable tones of the tonic triad.

---

(1) I^6

(2) I$^6_4$

(3) arpeggio

34 Tonic harmony is often prolonged by its first inversion, (1) _____ (*chord symbol*), and may also be prolonged by its second inversion, (2) _____, which is called a(n) (3) _____ $^6_4$.

---

bass

35 Provide the AT, using the smoothest correct voice leading. Remember to double the _____ (*voice*) of the $^6_4$ chord.

E♭: I   I^6 I$^6_4$

---

6 The abbreviated figured bass symbols for inversions of 7th chords are as follows:

(1) $^6_5$

(2) $^4_3$

(3) $^4_2$

first inversion (1) _____

second inversion (2) _____

third inversion (3) _____

7 Add the abbreviated figured bass to the given Roman numeral for each of these V⁷ chords in inversion:

(1) $^4_2$

(2) $^6_5$

(3) $^6_5$

(4) $^4_3$

(1) E♭: V____ (2) b: V____ (3) F: V____ (4) g: V____

8

(1) $^4_3$

(2) $^4_2$

(3) $^4_3$

(4) $^6_5$

(1) B♭: V ____   (2) C: V ____   (3) e: V ____   (4) a: V ____

9 Write these 7th chords with the notes as close together as possible:

D: V^4_2 g: V^6_5 a: V^4_3

10

f#: V^4_3 c: V^4_2 A: V^6_5

11 Complete these 7th chords for SATB. Remember to follow the spacing rule of no more than an octave between SA and no more than an octave between AT.

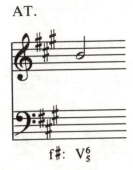

f#: V^6_5

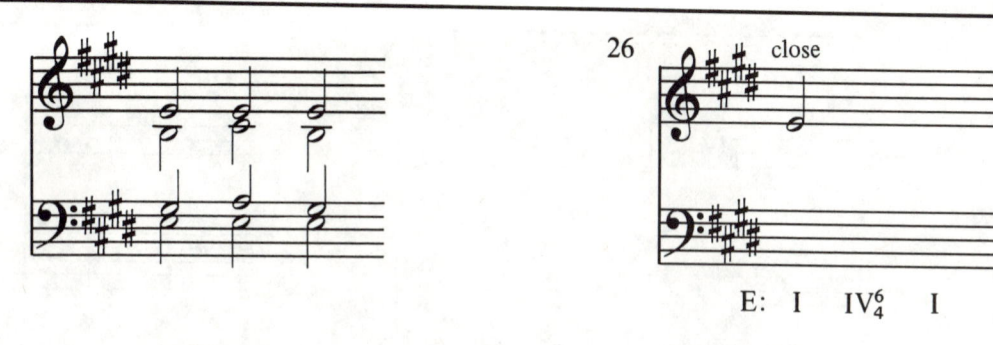

26

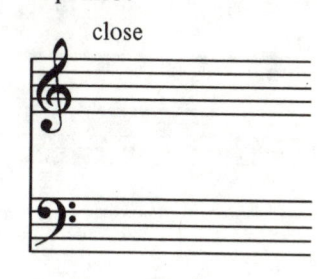

E: I   IV$^6_4$ I

OR

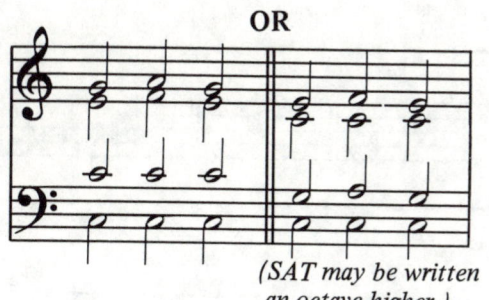

(SAT may be written an octave higher.)

27 Write each of the following with a neighboring soprano:

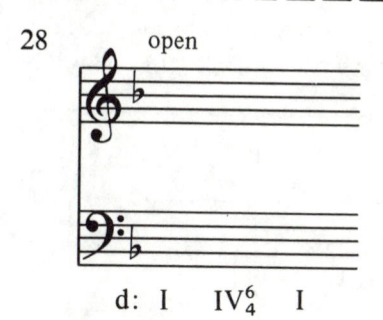

C: I   IV$^6_4$ I

OR

(SAT may be written an octave higher.)

28

d: I   IV$^6_4$ I

29 IV$^6_4$ may be used to prolong opening tonic and may also be used to prolong closing tonic in a way similar to a plagal cadence. Set the following figured bass. First give the Roman numeral analysis. Bracket and label each prolongation of tonic.

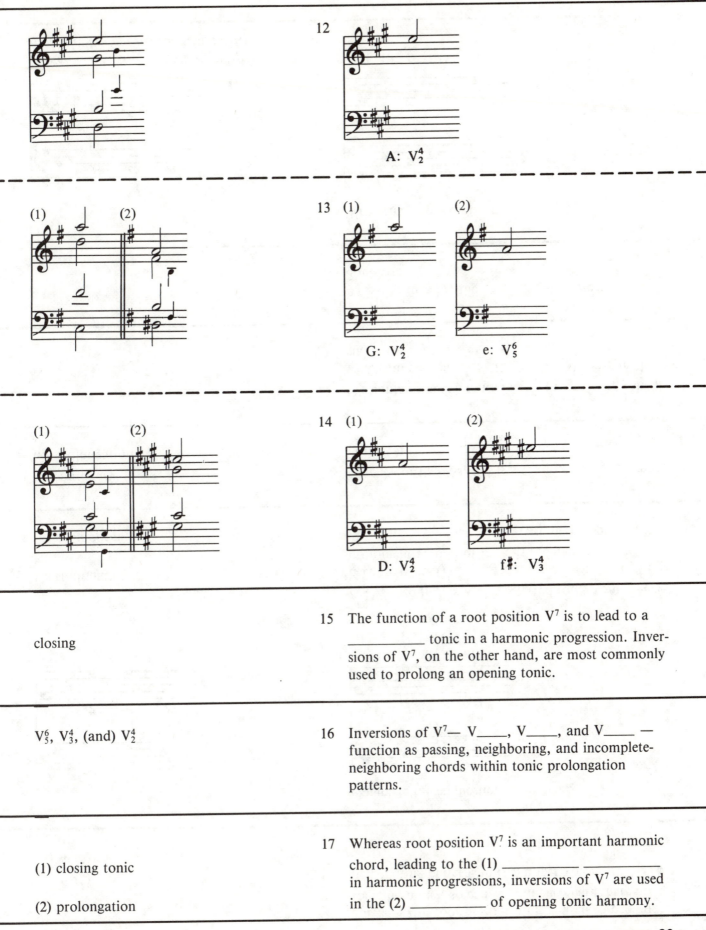

12   A: V_2^4

13 (1) G: V_2^4 (2) e: V_5^6

14 (1) D: V_2^4 (2) f#: V_3^4

closing	**15** The function of a root position V^7 is to lead to a _____ tonic in a harmonic progression. Inversions of V^7, on the other hand, are most commonly used to prolong an opening tonic.
V_5^6, V_3^4, (and) V_2^4	**16** Inversions of V^7— V____, V____, and V____ — function as passing, neighboring, and incomplete-neighboring chords within tonic prolongation patterns.
(1) closing tonic (2) prolongation	**17** Whereas root position V^7 is an important harmonic chord, leading to the (1) _____ _____ in harmonic progressions, inversions of V^7 are used in the (2) _____ of opening tonic harmony.

20 Just as IV in root position can be used to prolong tonic harmony, so can IV$^6_4$. In each case there are neighboring patterns in two upper voices: $\hat{5}$ _____ $\hat{5}$

$(\hat{5})\ \hat{6}\ (\hat{5})$
$(\hat{3})\ \hat{4}\ (\hat{3})$

$\hat{3}$ _____ $\hat{3}$

(1) stationary

(2) neighboring

21 Complete the connection:

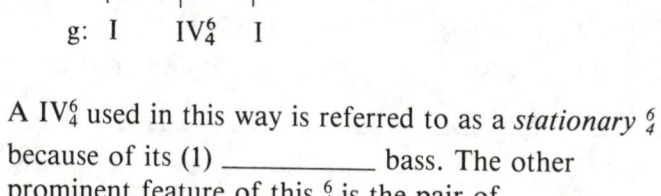

g: I IV$^6_4$ I

A IV$^6_4$ used in this way is referred to as a *stationary* $^6_4$ because of its (1) _____ bass. The other prominent feature of this $^6_4$ is the pair of
(2) _____ patterns in two of the upper voices.

---

(1) stationary

(2) prolongation

22 Named for its bass, IV$^6_4$ is a (1) _____ $^6_4$ chord in the (2) _____ of tonic harmony.

N

23 IV$^6_4$ contains active tones in two of its upper voices, which function as ____ (P, N, *or* IN) tones to the stable tones of I.

---

bass

24 As with other $^6_4$'s, the _____ (*voice*) of IV$^6_4$ is doubled.

---

25 Write these connections:

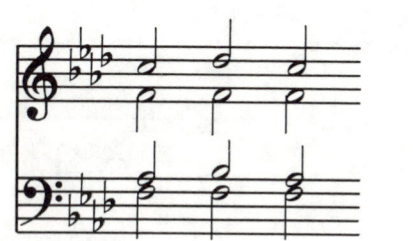

(Note: *The bass of a stationary* $^6_4$ *pattern may be repeated or sustained.*)

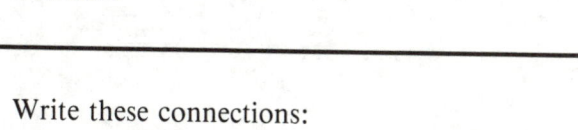

f: I IV$^6_4$ I

18 Give the Roman numeral analysis of the pattern below:

(1) B♭ :

(1) I V$_3^4$ I⁶

The second chord functions as a (2) _____

(2) passing chord

_____ between I and I⁶.

19 Write the Roman numeral analysis of this pattern:

(1) G:

(1) I V$_5^6$ I

The second chord functions as a (2) _____

(2) neighboring chord

_____ to I.

20 Give the Roman numeral analysis:

(1) c:

(1) I V$_2^4$ I⁶

The second chord functions as an (2) _____

(2) incomplete-neighboring

_____ chord.

(1) passing

(2) tonic

(3) voice exchange

16 In summary, the use of V_4^6 is very similar to that of VII^6, though V_4^6 occurs much less frequently in music than does VII^6. Both occur as (1) _____ chords in the prolongation of (2) _____ harmony. A typical SB pattern for both I VII^6 I^6 (or I^6 VII^6 I) and I V_4^6 I^6 (or I^6 V_4^6 I) is (3) _____ _____. Another common soprano for both is $\hat{1}$ $\hat{7}$ $\hat{1}$.

17 Set each figured bass. Provide the Roman numeral analysis, and bracket and label the prolongation of opening tonic.

18 *Use the typical soprano. (Note: Although the given AT in II^6 do not provide the smoothest connection of I^6 II^6, this voice leading is necessary in order to avoid faulty voice leading in subsequent chords.)*

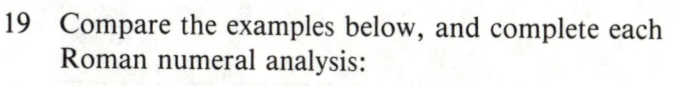

19 Compare the examples below, and complete each Roman numeral analysis:

(1) IV

(2) IV_4^6

21 For the following patterns give the Roman numeral analysis and label with P, N, or IN the function of the inversion of V^7:

g: (1)　　　　　　　(2)

(1) I^6 V^6_5 I
　　　IN

(2) I V^4_3 I^6
　　　P

22

F: (1)　　　　　　　(2)

(1) I V^4_2 I^6
　　　IN

(2) I V^6_5 I
　　　N

---

23 There are two active tones in V^7 (and its inversions):

$\hat{7}$, the leading tone, which if in S or B must resolve to (1) _____ (*scale degree*), and

$\hat{4}$, the seventh of the chord, which must resolve down by step to (2) _____.

(1) $\hat{1}$

(2) $\hat{3}$

---

24 Unlike V^7, which may be complete or incomplete, inversions of V^7 are always complete chords, having a root, _____, _____, and _____. They almost always lead to complete I or I^6 chords.

third, fifth, (and) seventh

---

25 V^6_5 and V^6 are both (1) _____ inversion chords, having the leading tone, (2) _____ (*scale degree*), in the bass.

(1) first

(2) $\hat{7}$

---

26 Because of the strong resolution tendency of $\hat{7}$ to (1) _____, V^6_5 and V^6 are always followed by (2) _____.

(1) $\hat{1}$

(2) I

(SAT may be written an octave higher.)

12 Write the following for four voices, using SB voice exchange:

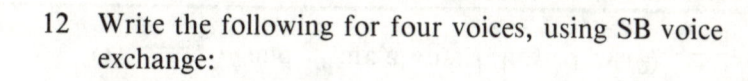

D: I V_4^6 I^6

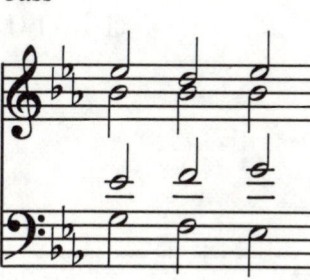

13

open

c: I V_4^6 I^6

bass

14 V_4^6 is also used as a passing chord between I and I^6 (or I^6 and I) with the soprano $\hat{1}$ $\hat{7}$ $\hat{1}$. Complete the following using the smoothest correct voice leading. Remember to double the _____ (*voice*) of V_4^6.

E♭: I^6 V_4^6 I

15

close

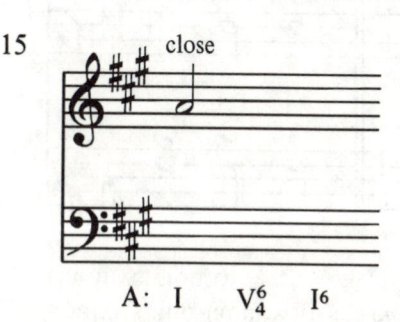

A: I V_4^6 I^6

N

27 As is illustrated in this example, V^6_5, like V^6, most commonly occurs as a(n) _____ (P, N, *or* IN) chord to I.

F:

down

28 There are a number of soprano patterns (which are themselves P, N, or IN patterns) that may occur with I V^6_5 I. The following frames contain problems using some of the most typical soprano lines.

Remember, in completing these and subsequent connections, to fill in the AT in the smoothest correct way. (You will find that common tone-stepwise voice leading is often possible.) Be sure to check for correct doubling in the I chords and for the presence of all chord tones in the V^6_5, and be certain to resolve the seventh of V^7, $\hat{4}$, _____ by step.

G: I V^6_5 I

29

d: I V^6_5 I

voice exchange

(*Soprano may be written an octave higher*.)

7   As is the case with I VII^6 I^6, a typical SB pattern with I V$^6_4$ I^6 is _____ _____. Write the soprano illustrating this typical pattern:

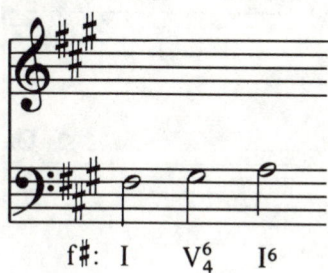

f♯: I   V$^6_4$ I^6

V$^6_4$

8   The usual procedure for $\frac{6}{4}$ chords, *no matter what their usage*, is to double the bass. This doubling occurs automatically in a ____ (*chord symbol*) connecting the voice exchange of I I^6 (or I^6 I).

9   Write the SB, using voice exchange:

g: I^6 V$^6_4$ I

D (and) F♯

10   In the example below, the notes to be added in the AT of V$^6_4$ are ____ and ____. Complete the AT using common tone-stepwise voice leading.

g: I^6 V$^6_4$ I

---

(1) passing

(2) tonic

(3) bass

11   V$^6_4$ is typically used as a (1) _____ chord in the prolongation of (2) _____ harmony. As is the case with all $\frac{6}{4}$ chords, the (3) _____ (*voice*) is doubled.

30

close

c: I V_5^6 I

31   (*Note: Common tone-stepwise voice leading in all voices is not possible.*)

open

E♭:   I V_5^6 I

32   (*Reminder: Give the smoothest possible solution.*)

open

D: I V_5^6 I

(1) N

(2) tonic

(3) IN

33   V_5^6 is most commonly used as a(n) (1) _____ (P, N, *or* IN) chord in the prolongation of (2) _____ harmony. As illustrated in the example below, V_5^6 may also be used as a(n) (3) _____ (P, N, *or* IN) chord.

F: I⁶ V_5^6 I

second

3 In the previous frame the label for the passing $^6_4$ which connects I and I^6 is V$^6_4$; it is a _____ (first *or* second) inversion dominant triad. Note that this label has a very different meaning from the label V($^{6-5}_{4-3}$). While the label for a cadential $^6_4$ differs from the usual convention, the labels for the $^6_4$ chords that prolong tonic follow the procedure we have employed with all $^5_3$ and $^6_4$ chords.

4 Give the Roman numeral analysis of the following:

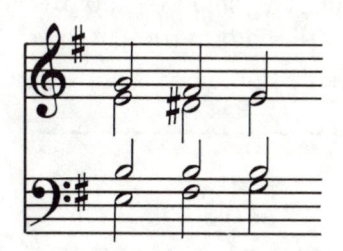

(1) I V$^6_4$ I^6

(1) e:

The second chord contains active tones that lead

(2) stable

from the (2) _____ (active *or* stable) tones of

(3) stable

I to the (3) _____ tones of I^6. Because of the passing function of the *bass*, this chord is referred

(4) passing

to as a (4) _____ $^6_4$ chord.

5 Write the Roman numeral analysis of the examples below. (The second chord is different in each case.)

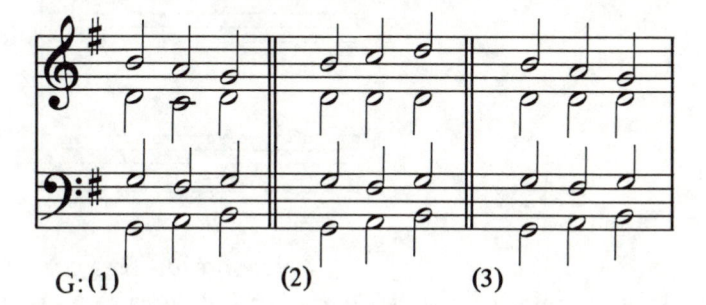

G:(1)   (2)   (3)

(1) I VII^6 I^6
(2) I V$^4_3$ I^6
(3) I V$^6_4$ I^6

(4) passing

The second chord of each is a (4) _____ chord connecting I with I^6.

6 VII^6 and V$^4_3$ are much more commonly used as passing chords between I and I^6 (or I^6 and I) than is V$^6_4$. A typical SB pattern in I VII^6 I^6 is

(1) voice exchange

(1) _____ _____; a typical SB pattern

(2) parallel 10ths

in I V$^4_3$ I^6 is (2) _____ _____.

y

34   Which of the two bass patterns below is correct?
_____

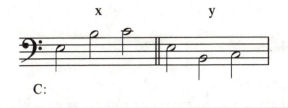

C:

opposite

35   In relation to the direction of its resolution, the leap to an IN should be from the _____ (same *or* opposite) direction.

36   Complete the I⁶ V⁶₅ I connections below:

A: I⁶   V⁶₅   I

37

E♭:   I⁶   V⁶₅   I

2̂

38   V⁴₃ and VII⁶ both have ____ (*scale degree*) in the bass. Like VII⁶, V⁴₃ most commonly functions as a passing chord between I and I⁶.

39   Although I V⁴₃ I⁶ and I VII⁶ I⁶ share the same bass movement, there are differences in the upper voice patterns that occur with them. The most common usage of VII⁶ is as a P chord with _____
voice exchange
_____ in SB. Complete this connection:

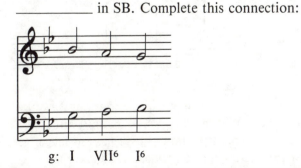

g: I   VII⁶   I⁶

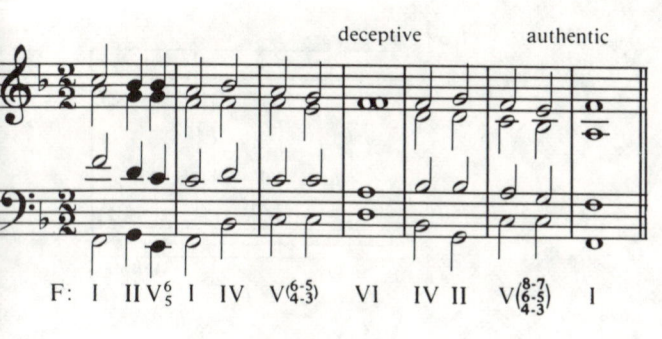

F: I   II V$^6_5$ I IV V$\left(^{6\text{-}5}_{4\text{-}3}\right)$ VI IV II V$\left(^{8\text{-}7}_{^{6\text{-}5}_{4\text{-}3}}\right)$ I

52 A cadential $^6_4$ may occur at a half or deceptive cadence, as well as at an authentic cadence. Set the following figured bass. Provide the Roman numeral analysis and label each cadence.

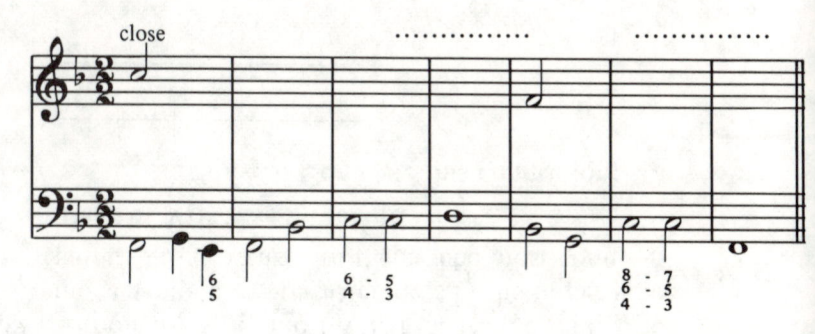

Set 18 / $^6_4$ CHORDS IN TONIC PROLONGATION

1 The cadential $^6_4$, which is by far the most common $^6_4$ chord, prolongs _____ harmony.

There are three types of $^6_4$ chord that are typically used to prolong *tonic* harmony: the *passing* $^6_4$, the *stationary* $^6_4$, and the *arpeggio* $^6_4$. We will consider each in turn.

dominant

2 Study the examples below. In example **x**, I and I⁶ are connected by means of a passing $^6_3$ chord. In example **y**, I and I⁶ are connected by means of a _____ $^6_4$ chord. Observe that the two passing chords differ in only one note (which is circled).

passing

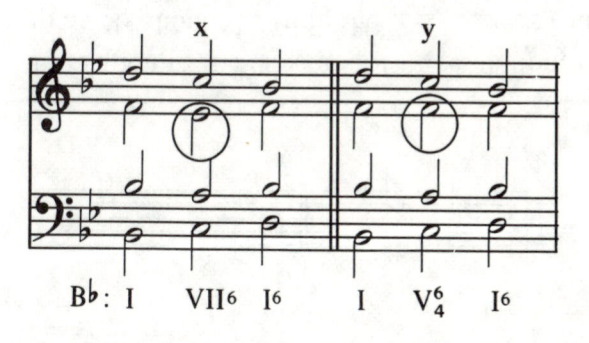

B♭: I   VII⁶ I⁶   I V$^6_4$ I⁶

10ths

40 V_3^4, which must have all chord members present, obviously can not be used when the given SB result in a doubled $\hat{2}$, as in the example in the previous frame. The idiomatic usage of V_3^4 is shown in the example below. The relation between SB is parallel _____.

g: I V_3^4 I⁶

---

(1) P (passing)

(2) voice exchange

(3) parallel 10ths

41 VII⁶ and V_3^4 are primarily used as (1) _____ chords between I and I⁶. VII⁶ is typically used with a (2) _____ _____ pattern in SB. V_3^4 is typically used with a (3) _____ _____ pattern in SB.

---

(1) soprano
(2) $\hat{5}$

42 I V_3^4 I⁶ with SB parallel 10ths contains an exception to the rule that the seventh of V⁷ must resolve down by step. Note that the seventh in the V_3^4, $\hat{4}$, in the (1) _____ voice, goes up to (2) _____, rather than down to $\hat{3}$. (The likely reason for this idiomatic usage is that the resolution of $\hat{4}$ is heard prominently in the bass of I⁶, which is $\hat{3}$.)

g: I V_3^4 I⁶

$\hat{3}$

43 The nonresolution of the seventh of V⁷, the movement of $\hat{4}$ to $\hat{5}$ rather than $\hat{4}$ to $\hat{3}$, is permissible *only* in the succession I V_3^4 I⁶. In all other cases, you must continue to resolve the seventh of V⁷, $\hat{4}$, down by step to _____.

48 Set each figured bass below. First give the Roman numeral analysis. *Where indicated by *, take care to use the typical soprano.*

d: I   IV⁶ I⁶ IV   V(⁶⁻⁵₄₋₃)   I

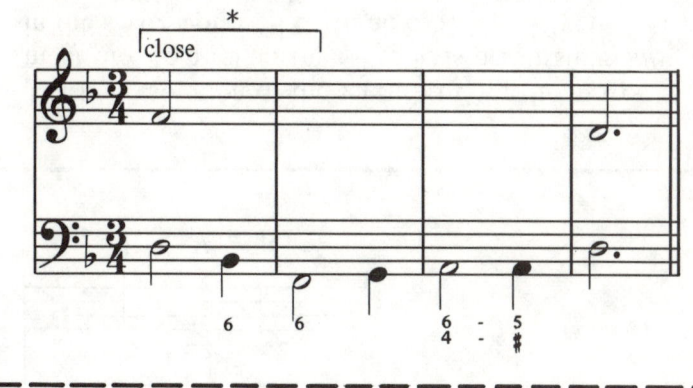

49

E♭: I   IV VII⁶ I⁶ II⁶ V(⁶⁻⁵₄₋₃)   I

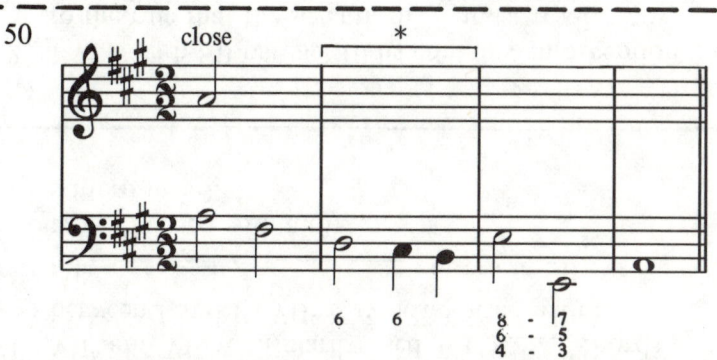

50

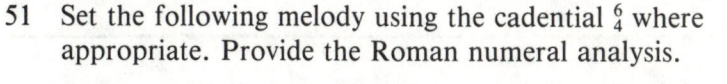

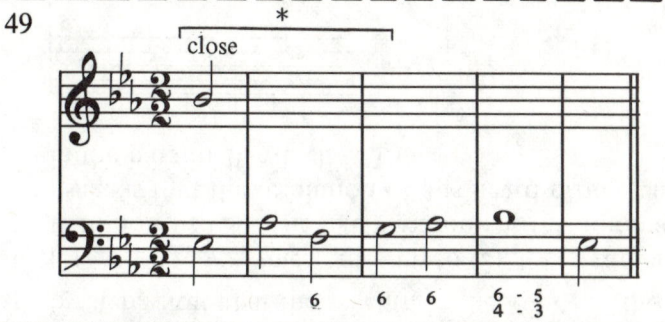

A: I   VI   II⁶ I⁶ II   V(⁸⁻⁷₆₋₅₄₋₃)   I

51 Set the following melody using the cadential $^6_4$ where appropriate. Provide the Roman numeral analysis.

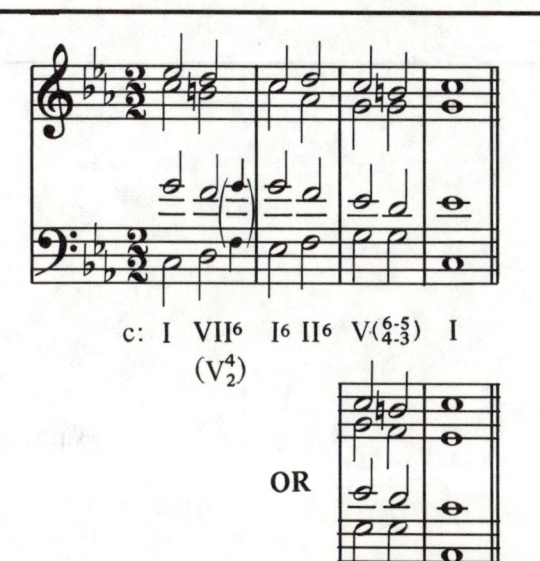

c: I   VII⁶   I⁶ II⁶   V(⁶⁻⁵₄₋₃)   I
   (V⁴₂)

OR

V(⁸⁻⁷₆₋₅₄₋₃)   I

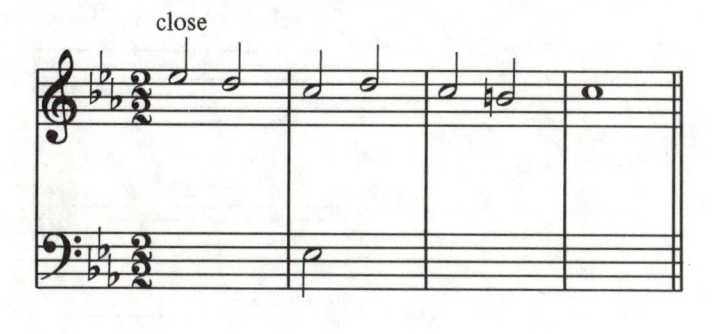

(1) parallel

(2) root (or the) fifth

44 In summary, an important idiomatic usage for V_3^4 is in the pattern I V_3^4 I⁶ with (1) _____ 10ths in the SB. Complete the inner voices of the problem below, using the smoothest possible (common tone-stepwise) voice leading. (Remember that correct doubling in I⁶ is either the (2) _____ or the _____, whichever gives the smoother voice leading.)

d: I V_3^4 I⁶

45 Write the following, using a SB pattern of parallel 10ths:

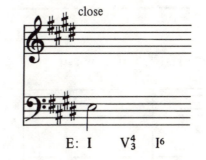

close

E: I V_3^4 I⁶

46

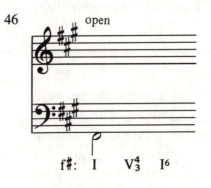

open

f♯: I V_3^4 I⁶

(1) smoothest

(2) IV

(3) II or II⁶

44 In connecting a pre-dominant to the cadential $^6_4$, the (1) _____ correct voice leading should be used. In this way the dissonant 4th above the bass will either be prepared by common tone, if the pre-dominant chord is (2) .... (*chord symbol(s)*), or will be approached by step from above, if the pre-dominant chord is (3) ....

45 Write each of the following in the smoothest correct way:

B♭: I   II   V($^6_4$: $^5_3$)   I

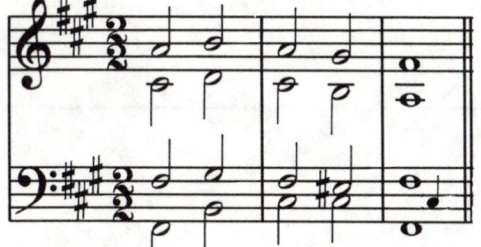

46

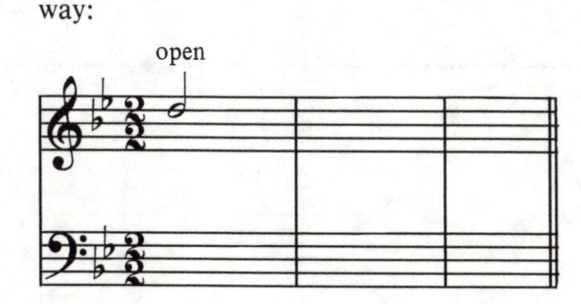

f♯: I   II⁶   V($^8_6$: $^7_5$: $^{}_3$)   I

47

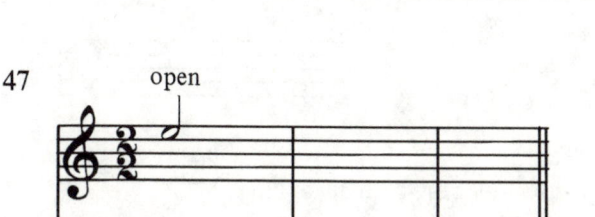

a: I   IV   V($^8_6$: $^7_5$: $^{}_3$)   I

47   I⁶ V$_3^4$ I (the reverse of the pattern introduced above) is also commonly found with SB parallel 10ths. Note that in this case $\hat{4}$ resolves regularly (see example **x**). Complete example **y** using SB parallel 10ths:

g: I⁶   V$_3^4$ I   D: I⁶   V$_3^4$ I

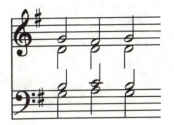

48   As is the case with VII⁶, V$_3^4$ is sometimes used as a N chord to I (and occasionally to I⁶). Complete these connections:

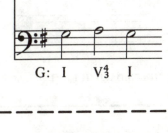

G: I   V$_3^4$ I

49   open

b: I   V$_3^4$ I

50   Other than the single exception in the idiomatic pattern for I V$_3^4$ I⁶, the seventh of V⁷ must resolve

down (by) step   _____ by _____.

(1) seventh   51   V$_2^4$ has the (1) _____ (*chord member*) in the bass. Therefore, the bass of V$_2^4$ must resolve

(2) down (by) step   (2) _____ by _____.

39 Complete the soprano line in each case:

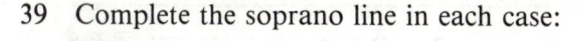

$g{:}$ I   IV   V$\left(\begin{smallmatrix}8\ -\ 7\\6\ -\ 5\\4\ -\ 3\end{smallmatrix}\right)$ I

40

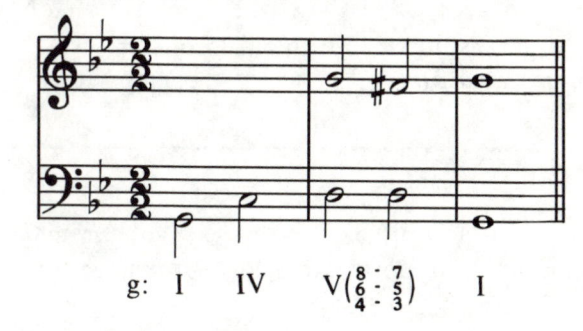

D: I   II^6 V$\left(\begin{smallmatrix}6\ -\ 5\\4\ -\ 3\end{smallmatrix}\right)$ I

41 Write the inner voices in the smoothest correct way:

close

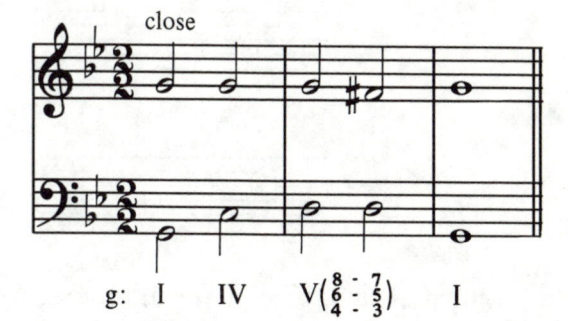

$g{:}$ I   IV   V$\left(\begin{smallmatrix}8\ -\ 7\\6\ -\ 5\\4\ -\ 3\end{smallmatrix}\right)$ I

42

open

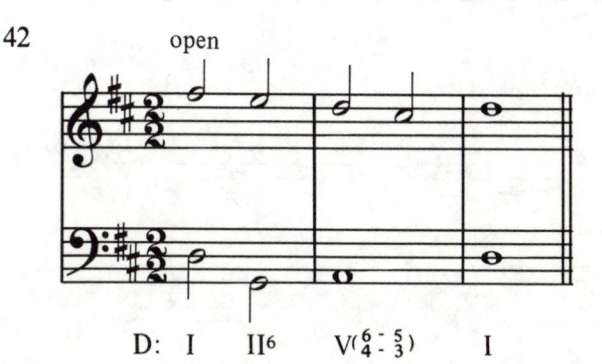

D: I   II^6 V$\left(\begin{smallmatrix}6\ -\ 5\\4\ -\ 3\end{smallmatrix}\right)$ I

43 In a basic harmonic progression the cadential $^6_4$ is typically preceded by one of the most common _____ chords, IV, II, or II^6.

pre-dominant

I^6

52 Resolve the seventh in this V_2^4. If $\hat{3}$ is in the bass, the chord of resolution must be _____ (*chord symbol*).

C: V_2^4

(1) I

(2) up (by) step

(3) down (by) step

53 Just as V_5^6 is always followed by (1) _____, V_2^4 is always followed by I^6. In V_5^6, the leading tone, which requires resolution (2) _____ by _____, is in the bass. In V_2^4, the seventh, which requires resolution (3) _____ by _____, is in the bass.

(1) I

(2) I^6

54 V_5^6 is always followed by (1) _____.
V_2^4 is always followed by (2) _____.

x

55 V_2^4 is commonly used as an IN chord in I V_2^4 I^6. Which of the bass patterns below is correct? _____

x   y

g: I V_2^4 I^6 I V_2^4 I^6

56 Complete this connection, using common tone-stepwise voice leading in the AT. (*Remember to check for correct doubling in I^6.*)

close

B♭: I V_2^4 I^6

(1) tonic
(2) pre-dominant
(3) closing tonic

35 A basic harmonic progression consists of an opening (1) _____ which leads to a (2) _____, to a dominant, and then to a (3) _____ _____.

(1) dominant

(2) pre-dominant

36 The cadential $^6_4$ prolongs (1) _____ harmony; therefore, in a basic harmonic progression a cadential $^6_4$ is preceded by a (2) _____ chord.

37 Of the pre-dominant chords that we have studied, those which most often precede the cadential $^6_4$ are IV, II, and II⁶. Study the voice leading in the examples below, and complete each Roman numeral analysis. Note in all cases the smooth approach to the cadential $^6_4$; all upper voice leading is common tone or stepwise.

(1) C: I ___ V$\left(^{8\,-\,7}_{^6\,-\,5}_{4\,-\,3}\right)$ I   (2) I ___ V$\left(^{6\,-\,5}_{4\,-\,3}\right)$ I

(1) II⁶
(2) IV

(3) II

(3) C: I ___ V$\left(^{6\,-\,5}_{4\,-\,3}\right)$ I

$\hat{1}$

38 The principal active tone in the cadential $^6_4$ is the 4th above the bass, namely, _____ (*scale degree*). This dissonance must either be prepared by common tone, if preceded by IV ($\hat{1}$ $\hat{1}$), or approached by step from above, if preceded by II⁶ or II ($\hat{2}$ $\hat{1}$).

voice exchange

57 Note the _____ _____ pattern in the SB between I and I⁶. Complete the connection:

58 V_2^4 is also used as a N chord to I⁶. Complete these connections:

59

60 In summary:

(1) N

V_5^6 most often occurs as a(n) (1) _____ (P, N, *or* IN) chord to I in I V_5^6 I, and also as a(n) (2) _____ in I⁶ V_5^6 I.

(2) IN

(3) P

V_3^4 occurs most often as a(n) (3) _____ chord between I and I⁶ (or I⁶ and I) with parallel 10ths in SB, and sometimes as a N to I or I⁶.

(4) IN

V_2^4 occurs most often as a(n) (4) _____ chord in I V_2^4 I⁶, and sometimes as a N to I⁶.

In all of these tonic prolongation patterns the smoothest AT connections are usually common tone-stepwise.

bb: V$\left(^{8\ :\ 7}_{^6\ :\ 5}_{4\ :\ 3}\right)$ I

31

close

8 : 7
6 : 5
4 :

(1) dominant

(2) V$\left(^{6-5}_{4-3}\right)$

(3) V$\left(^{8-7}_{6-5}_{4-3}\right)$

32 The cadential $^6_4$ delays chord tones of V$^{(7)}$ in the upper voices and thus prolongs (1) _____ harmony. The cadential $^6_4$ and its resolution to V is labeled (2) ....
The cadential $^6_4$ and its resolution to V$^{(7)}$ is labeled (3) ....

33 Give the Roman numeral analysis:

(1)

As shown in the example above, the cadential $^6_4$ always occurs on a beat that is metrically (2) _____ (stronger *or* weaker) than the beat of its resolution.

(1) F: I IV | V$\left(^{8-7}_{6-5}_{4-3}\right)$ | I ‖

(2) stronger

34 Provide the Roman numeral analysis:

(1)

The cadential $^6_4$ occurs on a (2) _____ (strong *or* weak) beat.

(1) b: I II^6 | V$\left(^{6-5}_{4-3}\right)$ | I ‖

(2) strong

1 The following ways of prolonging tonic using inversions of V^7 were introduced in the last set:

$$I \ V^6_5 \ I \qquad I^6 \ V^6_5 \ I$$
$$I \ V^4_3 \ I^6 \qquad I^6 \ V^4_3 \ I \qquad I \ V^4_3 \ I \qquad I^6 \ V^4_3 \ I^6$$
$$I \ V^4_2 \ I^6 \qquad I^6 \ V^4_2 \ I^6$$

In writing these tonic prolongation patterns, remember to use the smoothest possible voice leading in the AT. Check for:

1. Correct doubling in I and I^6.
2. The presence of all chord tones in the inversion of V^7.
3. Correct spacing.
4. Resolution of the active tones in the inversion of V^7: $\hat{7}$ to (1) ____; $\hat{4}$ to (2) ____. Reminder: There is a single exception to the resolution of $\hat{4}$. In I V^4_3 I^6 the soprano typically moves in parallel 10ths, $\hat{3} \ \hat{4} \ \hat{5}$.

(1) $\hat{1}$
(2) $\hat{3}$

2 Complete the following. (*Bear in mind the soprano scale degrees that are being used.*)

D: I V^4_2 I^6

3

D: I V^6_5 I

4

D: I V^4_3 I^6

27 Resolve the following:

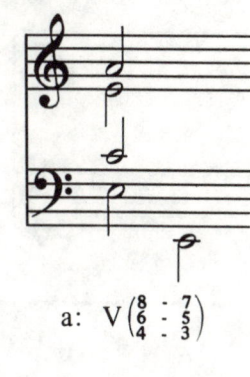

a: $V\begin{pmatrix}8 & - & 7\\6 & - & 5\\4 & - & 3\end{pmatrix}$

28 Write each for four voices as indicated:

E: $V\begin{pmatrix}8 & - & 7\\6 & - & 5\\4 & - & 3\end{pmatrix}$

29 close

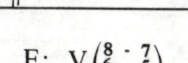
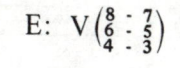

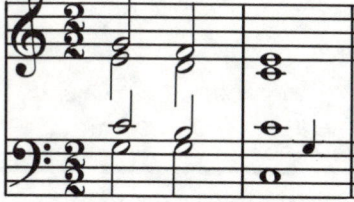
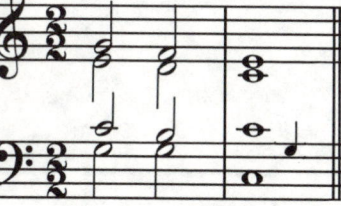
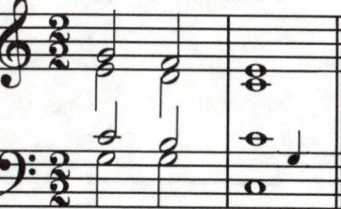

C: $V\begin{pmatrix}8 & - & 7\\6 & - & 5\\4 & - & 3\end{pmatrix}$ I

30 Given the figured bass, provide the Roman numeral analysis and set for four voices:

open

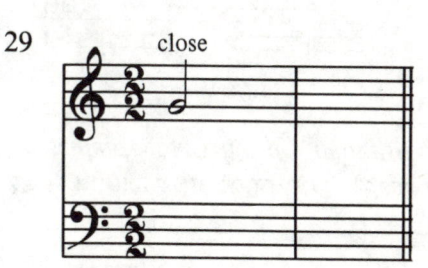

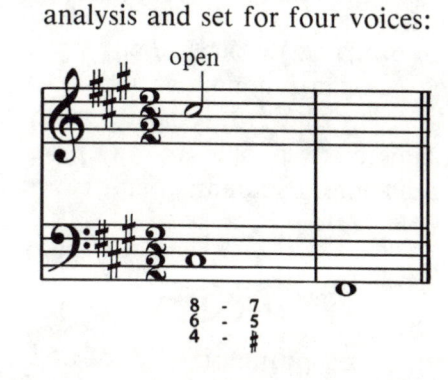

f#: $V\begin{pmatrix}8 & - & 7\\6 & - & 5\\4 & - & 3\end{pmatrix}$ I

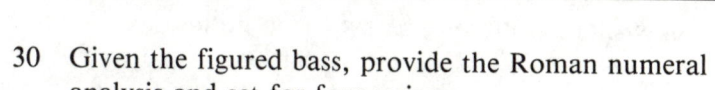

$\begin{matrix}8 & - & 7\\6 & - & 5\\4 & - & \#\end{matrix}$

5

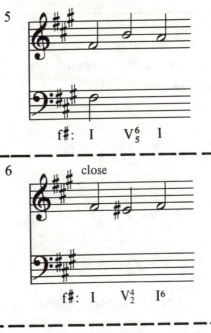

f#:   I   V$_5^6$ I

- -

6

close

f#:   I   V$_2^4$ I⁶

- -

7   (*Use the typical SB pattern.*)

open

f#:   I   V$_3^4$ I⁶

8   Sometimes it is necessary to write the SAT (given the bass) or to write the ATB (given the soprano). In problems in which only one outer voice is given, first determine the chords to be used and write the remaining outer voice.

Consider the following in completing a tonic prolongation pattern:

    1. A P, N, or IN pattern should be used in each of the outer voices. (The next two points will help to narrow the possibilities.)

    2. No tone is to be doubled in the inversions of V⁷. Double the third of VII⁶; double the root or fifth of V⁶.

    3. Root position I should have the root doubled. It is best to avoid a doubled third in I⁶.

Bear in mind these principles and refer to this frame and frame 1 as necessary, as you work on the problems below. In some cases trial and error may be needed before you discover the correct solution(s). You may wish to have some music manuscript paper handy.

23

open

g: V ($^6_4$: $^5_3$)

24 In the resolution of a cadential $^6_4$, the bass need not repeat. It may sustain its note or fall an octave. Set each figured bass below. First provide the Roman numeral analysis.

open

$^6_4$: $^5_♮$

f: V ($^6_4$: $^5_3$)

25

close

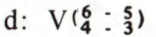

$^6_4$: $^5_♯$

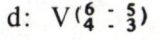

d: V ($^6_4$: $^5_3$)

26 Study the example below:

B♭: V ($^8_6_4$: $^7_5_3$)

Sometimes, as illustrated above, the cadential $^6_4$ resolves to (1) _____ rather than to V. The specific voice leading is given in the figured bass, $^{8-7}_{6-5}_{4-3}$. All upper voices in the cadential $^6_4$ move down by (2) _____.

(1) V^7

(2) step

9 The soprano below is to be set in two ways. Determine the chords to be used and write the bass lines, choosing from the following: I V₅⁶ I, I V₃⁴ I⁶, I V₂⁴ I⁶. (One of these chord successions will not work with the given soprano.) Then fill in the inner voices.

I V₅⁶ I   I V₂⁴ I⁶

(*Note: V₃⁴ cannot be used because it would give a doubled B♭. Inversions of V⁷ must be complete chords with no tones doubled.*)

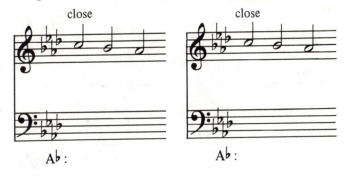

close   close

A♭:   A♭:

10 Set the soprano below three ways. Choose appropriate chord successions from the following: I V⁶ I, I VII⁶ I⁶, I V₅⁶ I, I V₃⁴ I, I V₂⁴ I⁶. (*First determine the key and chords to be used and write the bass lines. Then write the AT.*)

c: I VII⁶ I⁶

c: I V₃⁴ I

c: I V₂⁴ I⁶

(*Note: V⁶ and V₅⁶ cannot be used because they would give a doubled leading tone and parallel octaves in SB.*)

open

open

open

19 Give the Roman numeral analysis of the example below:

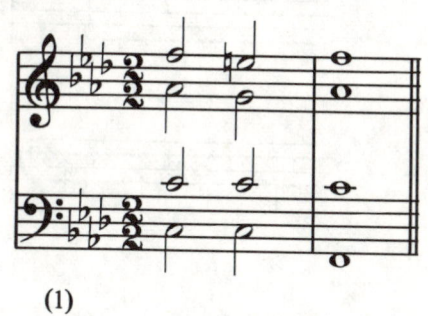

(1)

(1) f: V($^{6-5}_{4-3}$) I

As illustrated above, in writing the cadential $^6_4$ for four voices the *bass* is doubled, and in the resolution to the dominant triad the doubled bass note is kept as a (2) _____ tone in one of the upper voices and in the bass.

(2) common

bass

20 In a cadential $^6_4$ the _____ (*voice*) is doubled.

21 Write V($^{6-5}_{4-3}$) for four voices.
The procedure is:

1. Write the dominant note in the bass.
2. Complete the upper voices as indicated. Be sure to include the doubled bass note and a 6th and 4th (or corresponding compound intervals) above the bass. (*Take care to use correct spacing.*)
3. Resolve the 6th and the 4th above the bass down by step as indicated by the symbols $^{6-5}_{4-3}$.
4. Keep the doubled bass note as a common tone.

E$\flat$: V($^6_4$: $^5_3$)

22

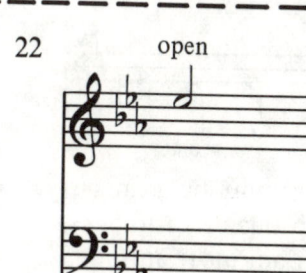

c: V($^6_4$: $^5_3$)

11 Set this pattern in E minor two ways, using an inversion of V⁷ as the second chord. Follow the procedure given in previous frames.

I V^6_5 I

I V^4_3 I

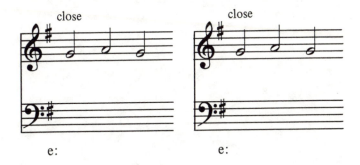

close   close

e: e:

(*Note: I⁶ cannot be used; a doubled third would result. V^4_2 cannot be used because it would give a doubled 4̂.*)

12 Set this pattern in G major four ways, using the given first chords and an inversion of V⁷ as the second chord:

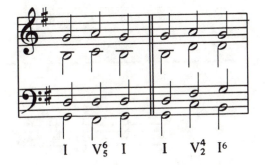

I V^6_5 I   I V^4_2 I⁶

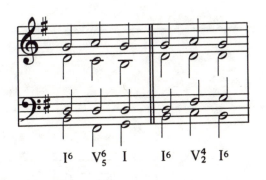

I⁶ V^6_5 I   I⁶ V^4_2 I⁶

G: I   G: I

G: I⁶   G: I⁶

13 Write the cadential $^6_4$ in the key of E minor:

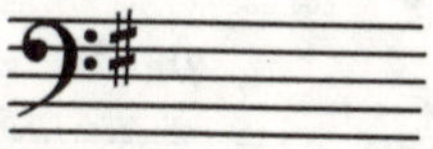

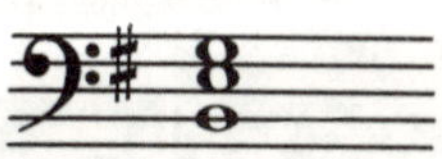

$V\binom{6\text{-}5}{4\text{-}3}$

14 The label for the cadential $^6_4$ and its resolution is:

....

$V\left(\begin{smallmatrix}6-5\\4-3\end{smallmatrix}\right)$

15 Write and resolve each cadential $^6_4$:

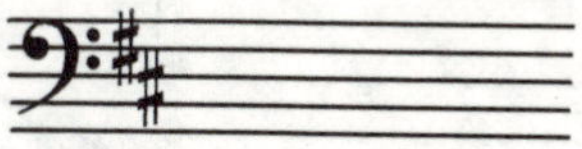

D: $V\left(\begin{smallmatrix}6\\4\end{smallmatrix} : \begin{smallmatrix}5\\3\end{smallmatrix}\right)$

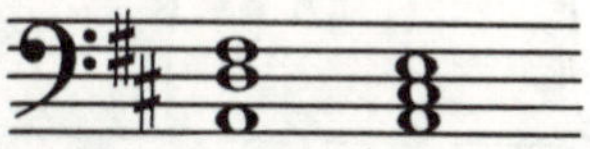

16

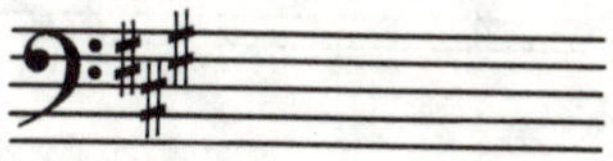

f#: $V\left(\begin{smallmatrix}6\\4\end{smallmatrix} : \begin{smallmatrix}5\\3\end{smallmatrix}\right)$

17 Given the figured bass, write and resolve each cadential $^6_4$. First give the key and Roman numeral analysis. (*Remember to use parentheses to indicate the prolongational function of the $^6_4$.*)

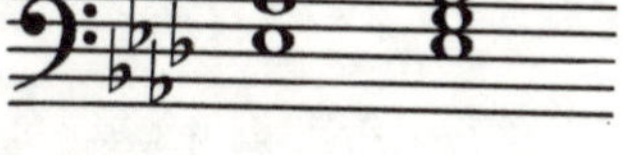

$\begin{smallmatrix}6\\4\end{smallmatrix} : \begin{smallmatrix}5\\3\end{smallmatrix}$

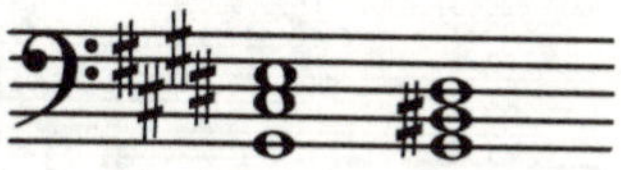

A♭: $V\left(\begin{smallmatrix}6\\4\end{smallmatrix} : \begin{smallmatrix}5\\3\end{smallmatrix}\right)$

18

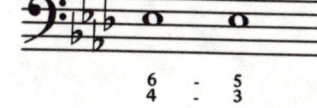

$\begin{smallmatrix}6\\4\end{smallmatrix} : \begin{smallmatrix}5\\ \sharp\end{smallmatrix}$

c#: $V\left(\begin{smallmatrix}6\\4\end{smallmatrix} : \begin{smallmatrix}5\\3\end{smallmatrix}\right)$

The usual procedure for writing the Roman numeral analysis, given the figured bass, includes the recopying of figures, deleting any indication of an altered interval above the bass and substituting the Arabic numeral "3" for a "♯" or a "♮" standing alone. However, in this and subsequent frames, you should not consider your answer wrong if you added the Roman numeral and parentheses to the given figures and thus have $V\left(\begin{smallmatrix}6-5\\4-\sharp\end{smallmatrix}\right)$ as your answer.

13 Set the given soprano, using an inversion of V⁷ as the second chord. *Hint: Pay particular attention to the soprano scale degrees. There is only one correct way of setting this pattern. (If you are in doubt, refer to frame 1.)*

I   V$_3^4$ I⁶

close

E♭ :

---

sharp (or) natural

14 Now that you have had practice in setting a given soprano, we will review some figured bass rules and set a few figured bass patterns.

In a figured bass in minor keys, the leading tone in a V$_3^4$ or V$_2^4$ is indicated by a slash through a figure or by a _____ or _____ sign with a figure. (*See examples below, if necessary.*)

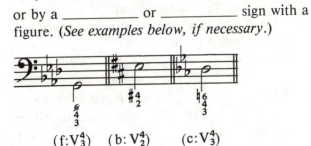

(f: V$_3^4$)   (b: V$_2^4$)   (c: V$_3^4$)

---

(1) 6th

(2) 4th

15 In a V$_3^4$ the leading tone is the (1) ____ above the bass (example **x**). In a V$_2^4$ the leading tone is the (2) ____ above the bass (example **y**).

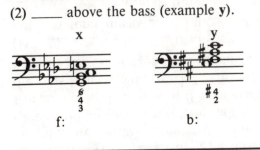

f: b:

---

(1) e: I V$_3^4$ I⁶

(2) g: I V$_2^4$ I⁶

16 Give the Roman numeral analysis of each figured bass below:

(1)   (2)

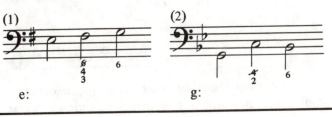

e: g:

7 Write the 6th and 4th above the bass and then resolve them down to the 5th and 3rd above the bass.

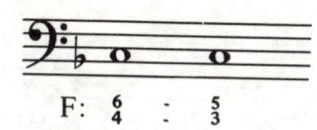

F: $^6_4$: $^5_3$

(1) 1̂, 3̂, (and) 5̂

(2) dominant

8 The procedure we will follow in giving the Roman numeral analysis of a cadential $^6_4$ is different from anything previously encountered in this book. If we were to follow the usual rules of labeling, the Roman numeral analysis of the pattern from the previous frame would be: I$^6_4$ V. This labeling is problematic. Although the cadential $^6_4$ contains

(1) ____, ____, and ____ (*scale degrees*), it does not have tonic function. Its function is to prolong

(2) _____ harmony through the delaying of dominant chord tones in the upper voices, and the Roman numeral analysis reflects this function.

(1) dominant

(2) 5th
(3) 3rd

9 The symbol that we will use for the cadential $^6_4$ and its resolution is: V($^{6-5}_{4-3}$).

The V indicates that it is (1) _____ harmony which is being prolonged. The $^{6-5}_{4-3}$ in parentheses shows the specific way that the prolongation is effected, and it gives the specific voice leading for the resolution of the cadential $^6_4$. The bass remains stationary while the 6th above the bass resolves to the (2) ____ above the bass, and the 4th above the bass resolves to the (3) ____ above the bass.

(1) cadential
(2) dominant

10 The (1) _____ $^6_4$ occurs above a bass of 5̂, prolonging (2) _____ harmony at a cadence.

$^5_3$

11 Complete this symbol (by filling in the box), showing the resolution of the cadential $^6_4$: V($^6_{4-}$ □).

5̂

12 The cadential $^6_4$ occurs above ____ (*scale degree*) in the bass. Write the cadential $^6_4$ in the key of A major. (*Do not resolve it*.)

(*May be written an octave lower*.)

17 Set this figured bass for four voices. Use the typical soprano found with this pattern. (*First give the key and Roman numeral analysis*.)

b: I V⁴₃ I⁶

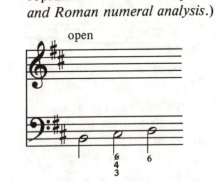

open

18 Set each figured bass below for four voices. Give the key and Roman numeral analysis; then choose an appropriate P, N, or IN soprano pattern, referring to frame 8 as necessary.

b: I V⁶₅ I

OR

b: I V⁶₅ I

close

19

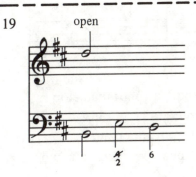

open

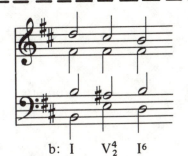

b: I V⁴₂ I⁶

OR

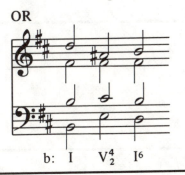

b: I V⁴₂ I⁶

1 In previous parts we have dealt with $\begin{smallmatrix}5\\3\end{smallmatrix}$ and $\begin{smallmatrix}6\\3\end{smallmatrix}$ chords and with V^7 and its inversions. In this part we will focus on $\begin{smallmatrix}6\\4\end{smallmatrix}$ chords. Although there are many typical usages of $\begin{smallmatrix}5\\3\end{smallmatrix}$, $\begin{smallmatrix}6\\3\end{smallmatrix}$, and V^7 chords, there are only a few typical $\begin{smallmatrix}6\\4\end{smallmatrix}$ chord usages. In this set we will deal with the most common $\begin{smallmatrix}6\\4\end{smallmatrix}$ chord, the *cadential* $\begin{smallmatrix}6\\4\end{smallmatrix}$.

---

(1) **y**

(2) dominant

2 Compare examples **x** and **y** below. In example (1) _____, the dominant is prolonged by the $\begin{smallmatrix}6\\4\end{smallmatrix}$ chord that precedes it. This $\begin{smallmatrix}6\\4\end{smallmatrix}$ chord delays chord tones of the dominant triad and thus prolongs (2) _____ harmony.

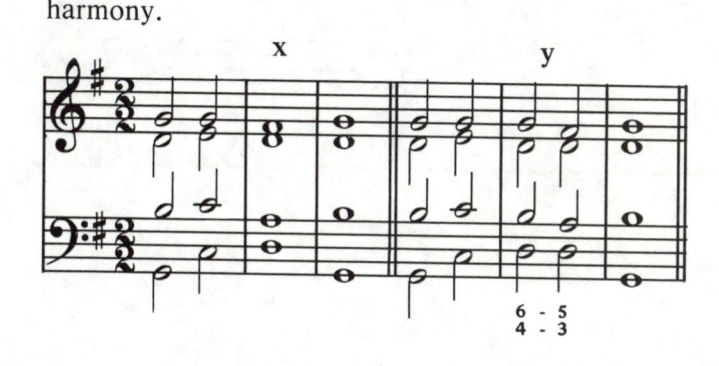

---

bass

3 As in all figured bass symbols, the numerals in the symbol $\begin{smallmatrix}6\\4\end{smallmatrix}$ refer to intervals above the _____.

---

cadential

4 The usage of $\begin{smallmatrix}6\\4\end{smallmatrix}$ chord illustrated in frame 2 is typically found prolonging the dominant at a cadence (most often, an authentic cadence) and is, therefore, called a _____ $\begin{smallmatrix}6\\4\end{smallmatrix}$.

$\hat{5}$

5 The cadential $\begin{smallmatrix}6\\4\end{smallmatrix}$ occurs over a bass of ____ (*scale degree*) at a cadence. (*Refer to frame 2, if necessary.*)

---

(1) 4th

(2) 5th
(3) 3rd

6 The cadential $\begin{smallmatrix}6\\4\end{smallmatrix}$ consists of the intervals of a 6th and a (1) ____ above the bass, $\hat{5}$.
The 6th and 4th above the bass are active tones—they are not part of the dominant chord, and they require resolution down by step to the stable tones which are, respectively, a (2) ____ and a (3) ____ above the bass. (*See example below.*)

$$\text{B}\flat: \begin{smallmatrix}6\\4\end{smallmatrix} - \begin{smallmatrix}5\\3\end{smallmatrix}$$

20 In this part of the book (Sets 4–8) the following tonic prolongation patterns have been studied:

$$I \ I^6 \qquad\qquad I^6 \ I$$
$$I \ VII^6 \ I^6 \qquad I^6 \ VII^6 \ I \qquad I \ VII^6 \ I \qquad I^6 \ VII^6 \ I^6$$
$$I \ V^6 \ I \qquad\qquad I^6 \ V^6 \ I$$
$$I \ V^6_5 \ I \qquad\qquad I^6 \ V^6_5 \ I$$
$$I \ V^4_3 \ I^6 \qquad\ I^6 \ V^4_3 \ I \qquad I \ V^4_3 \ I \qquad I^6 \ V^4_3 \ I^6$$
$$I \ V^4_2 \ I^6 \qquad\ I^6 \ V^4_2 \ I^6$$

(1) prolongation

21 The bracket and Roman numeral under the first three chord symbols below indicate that they are a

(1) _____ of tonic harmony.

$$I \ V^4_3 \ I^6 \ II^6 \ V^7 \ I$$
$$\underbrace{}_{I}$$

Show, in like manner, the prolongation of tonic in the following:

(2) $I \ V^4_2 \ I^6 \ IV \ V \ I$
$\underbrace{}_{I}$

(2) $\qquad\qquad I \ V^4_2 \ I^6 \ IV \ V \ I$

22 Patterns prolonging the opening tonic may be strung together to form a larger tonic prolongation pattern, as indicated by the brackets in the example below:

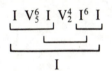

Note that each of these overlapping bracketed patterns is one of those listed in frame 20. The long bracket and Roman numeral I at the bottom indicate that the whole series of chords can be thought

tonic prolongation

of as a single _____ _____ pattern.

23 Using the example in the previous frame as a model, show with brackets how tonic is prolonged in the following:

$$I \ VII^6 \ I^6 \ V^6_5 \ I$$

$I \ VII^6 \ I^6 \ V^6_5 \ I$
(with brackets)
I

$I \ I^6 \ V^4_2 \ I^6 \ V^4_3 \ I$
(with brackets)
I

24 $\quad I \ I^6 \ V^4_2 \ I^6 \ V^4_3 \ I$

2. Set this melody for four voices, using the series of descending 5ths. Provide the Roman numeral analysis.

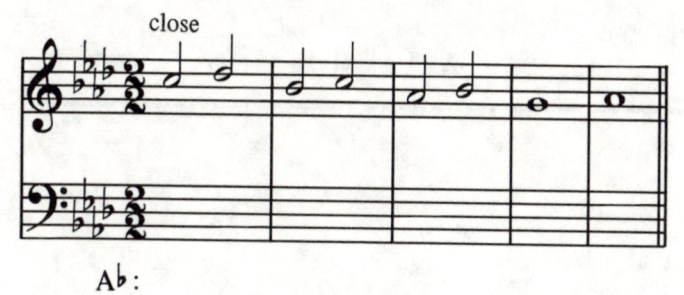

Ab:

3. Write the following progression. Bracket and label the prolongation of opening tonic.

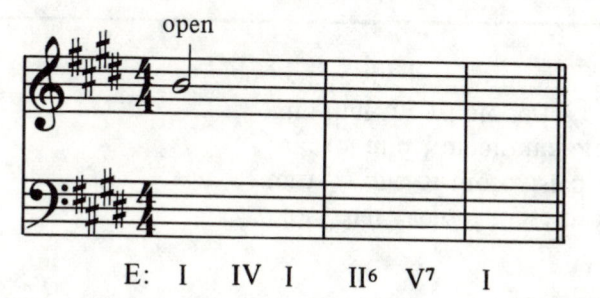

E: I IV I   II⁶ V⁷   I

4. Set this figured bass. First give the Roman numeral analysis.

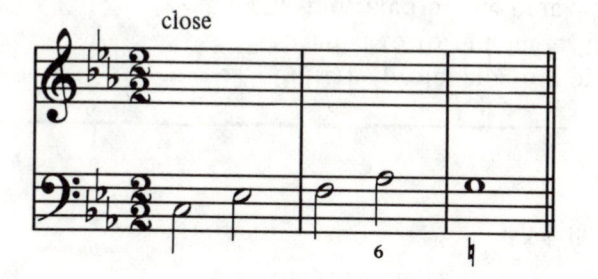

5. Give the cadence term associated with each progression:

IV⁶ V (in minor)   (1) _____

V⁽⁷⁾ VI   (2) _____

V⁽⁷⁾ I   (3) _____

IV I   (4) _____

→ V   (5) _____

25 Set the following for four voices as indicated. First write the bass; then the AT. Show with brackets (as in previous frames) how tonic harmony is prolonged.

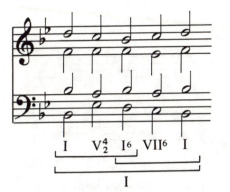

open

$B\flat$: I V^4_2 I^6 VII^6 I

26

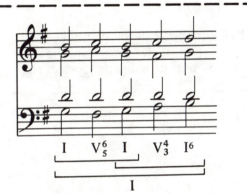

close

G: I V^6_5 I V^4_3 I^6

27

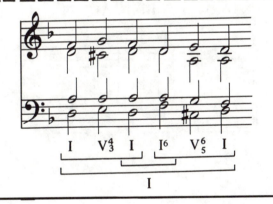

d: I V^4_3 I I^6 V^6_5 I

---

28 A prolonged opening tonic typically leads to a pre-dominant, followed by a root position dominant, and then to a closing tonic. Bracket and label the tonic prolongation in the following:

I V^4_2 I^6 VII^6 I IV V^7 I

I V^4_2 I^6 VII^6 I IV V^7 I

---

29 I I^6 V^6 I V^4_3 I^6 II^6 V I

I I^6 V^6 I V^4_3 I^6 II^6 V I

49 Write the Roman numerals and bass line for the series of descending 5ths in A minor:

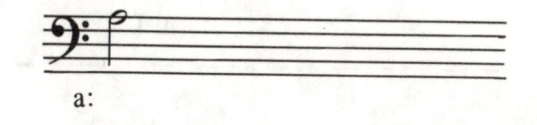

a:

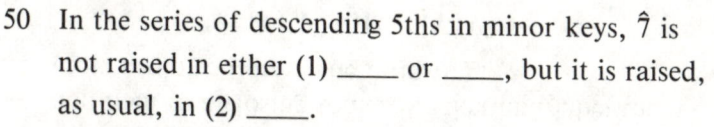

a: I   IV VII III VI II V I

(1) VII (or) III

(2) V

50 In the series of descending 5ths in minor keys, $\hat{7}$ is not raised in either (1) ____ or ____, but it is raised, as usual, in (2) ____.

51 Set the following melody for four voices, using the series of descending 5ths. Remember to double the root of each chord.

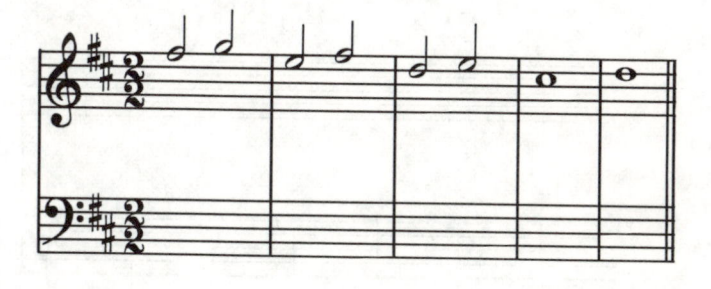

b:

b: I IV VII III VI II   V   I

TEST COVERING PART 4

The questions below will test your mastery of the material in Part 4. Complete the entire test, then check your answers with the correct ones on page 167. For each question that you miss, the corresponding material may be reviewed in the set whose number is given with the correct answer.

Reminder: In all writing problems use typical soprano patterns, doubling, and voice leading.

1. Write the following connections. Identify the function of each IV⁶.

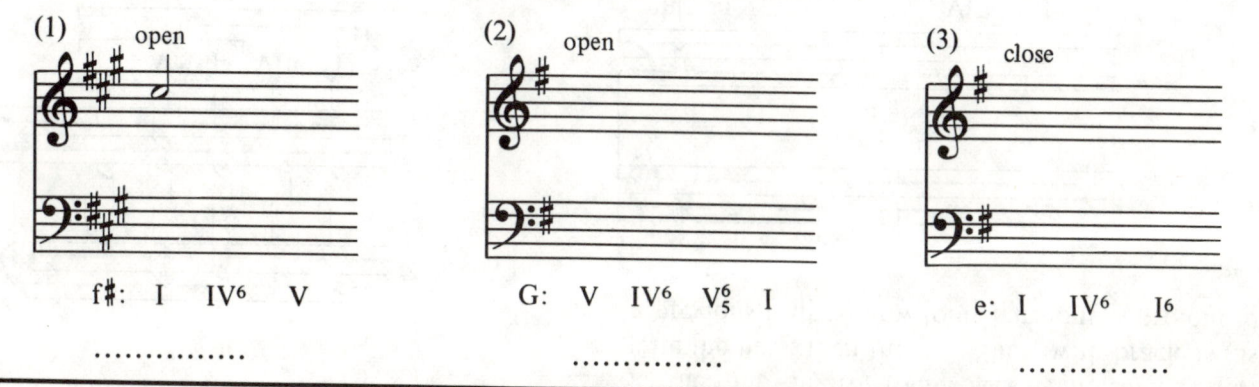

(1) open

f#: I   IV⁶ V

....

(2) open

G: V IV⁶ V⁶₅ I

....

(3) close

e: I   IV⁶   I⁶

....

30 The following are harmonic progressions beginning with a prolonged tonic. Complete these progressions for four voices as indicated, based on the chord vocabulary studied thus far. Remember to use the smoothest correct voice leading in all cases. Bracket and label the prolongation of opening tonic as in the previous frames.

(First write the soprano, then the AT.)

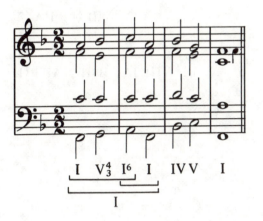

I V$^4_3$ I^6 I IV V I

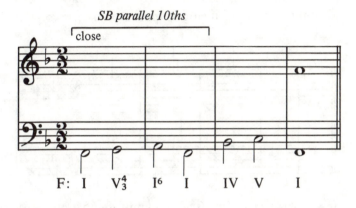

F: I V$^4_3$ I^6 I IV V I

31 *(First give the Roman numeral analysis. Then fill in the AT.)*

I V$^4_2$ I^6 V$^6_{(5)}$ I II^6 V$^{(7)}$ I

a:

32 Note: SB voice exchange is indicated by ✕. *(Suggestion: First complete the soprano; then complete the Roman numeral analysis; then fill in the AT.)*

I V$^6_5$ I VII^6 I^6 I V$^4_3$ I^6 IV V^7 I

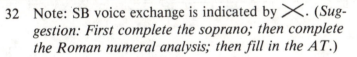
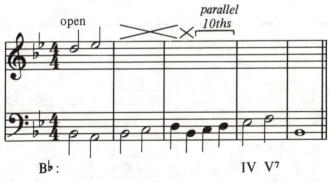

B♭: IV V^7

I IV VII III VI II V I

45 close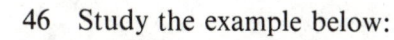

G:

46 Study the example below:

c: I IV VII III VI II V I

When the series of descending 5ths is written in minor keys, $\hat{7}$ is not raised in either VII or III. VII and III, in this case, are both _____ (*structural type*) triads.

major

47 Give the Roman numeral analysis:

(1) f:

In the series of descending 5ths in minor, $\hat{7}$ is not raised in (2) ____ or ____, but the leading tone is used, as usual, in V.

(1) I IV | VII III | VI II | V | I ‖

(2) VII (or) III

diminished

48 In minor keys, II, a _____ (*structural type*) triad, does not frequently occur in root position. The series of descending 5ths is, however, a case in which root position II in a minor key is used.

(1) tonic

(2) opening tonic

1 The function of root position V and V⁷ is to lead to the closing (1) _____ in a harmonic progression. The usual function of inversions of V⁷, as well as VII⁶ and V⁶, is to prolong the (2) _____ _____.

pre-dominant

2 In a basic harmonic progression root position V and V⁷ are preceded by a _____ chord.

3 Inversions of V⁷, VII⁶, and V⁶ may also be preceded by a pre-dominant, as illustrated in the examples of tonic prolongation below. Study these examples and complete the Roman numeral analysis of examples **y** and **z**:

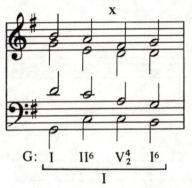

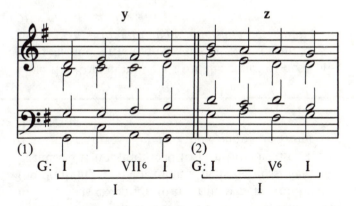

(1) I IV VII⁶ I
(2) I II V⁶ I

pre-dominant

4 VII⁶, V⁶, and inversions of V⁷ may be preceded by a _____ chord in a tonic prolongation pattern.

III

40 In a series of descending 5ths, VII leads to ____.

root

41 In writing the series of descending 5ths for four voices, the usual doubling for root position chords is used: The _____ of each chord is doubled. In major keys this results in a doubled leading tone in VII. This exception to the rule which prohibits the doubling of the leading tone is permissible because VII does not lead to I and the leading tone does not resolve. (Refer to the example in frame 36, if necessary.)

42 Give the Roman numerals for the series of descending 5ths and write the bass line in each example below. (*In writing the bass, alternate descending 5ths and ascending 4ths.*)

43

44 Set each of the following melodies for four voices, using the series of descending 5ths. First write the Roman numerals and fill in the bass. Then write the AT in the smoothest correct way, remembering to double the root of each chord.

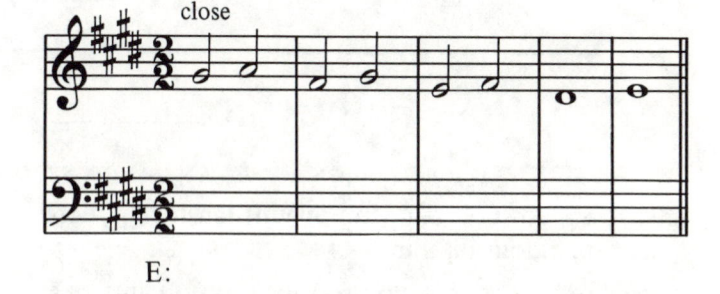

5 Write the Roman numeral analysis:

(1) I IV V$_2^4$ I^6

(1)   c:

(2) prolongation

This example illustrates (2) _____ of tonic harmony.

6 There are many possible ways of using a pre-dominant chord in preceding a VII^6, V^6, or inversion of V^7 in the prolongation of tonic harmony. In this set we will discuss some of the most typical usages.

The tonic prolongation patterns, I IV VII^6 I and I IV VII^6 I^6, are quite common, most often occurring with an ascending soprano, $\hat{5}$ $\hat{6}$ $\hat{7}$ $\hat{1}$. Complete the connections below (and all others in this set) following the usual doubling and voice-leading procedures. (*Hint: Be particularly careful to use correct doubling in VII^6.*)

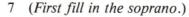

B♭ : I   IV   VII^6 I

7 (*First fill in the soprano.*)

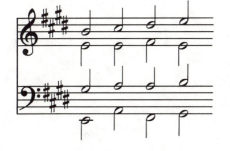

open

$\hat{5}$ $\hat{6}$ $\hat{7}$ $\hat{1}$

E: I   IV   VII^6 I^6

35 Give the Roman numeral analysis of the following example:

C: I IV | VII III | VI II | V | I ||

A common use of III and VII, as illustrated above, is in a progression consisting of a series of *descending 5ths*. Observe that although we generally speak of this root movement as descending 5ths, the bass actually alternates descending 5ths with ascending 4ths.

36 Write the Roman numeral analysis of the example below:

(1) A : I IV | VII III | VI II | V | I ||

(1)

This example consists of a series of descending

(2) 5ths

(2) _____. (Note that in the above example, as in many descending 5th progressions, there is a consistent voice-leading pattern between chord pairs.)

37 As shown in the example in the previous frame, the series of descending 5ths starting on I will lead back

(1) I   (2) authentic

to (1) ____ through a(n) (2) _____ cadence.

38 Give the Roman numerals to complete the series of descending 5ths:

(I IV) VII III (VI) II V (I)

I IV ____ ____ VI ____ ____ I

diminished

39 In major keys, VII is a _____ (*structural type*) triad, which occurs in first inversion quite commonly, but which is found in root position infrequently. VII in root position is most often used as part of a series of root position chords moving by descending 5th.

8 Observe that the examples above of I IV VII⁶ I (or I⁶) with a soprano of $\hat{5}$ $\hat{6}$ $\hat{7}$ $\hat{1}$ are in major keys. When the ascending line $\hat{5}$ $\hat{6}$ $\hat{7}$ $\hat{1}$ is harmonized in minor keys, $\hat{6}$ is raised a half step by means of an accidental in order to avoid an augmented 2nd between $\hat{6}$ and $\hat{7}$. The raising of $\hat{6}$, as illustrated in the example below, corresponds to the .... (*what specific type?*) scale.

melodic minor ascending

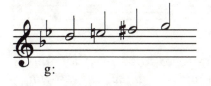

g:

---

(1) **x**

(2) **y**

9 Example (1) ____ below is incorrect; there is an augmented 2nd in the soprano of IV VII⁶. The soprano of example (2) ____ is correct; $\hat{6}$ has been raised to avoid the augmented 2nd.

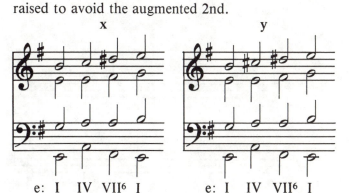

e: I IV VII⁶ I   e: I IV VII⁶ I

---

10 Write the soprano line for the following tonic prolongation pattern:

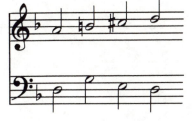

$\hat{5}$ $\hat{6}$ $\hat{7}$ $\hat{1}$

d: I   IV   VII⁶   I

---

11 Now, write the inner voices following the usual doubling and voice-leading rules:

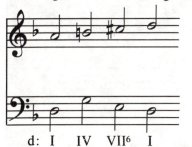

d: I   IV   VII⁶   I

32 Give the Roman numeral analysis of the example below:

e: I III IV IV⁶ V

(*Note that although $\hat{7}$ is not raised in measure 1 because it is part of the descending line, $\hat{1}\,\hat{7}\,\hat{6}$, it is raised, as usual, in V.*)

33 Set each figured bass below, following procedures given in previous frames. (*First give the Roman numeral analysis.*)

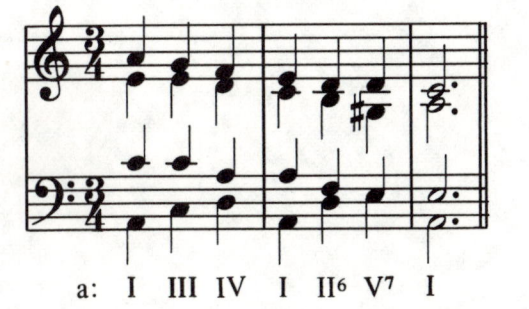

a: I III IV I II⁶ V⁷ I

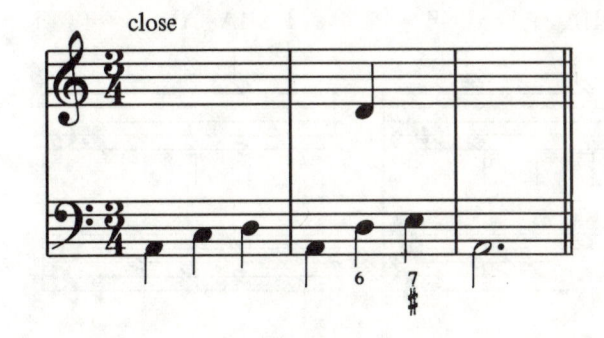

close

34 (*Hint: Use the typical soprano, doubling, and voice leading for this type of cadence.*)

d: I III IV IV⁶ V

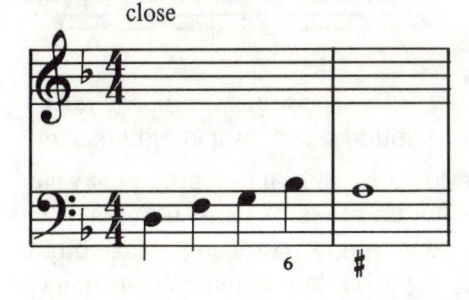

close

12 Note: Raising $\hat{6}$ to avoid an augmented 2nd in minor keys is done in only a very few situations—those in which an ascending line is specifically called for. *Do not* use this technique for avoiding an augmented 2nd in other problems in chord connection. Usually an augmented 2nd in minor keys is avoided by avoiding an ascending line. For example, in the progressions below, the faulty augmented 2nd of case (1) _____ can be eliminated by moving the SA in contrary motion to the bass as in case (2) _____.

(1) **y**

(2) **x**

13 When V^7 is preceded by one of the pre-dominant chords IV, II⁶, or II, the seventh of V^7 ($\hat{4}$) is prepared by (1) _____ _____. Likewise, when an inversion of V^7 is preceded by IV, II⁶, or II, the seventh in the inversion of V^7 is (2)_____ by (3) _____ _____.

(1) common tone

(2) prepared

(3) common tone

14 V^4_2 is often preceded by IV or II⁶, as in the examples below. In these patterns the seventh, which is in the (1) _____ (*voice*) of the V^4_2 is (2) _____ by _____ _____.

(1) bass

(2) prepared (by) common tone

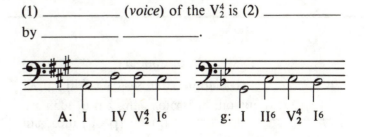

(1) root

(2) common tones

(3) nearest chord tones

(4) contrary

28 As is generally the case with root position triads, the (1) _____ of III should be doubled. In moving from I to III the (2) _____ _____ are kept in the same voices. In moving from III to IV the upper voices move to the (3) .... in (4) _____ motion to the bass.

29 Complete the following connections:

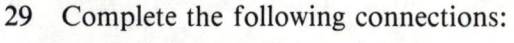

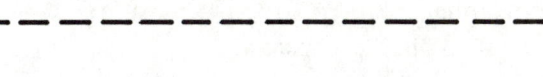

g: I   III   IV

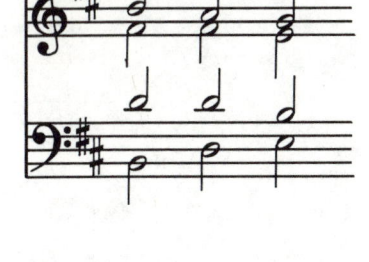

30 (*Remember to use the typical soprano.*)

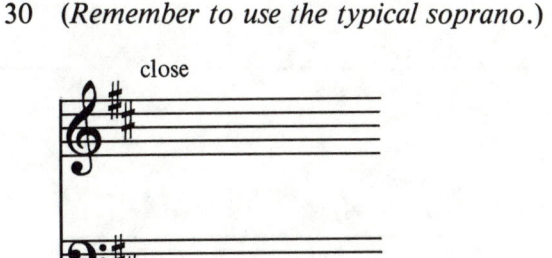

b: I   III   IV

31

f♯:   I   III   IV

15 Complete the following connections. Remember, in these and all other problems, to:
   1. Use the smoothest correct voice leading.
   2. Double check each chord for correct doubling.
   3. Bear in mind the soprano scale degrees being used.

open

A: I   IV   V$^4_2$ I^6

16

close

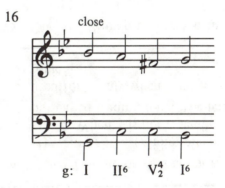

g: I   II^6 V$^4_2$ I^6

17 V^6 or V$^6_5$ may be preceded by II. Complete the following connections:

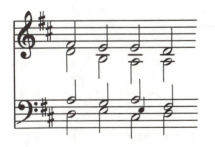

close

D: I   II   V^6 I

22   In a descending line in minor, $\hat{1}$ $\hat{7}$ $\hat{6}$ $\hat{5}$, the augmented 2nd between $\hat{7}$ and $\hat{6}$ (example **x**) is avoided by not raising (1) _____, corresponding to the (2) .... scale (example **y**).

e:

(1) $\hat{7}$

(2) melodic minor descending

---

23   Write the indicated soprano correctly. (*Be sure to avoid an augmented 2nd.*)

$\hat{1}$ $\hat{7}$ $\hat{6}$ $\hat{5}$

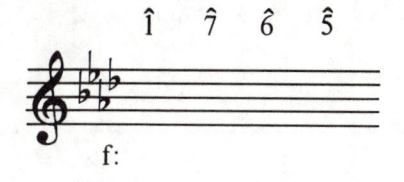

f:

(*May be written an octave lower.*)

---

24   When $\hat{7}$ in minor keys is not raised, there is a (1) .... (whole tone *or* semitone) between $\hat{1}$ and $\hat{7}$. When $\hat{7}$ is not a semitone below tonic, it is not called leading tone. The term *leading tone* is used for $\hat{7}$ only when it is a (2) .... below tonic.

(1) whole tone

(2) semitone

---

25   Give the Roman numeral analysis:

f:

The structural type of the III chord in the above example is (2) _____.

(1) I III IV V$^{8-7}$ I

(2) major

---

26   In a minor key, when $\hat{7}$ is not raised, the structural type of III is _____.

major

---

27   In both major and minor keys, III is typically used to support (1) ____ (*scale degree*) in a(n) (2) _____ (ascending *or* descending) soprano line, in leading from I to IV.

(1) $\hat{7}$
(2) descending

18 (*Note that in the given soprano the seventh of V$^6_5$ is prepared and resolved.*)

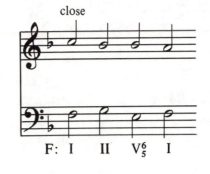

F: I II V$^6_5$ I

19 Although there are many possible ways of using a pre-dominant chord in preceding a VII⁶, V⁶, or inversion of V⁷ in the prolongation of tonic harmony, some are more common than others. In this set we have dealt with the following typical patterns:

$$
\begin{array}{l}
\qquad\quad\ \text{I} \\
\text{I\ \ IV\ \ VII}^6\ \text{or}\quad\text{with soprano } \hat{5}\ \hat{6}\ \hat{7}\ \hat{1} \\
\qquad\quad\ \text{I}^6
\end{array}
$$

$$
\begin{array}{l}
\ \ \ \ \text{IV} \\
\text{I\ \ or\ \ V}^4_2\ \text{I}^6 \\
\ \ \ \text{II}^6
\end{array}
$$

$$
\begin{array}{l}
\qquad\ \ \text{V}^6 \\
\text{I\ \ II\ \ or\ \ I} \\
\qquad\ \ \text{V}^6_5
\end{array}
$$

(1) $\hat{5}\ \hat{6}\ \hat{7}\ \hat{1}$

(2) IV (and) II⁶

(3) II

20 The soprano that typically occurs with I IV VII⁶ I (or I⁶) is: (1) ____ ____ ____ ____.
Pre-dominant chords that often precede V$^4_2$ are
(2) ____ and ____.
V$^6_5$ and V⁶ are often preceded by the pre-dominant chord (3) ____.

prepared (by common tone)

21 When an inversion of V⁷ is preceded by one of the pre-dominant chords, IV, II⁶, or II, the seventh of the inversion of V⁷ must be ....

19   The previous examples have dealt with III in major keys. We will now consider the use of III as support for $\hat{7}$, in a descending line in minor keys.

Up to this point in our work in four-part writing, all triads in minor keys containing $\hat{7}$ have contained the leading tone, which requires an accidental raising $\hat{7}$. However, there are some cases in which $\hat{7}$ in minor keys is not raised. As illustrated below, when a descending line, $\hat{1}$ $\hat{7}$ $\hat{6}$, is used in minor keys, it corresponds to the .... (*what specific type*?) scale.

melodic minor descending

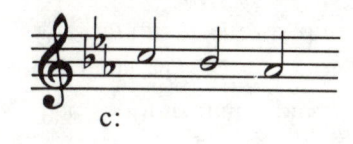

c:

20   The soprano line given below is faulty because of the (1) _____ _____ between $\hat{7}$ and $\hat{6}$.

(1) aug 2nd

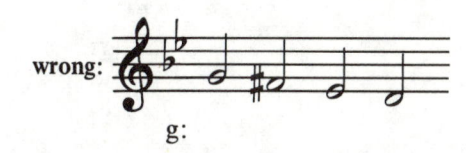

wrong: g:

In a descending line, the augmented 2nd is avoided by *not raising* $\hat{7}$. The resulting line corresponds to the (2) .... scale. Rewrite the above example correctly:

(2) melodic minor descending

correct: g:

21   In an ascending line in minor, $\hat{5}$ $\hat{6}$ $\hat{7}$ $\hat{1}$, the augmented 2nd between $\hat{6}$ and $\hat{7}$ (example **x**) is avoided by raising (1) ____, corresponding to the (2) .... scale (example **y**).

(1) $\hat{6}$
(2) melodic minor ascending

x   y

e:

(1)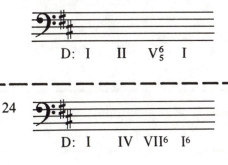

(2)

22 In writing the bass line for one of the tonic prolongation patterns under consideration, bear in mind the direction (and octave placement) that the bass line would have in a simpler prolongation of tonic (that is, one without a pre-dominant chord). For example, in determining the correct bass line for I IV V_2^4 I^6, first write the bass for I V_2^4 I^6:

(1)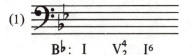

$B\flat$: I $\quad$ V_2^4 $\quad$ I^6

Now, insert the pre-dominant chord:

(2)

$B\flat$: I $\quad$ IV $\quad$ V_2^4 $\quad$ I^6

---

23 Following the procedure outlined above, write these bass lines:

D: I $\quad$ II $\quad$ V_5^6 $\quad$ I

*

24 D: I $\quad$ IV $\quad$ VII^6 $\quad$ I^6

(*Note: A descent to G creates a bass with unnecessary large leaps.)

---

25 Set each of the following soprano lines. First complete the Roman numeral analysis and write the bass line, choosing as your setting one of the tonic prolongation patterns introduced in this set. Then write the AT. (*Hint: Which of the pre-dominant chords which commonly precede V_2^4 will support $\hat{1}$ in the soprano?*)

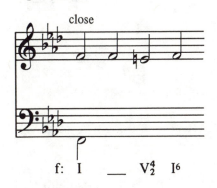

I $\quad$ IV $\quad$ V_2^4 $\quad$ I^6

close

f: I $\quad$ ___ $\quad$ V_2^4 $\quad$ I^6

16   Complete the Roman numeral analysis of each
example below:

(1) C: I   III   IV   ___   ___

(2) C: I   III   IV   ___   ___ ___ ___
                                I

The IV to which III leads may function as a pre-
dominant, leading to V, as in example (3) ____
above, or it may lead to I or I⁶, having the function
of prolonging tonic, as in example (4) ____.

(1) V^{8-7} I

(2) I⁶ II⁶ V I

(3) x

(4) y

---

17   Complete each of the following, illustrating the
typical use of III:

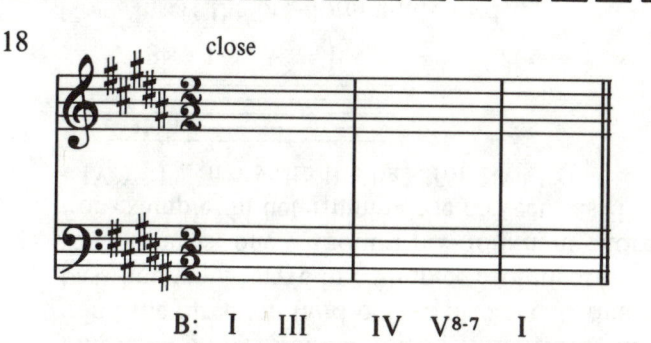

close

E♭: I   III   IV   I   IV   V⁷   I

18

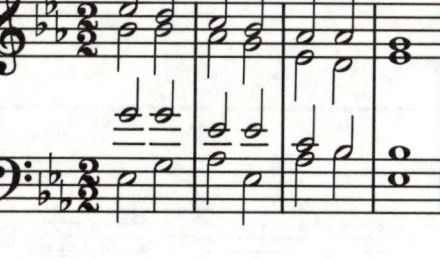

close

B: I   III   IV V^{8-7} I

I   IV   VII⁶   I⁽⁶⁾

OR

I   IV   V$\frac{4}{2}$ I⁶

26

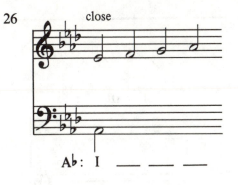

A♭: I ___ ___ ___

---

27 (*Remember to prepare and resolve the seventh of V$^6_5$.*)

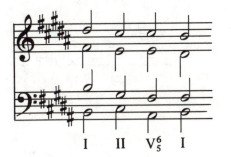

I   II   V$^6_5$ I

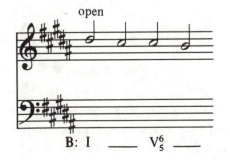

B: I ___ V$^6_5$ ___

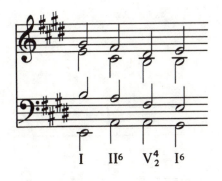

I   II⁶   V$\frac{4}{2}$ I⁶

28

E: I ___ V$\frac{4}{2}$ ___

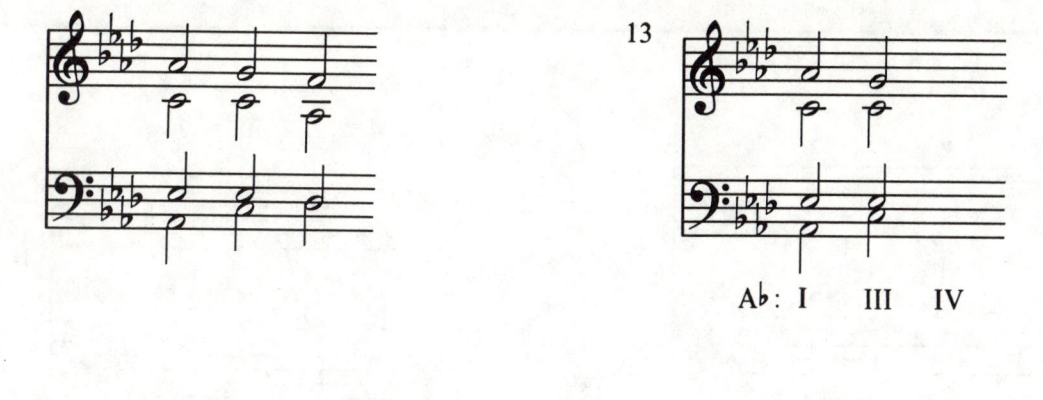

13

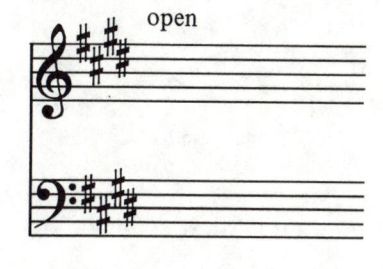

Ab: I   III   IV

7̂ 6̂

14 The typical soprano line in I III IV is 1̂ ____ ____.
(*Refer to examples in previous frames, if necessary*.)
Complete these connections using the typical soprano:

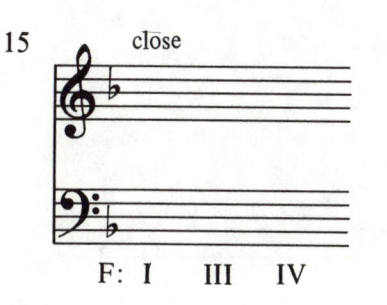

E: I   III   IV

(*SAT may be written an octave higher.*)

15

F: I   III   IV

29 Given below are figured bass patterns and beginning soprano notes. Set each figured bass. First give the Roman numeral analysis. (*Remember, a figured bass tells you precisely what chords to use.*)

F: I   IV   VII⁶ I⁶

30 (*Be careful to avoid an augmented 2nd.*)

c: I   II⁶   V⁴₂   I⁶

OR

Eb: I   II   V⁶₅   I

31 (*Remember to prepare and resolve the seventh.*)

(1) $\hat{7}$

(2) descending

8 A typical usage of III is to support (1) _____ (*scale degree*) in a(n) (2) _____ soprano line. In this context, III usually leads from I to IV.

root

9 As is generally the case with root position triads, the _____ of III is doubled.

two

10 I and III have _____ (*how many?*) common tone(s). Complete the connection below in the smoothest correct way, doubling the root of each chord:

B♭: I   III

11 Complete this connection:

open

A♭: I   III

(1) do not

(2) contrary motion-nearest

12 III and IV (1) .... (do *or* do not) have a common tone. The smoothest correct connection is, therefore (2) .... Complete the following:

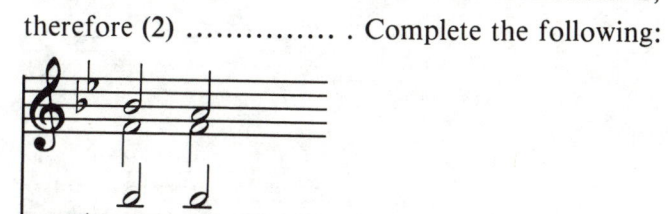

B♭: I   III   IV

32 *(Be careful to avoid parallel perfect 5ths and an augmented 2nd.)*

d: I   IV   V$^4_2$ I^6

open

A: I   II   V$^6_5$ I

33   open

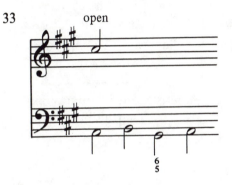

$^6_5$

b: I   II^6 V$^4_2$ I^6

34   open

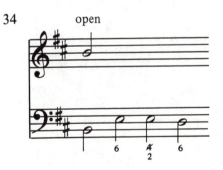

6    $^4_2$ 6

a: I   IV   V$^4_2$ I^6

35   close

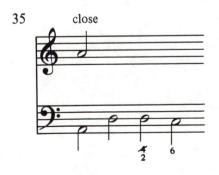

$^4_2$ 6

2 Give the Roman numeral analysis of the example
below:

G:

I III IV V$^{8-7}$ I

$\hat{7}$

3 The example in the previous frame illustrates a typical use of III: Supporting _____ (*scale degree*) in a
descending soprano line, in leading from I to IV.

---

4 Write the Roman numeral analysis of this example:

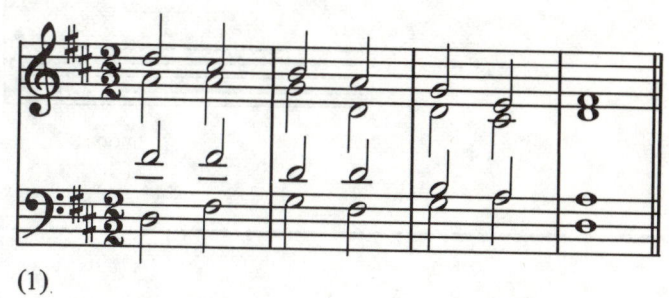

(1) D: I III IV I^6 IV V I

(1) .

(2) I (to) IV

(3) $\hat{7}$

III leads from (2) _____ (*chord symbol*) to _____,
while supporting (3) _____ (*scale degree*) in a
descending soprano line.

$\hat{1}$

5 In all previous sets in this book, we have followed
the rule that the leading tone, when in an outer
voice, must resolve to _____ (*scale degree*). Obviously,
when $\hat{7}$ is part of a descending line, $\hat{1}$ $\hat{7}$ $\hat{6}$, as in the
example in the previous frame, it does not resolve
to $\hat{1}$.

III

6 When $\hat{7}$ in the soprano ascends to $\hat{1}$, it is usually set
with a dominant triad or 7th chord or a VII^6. How-
ever, when $\hat{7}$ is part of a stepwise descending soprano
line, it is generally set with _____ (*chord symbol*).

---

(1) $\hat{1}$

(2) $\hat{6}$

7 As learned in previous sets, when the leading tone in
the soprano is set with a dominant triad or 7th
chord or a VII^6, $\hat{7}$ must resolve to (1) _____. But
when $\hat{7}$ in the soprano is set with III, it is generally
part of a descending line, (2) $\hat{1}$ $\hat{7}$ _____, and thus
does not resolve to $\hat{1}$.

36 Tonic prolongation patterns studied in this set are:

(1) I IV VII⁶ or $\begin{array}{c}\text{I}\\ \text{I}^6\end{array}$

(1) ＿＿ ＿＿ $\overline{}$ VII⁶ or $\overline{}$

(2) I or V$_2^4$ I⁶ $\begin{array}{c}\text{IV}\\ \text{II}^6\end{array}$

(2) ＿＿ or $\overline{}$ V$_2^4$ ＿＿ $\overline{}$

(3) I II or I $\begin{array}{c}\text{V}^6\\ \text{V}_5^6\end{array}$

(3) ＿＿ ＿＿ or ＿＿ $\begin{array}{c}\text{V}^6\\ \text{V}_5^6\end{array}$

These ways of prolonging tonic are more elaborate than those studied in previous sets in that VII⁶, V⁶, or an inversion of V⁷ is preceded by a (4) ＿＿＿＿＿＿ chord.

(4) pre-dominant

---

(1) root position
(2) inversion

37 Harmonic progressions contain a dominant chord in (1) ＿＿＿＿ ＿＿＿＿. Tonic prolongation patterns contain a(n) (2) ＿＿＿＿ of V or V⁷, or a VII⁶.

---

(1) harmonic progression
(2) tonic prolongation
(3) tonic prolongation

38 Label each of the following as either *harmonic progression* or *tonic prolongation*:

I II⁶ V⁷ I   (1) ＿＿＿ ＿＿＿＿

I IV V$_2^4$ I⁶   (2) ＿＿＿ ＿＿＿＿

I IV VII⁶ I   (3) ＿＿＿ ＿＿＿＿

- -

(1) harmonic progression
(2) tonic prolongation
(3) harmonic progression

39   I II V I   (1) ＿＿＿ ＿＿＿＿

I II V$_5^6$ I   (2) ＿＿＿ ＿＿＿＿

I IV V⁷ I   (3) ＿＿＿ ＿＿＿＿

---

40 Give the Roman numeral analysis of the following example. Bracket and label the prolongation of opening tonic.

f : I II⁶| V$_2^4$ I⁶| IV V⁷| I ‖
   ⌐‾‾‾‾‾‾‾⌐
      I

52 In summary, common usages of IV⁶ are:

1. In tonic prolongation (I IV⁶ I⁶ with soprano $\hat{3}$ $\hat{4}$ $\hat{5}$).
2. As a pre-dominant (IV⁶ V with soprano $\hat{4}$ $\hat{5}$).
3. In subdominant prolongation (IV IV⁶ or IV⁶ IV with SB voice exchange).
4. As a passing chord in the prolongation of dominant harmony (V IV⁶ V$^6_5$ with soprano $\hat{5}$ $\hat{4}$ $\hat{4}$).

53 Give the Roman numeral analysis of the following, and identify the function of each IV⁶:

F: I *IV⁶ | I⁶ II | V **IV⁶ V$^6_5$ | I ‖

*tonic prolongation
**passing chord in dominant
  prolongation

....

54

b: I V$^4_2$ | I⁶ VII⁶ | I *IV⁶ | V | I |
   **IV⁶ IV | V$^{8-7}$ | I ‖

 *pre-dominant (at Phrygian cadence)
**subdominant prolongation

....

Set 16 / III AND VII

1 In comparison to the other chords studied thus far, III and VII($^5_3$) occur relatively infrequently. In this set we will study a few of the most common usages.

OR

41 Complete the following progression as indicated:

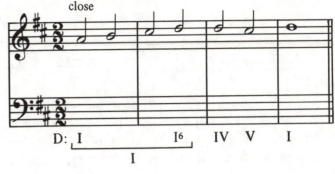

42 As illustrated in example **x**, patterns prolonging the opening tonic may overlap to form a longer tonic prolongation pattern. Bracket and label the tonic prolongation in example **y**.

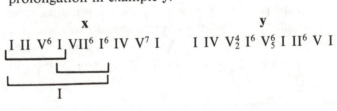

43 Write the Roman numeral analysis of the example below. Bracket and label the prolongation of opening tonic.

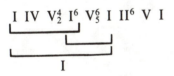

49 Set the following figured bass according to procedures outlined above. First give the Roman numeral analysis. Bracket and label the dominant prolongation.

D: I   IV   V   IV⁶ V⁶₅   I
                  └───V───┘

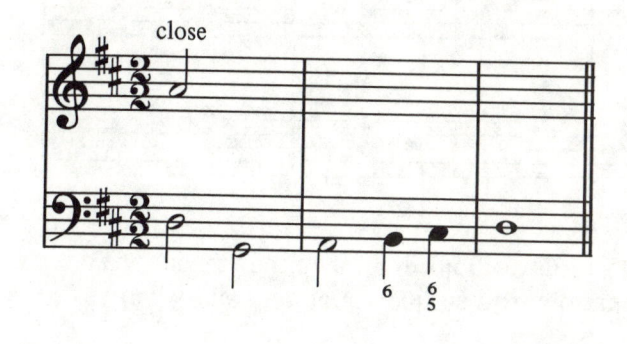

close

6   6
     5

50 In all of the examples above, IV⁶ has been used as a passing chord connecting V and V⁶₅ in *major* keys. Although this prolongation of dominant harmony is more commonly found in major keys than minor keys, a brief note concerning its use in minor is appropriate.

When this ascending bass pattern is used in minor keys, the bass of IV⁶ ($\hat{6}$) must be raised in order to eliminate the augmented 2nd between $\hat{6}$ and $\hat{7}$. The raising of $\hat{6}$, as illustrated in the example below, corresponds to the .... (*what specific type?*) scale.

melodic minor ascending

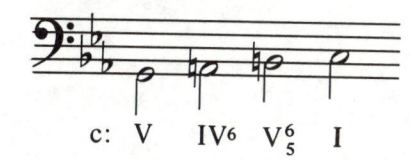

c: V   IV⁶   V⁶₅   I

(1) **x**

(2) **y**

51 Example (1) _____ below is incorrect; there is an augmented 2nd in the bass of IV⁶ V⁶₅. The bass in example (2) _____ is correct; $\hat{6}$ has been raised to avoid the augmented 2nd.

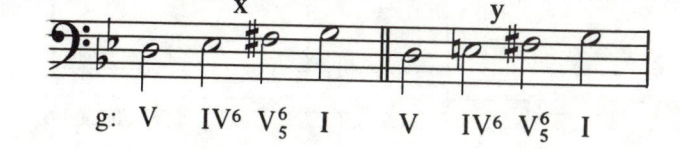

x   y

g: V   IV⁶ V⁶₅   I   V   IV⁶ V⁶₅   I

I II V$_5^6$ I V$_3^4$ I^6 IV V I

I

44 Complete the following progression as indicated. Bracket and label the prolongation of opening tonic.

open

G: I II V$_5^6$ I V$_3^4$ I^6 IV V I

---

(1) 7th

(2) $\hat{3}$

45 As shown in the example below, a V may be converted to a V^7 with the introduction of a passing seventh in an upper voice. As indicated by the symbol V$^{8-7}$, the octave above the bass moves to a

(1) _____ (*general interval*) above the bass, while other chord tones are sustained. The seventh ($\hat{4}$)

then resolves down by step to (2) _____ (*scale degree*) in the following I chord. Thus, the seventh of V^7 is part of a descending passing motion: $\hat{5}$ $\hat{4}$ $\hat{3}$.

B$\flat$: V$^{8-7}$ I

---

46 Convert the V in the example below to a V^7 through the introduction of a passing seventh. Change the value of the appropriate note to a quarter note. Then resolve the V^7 in the usual manner.

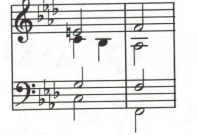

f: V$^{8-7}$ I

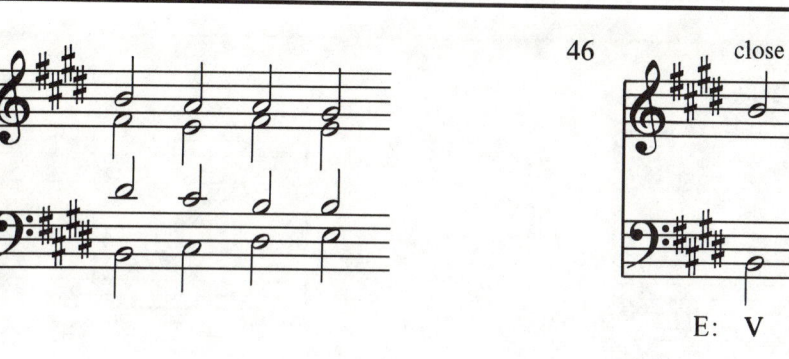

46

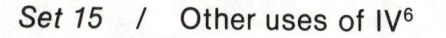

close

E: V   IV⁶   V⁶₅   I

47 Complete the connections below according to the following procedure:

1. Write the bass.
2. Write the typical soprano ($\hat5$ $\hat4$ $\hat4$ $\hat3$).
3. Write the AT, doubling the third of IV⁶ in order to achieve the smoothest voice leading.
4. Bracket and label (with V) the prolongation of dominant harmony.

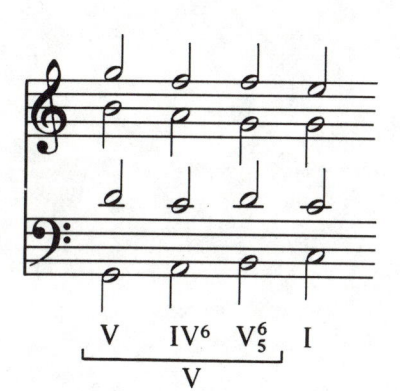

V   IV⁶   V⁶₅   I

V

open

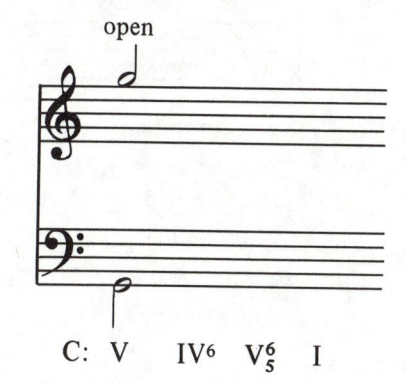

C: V   IV⁶   V⁶₅   I

48

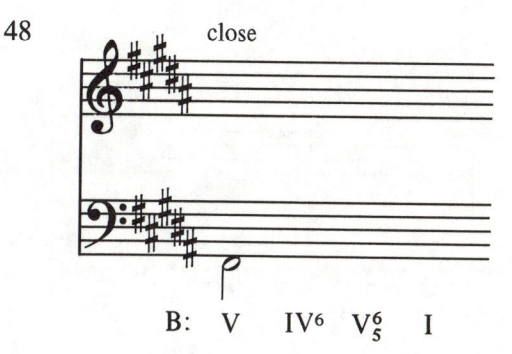

close

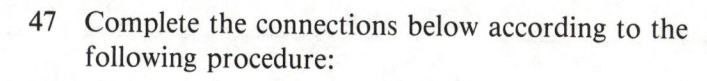

V   IV⁶   V⁶₅   I

V

B: V   IV⁶   V⁶₅   I

47   Study the examples below.
As illustrated in example **x**, a V may be converted to a V^7 with the introduction of a passing

(1) _____ in an upper voice. Similarly, as illustrated in example **y**, a V may be converted into a V_2^4 with the introduction of a passing seventh in the (2) _____ voice. In both cases the passing seventh forms a stepwise connection (3) $\hat{5}$ ____ $\hat{3}$.

(1) seventh

(2) bass

(3) $(\hat{5})$ $\hat{4}$ $(\hat{3})$

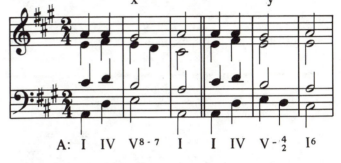

A: I   IV V^{8-7} I   I   IV $V-_2^4$ I^6

---

48   The addition of a passing seventh in an upper voice of a V chord is symbolized V.............. . The introduction of a passing seventh in the bass of a V chord is symbolized $V-_2^4$. Convert the V below to a V_2^4. Change the value of the appropriate note to a quarter note. Then resolve the V_2^4 in the usual manner and label the chord of resolution.

V^{8-7}

V $-$ $\frac{4}{2}$ I^6

E: V $-$ $\frac{4}{2}$ _____

---

49   A V_2^4 always leads to a ____ (*chord symbol*). Therefore, the introduction of the passing seventh in the bass changes the function of a chord succession from that of harmonic progression (root position dominant, leading to root position tonic) to that of tonic prolongation (inverted dominant, leading to inverted tonic).

I^6

---

50   Write the bass line:

(1)

(1)

g: I II^6 V $-$ $\frac{4}{2}$ I^6

(2) prolongation

The function of this pattern is tonic (2) _____.

42 Using the typical soprano, write the outer voices for each of the following:

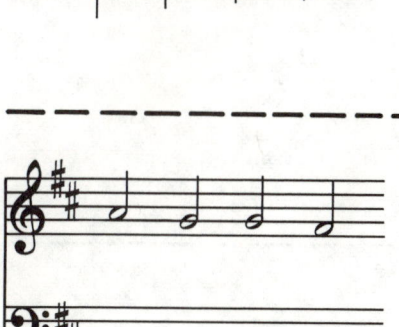

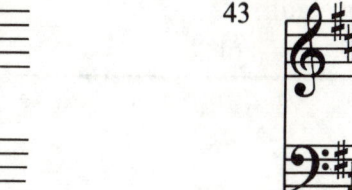

F: V   IV⁶   V$^6_5$ I

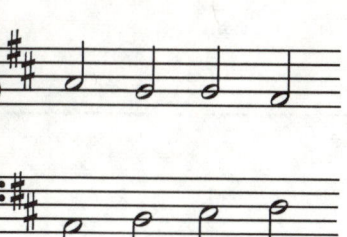

43

D: V   IV⁶   V$^6_5$ I

---

44 Study the voice leading in the example below. When IV⁶ is used as a passing chord leading from V to V$^6_5$, the smoothest voice leading, as shown in the example, is achieved by doubling the _____ of IV⁶.

third (*or* bass)

D: V   IV⁶   V$^6_5$ I

---

45 Complete the inner voices, being sure to double the third of IV⁶:

F: V   IV⁶   V$^6_5$ I

51 Write the AT:

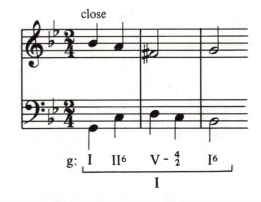

g: I   II⁶   V—$\frac{4}{2}$ I⁶

I

52 Complete this progression. Bracket the prolongation of opening tonic. (*First write the bass line.*)

I IV V—$\frac{4}{2}$ I⁶

I

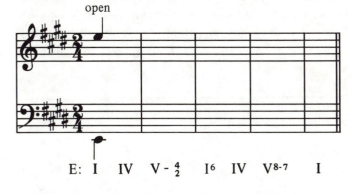

E: I   IV   V—$\frac{4}{2}$ I⁶   IV   V⁸⁻⁷   I

53 In Part 2 we have studied a variety of ways of prolonging opening tonic harmony, from the simple (I I⁶) to the more elaborate (I IV V—$\frac{4}{2}$ I⁶). In addition to the emphasis on understanding and writing these prolongation patterns in isolation, an effort has continually been made to show how the patterns typically function in music, that is, how the prolonged opening tonic leads to a pre-dominant, to a root position (1) _____, and then to a closing (2) _____.

(1) dominant
(2) tonic

54 I   pre-dominant   V⁽⁷⁾   I
is a typical structure for many phrases in tonal music, as well as the basic structure for exercises in this book. When a musical phrase ends with the progression V I or V⁷ I, this ending is termed an *authentic cadence*. The exercise in frame 52 concludes with an _____ cadence.

authentic

authentic

55 The formula for an _____ cadence is V⁽⁷⁾ I.

39 A very different usage of IV⁶ is as a passing chord connecting V with V$_5^6$ (or sometimes V with V⁶).

As shown below, the function of the passing IV⁶ is prolongation of _____ harmony.

dominant

A: V IV⁶ V$_5^6$ I
⎣_____⎦
V

40 Write the bass:

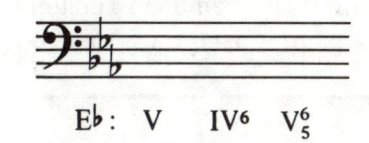

E♭: V IV⁶ V$_5^6$

V and V$_5^6$ are connected by means of a _____ IV⁶.

passing (*or* prolonging)

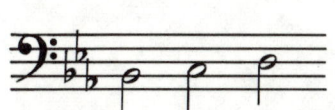

41 The soprano typically used with V IV⁶ V$_5^6$ is illustrated in example **x**. Note that the passing IV⁶ provides a smooth introduction of $\hat{4}$, the dissonant seventh of the dominant harmony, which eventually resolves down to ____ in the I chord.
Write the soprano for example **y**. (*Use the typical pattern.*)

$\hat{3}$

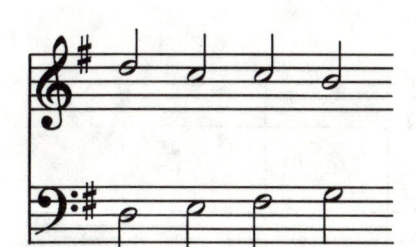

B♭: V IV⁶ V$_5^6$ I   G: V IV⁶ V$_5^6$ I

half

56 Not all cadences in music give a feeling of finality. The V triad may serve as a goal (though not a final goal) for a musical idea. When a phrase ends on V it is termed a *half cadence*. The example below concludes with a(n) _____ cadence.

(1) half

57 The term (1) _____ cadence is used to describe the ending of a phrase that concludes with a V triad. A V^7 chord, because of the added dissonance, is too unstable to serve as the concluding chord of a phrase. Therefore, only a root position V triad, and not a V^7 chord, is used at a (2) _____ cadence.

(2) half

58 Give the Roman numeral analysis of the following example. Label each cadence according to type.

(1) half
(2) authentic

(1) _____   (2) _____

B♭: I | IV VII⁶ | I⁶ VII⁶ | I IV | V | I V_3^4 |
I⁶ I | II⁶ V^7 | I ‖

TEST COVERING PART 2

The questions below will test your mastery of the material in Part 2. Complete the entire test, then check your answers with the correct ones on page 164. For each question that you miss, the corresponding material may be reviewed in the set whose number is given with the correct answer.

1. In writing tonic prolongation patterns for four voices, the following doubling rules should be observed:

I   —Double the (1) _____ .

VII⁶   —Double the (2) _____ .

I⁶ and V⁶   —Double the (3) _____ or _____ , whichever gives the smoothest correct voice leading.

Inversions of V^7—Use the (4) _____ (complete *or* incomplete) chord.

35 Write the Roman numeral analysis of the example below:

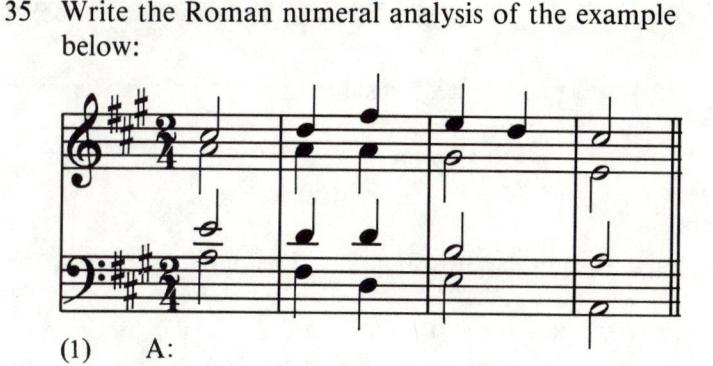

(1)   A:

In the second measure, subdominant harmony is

(2) _____ .

(1) I IV⁶ IV V⁸⁻⁷ I

(2) prolonged

---

36 As with the prolongation of other harmonies, a typical SB pattern in IV⁶ IV (or IV IV⁶), as illustrated in the previous frame, is _____ _____ .

voice exchange

---

37 Complete the soprano for the following progression, using voice exchange in prolonging IV. (*Do not write the inner voices yet.*)

b: I   IV   IV⁶   V

---

38 Now, continuing with the problem from above, write the AT. (*Hint: Use the usual doubling for IV and the doubling for IV⁶ that is typical in its use as a pre-dominant chord.*)

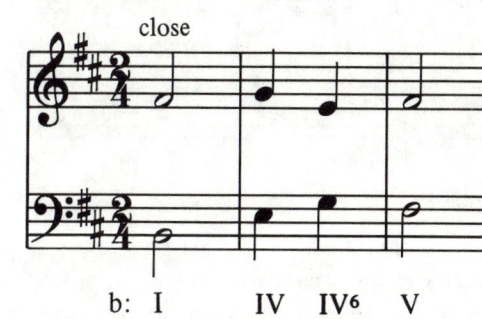

close

b: I   IV   IV⁶   V

2. Give a four-voice illustration of each of the common I I⁶ connections. Label each SB pattern.

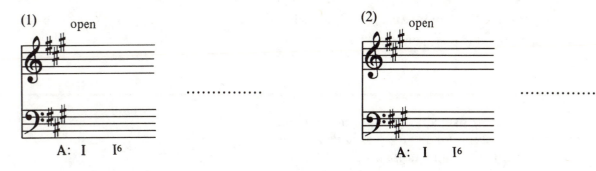

(1) open   ....   (2) open   ....

A: I   I⁶   A: I   I⁶

3. V_3^4 and VII⁶ are primarily used as (1) _____ chords between I and I⁶. V_3^4 is typically used with a SB pattern of (2) _____ _____. VII⁶ is typically used with a SB pattern of (3) _____ _____.

Write each for four voices, using the typical soprano:

(4) close   (5) close

f: I V_3^4 I⁶   c: I   VII⁶   I⁶

4. Complete the four-voice illustration of a typical usage of V_5^6 (in problem 1) and V_2^4 (in problem 2) in prolonging tonic. Provide the Roman numeral analysis, and label the function of the prolonging chord with P, N, or IN, as appropriate.

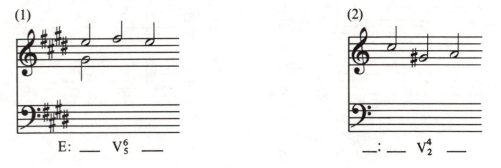

(1)   (2)

E: __ V_5^6 __   __: __ V_2^4 __

5. Set each figured bass. Provide the Roman numeral analysis and label as either *harmonic progression* or *tonic prolongation*.

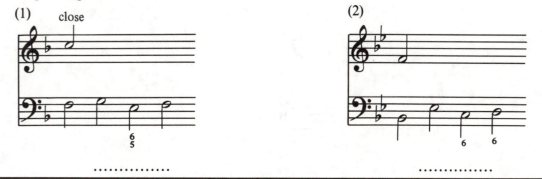

(1) close   (2)

          6   6   6
          5

....

30 (*Hint: Be sure to avoid any leap larger than a 4th.*)

close

d: I   IV⁶ V

---

31 Set each figured bass below and give the Roman numeral analysis:

open

G: I   IV⁶ V⁸⁻⁷   I

    6   8 - 7

- -

32

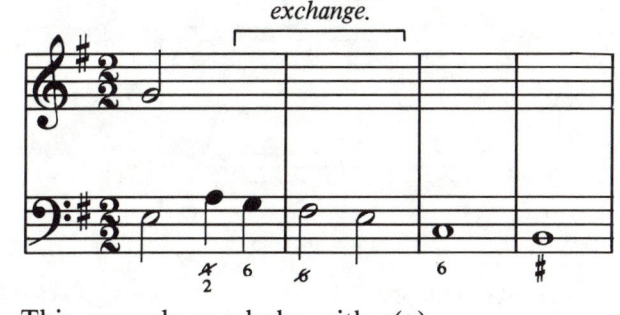

Use SB voice exchange.

e: I V⁴₂ I⁶ VII⁶ I   IV⁶ V

Phrygian

$\substack{4\\2}$ 6 6   6   ♯

This example concludes with a(n) _____ cadence.

---

(1) $\hat{5}$

(2) $\hat{2}$

33 As tonic is the name for $\hat{1}$, dominant the name for (1) ____, and supertonic the name for (2) ____, *subdominant* is the name for $\hat{4}$, and the name for the harmony whose symbol is IV.

---

subdominant

34 Just as other ⁶₃ chords, such as I⁶, V⁶, and II⁶, may prolong tonic, dominant, and supertonic harmony, respectively, IV⁶ may prolong _____ harmony.

6. Write the following progression. Bracket and label the prolongation of opening tonic.

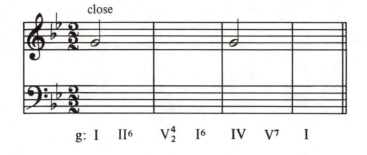

g: I   II⁶   V₂⁴   I⁶   IV   V⁷   I

The progression concludes with a(n) _____ cadence.

7. Given the SB, complete this progression for four voices based upon the chord vocabulary studied thus far. First provide the Roman numeral analysis; then fill in the AT. Bracket and label the prolongation of opening tonic.

D:

26 Connect I to IV⁶. (*Be sure to double the root of I and the fifth of IV⁶.*)

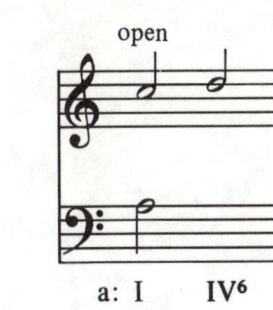

a: I   IV⁶

27

F: I   IV⁶

28 Complete the examples below following the procedures outlined in previous frames. (*Remember to use the typical soprano in IV⁶ V.*)

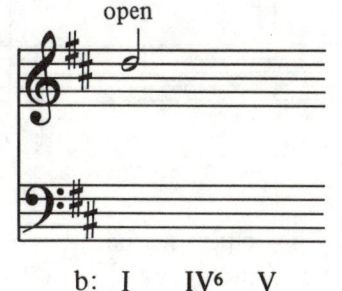

b: I   IV⁶   V

29

c: I   IV⁶   V

IV, II, and II^6

1 The pre-dominant chords that commonly lead to V are ____, ____, and ____.

I

2 Just as opening tonic harmony may be prolonged, so may pre-dominant harmony (though usually pre-dominant prolongation is not as extensive as tonic prolongation).

In the prolongation of opening tonic harmony, it is the ____ chord that is being prolonged. In the prolongation of pre-dominant harmony it is the *harmonic function* that is being prolonged, not necessarily a particular chord.

---

3 There are three common ways of prolonging pre-dominant harmony:

> IV II^6
> IV II
> II II^6 (or II^6 II)

We will consider each in turn.

---

4 Give the Roman numeral analysis of the progression below:

G: I IV II^6 V$^{8-7}$ I

---

(1) $\hat{4}$ (and) $\hat{6}$
(2) $\hat{1}$
(3) $\hat{2}$

5 Both IV and II^6 contain (1) ____ and ____ (*scale degrees*). They differ in only one note. IV contains (2) ____, whereas II^6 contains (3) ____.

6th

6 IV becomes II^6 simply by moving the 5th above the bass to a ____ above the bass (see example).

G: IV   II^6

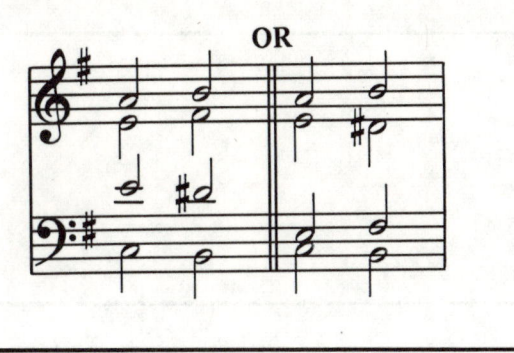

OR

22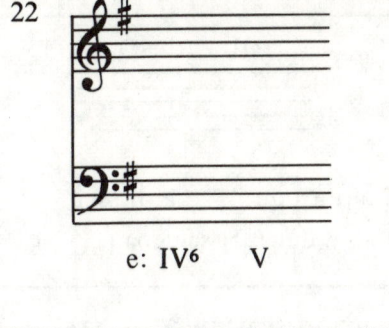

e: IV⁶   V

23 In minor keys, IV⁶ sometimes precedes V at a half cadence. There is a special name for this type of half cadence: *Phrygian* cadence. The cadence below is a _____ cadence.

Phrygian

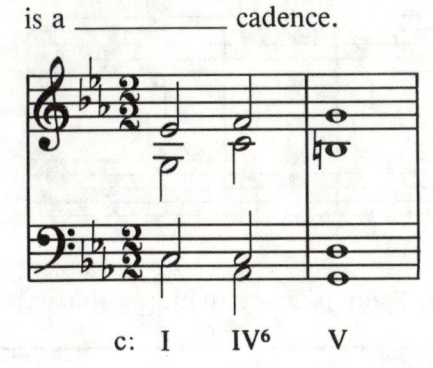

c: I   IV⁶   V

24 A _____ cadence is characterized by the movement, in minor keys, from IV⁶ to V, paired with a soprano of $\hat{4}\ \hat{5}$.

Phrygian

25 Study the voice leading in the examples below. In the connection of I to IV⁶, a common tone is kept, but one of the inner voices must move by

(1) _____ (step *or* leap) to achieve a IV⁶ with doubled (2) _____ (*chord member*).

(1) leap
(2) fifth

g: I   IV⁶   V   I   IV⁶   V

7 Convert this IV to a II⁶. (Change the value of the appropriate note to a half note.)

D: IV   II⁶

8 Follow the above instructions in converting IV to II⁶:

E♭: IV   II⁶

9

f: IV   II⁶

(1) 5th
(2) 6th

10 Although it would be possible to rearrange other voices in IV II⁶, usually just one voice moves from a

(1) _____ to a (2) _____ above the bass, that is from Î to 2̂, while the other voices remain stationary.

11 Complete the following progressions:

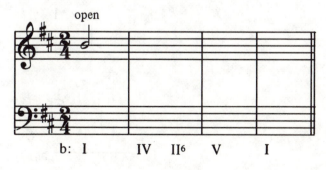

b: I   IV   II⁶   V   I

fifth

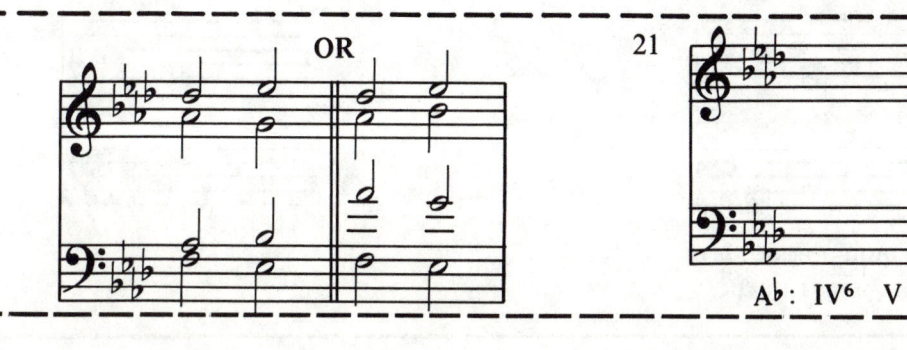

17 *First complete the IV⁶. Remember, the best doubling is the _____.*

a: IV⁶   V

18

c♯: IV⁶   V

(1) 4̂ 5̂
(2) fifth

19 In a IV⁶ V connection, the typical soprano is
(1) ____ ____ (*scale degrees*); the best doubling for
IV⁶ is the (2) _____.

20 Write the IV⁶ V connections below, following this procedure:

   1. Write the bass.
   2. Write the typical soprano.
   3. Complete the IV⁶, doubling the fifth.
   4. Move the AT stepwise to the chord tones of V, being sure to avoid voice crossing and spacing errors.

OR

f: IV⁶   V

OR

21

A♭: IV⁶   V

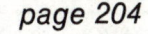

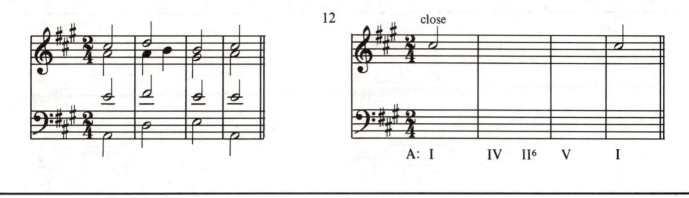

12

A: I   IV   II⁶   V   I

13 Complete the Roman numeral analysis of each progression below:

(1) II⁶
(2) II

(1) E: I   IV __ V⁷   I (2) I   IV __ V⁷   I

14 A prolongation of pre-dominant harmony similar to IV II⁶ occurs in the movement from IV to II. The usual voice leading is indicated in the example below. An upper voice moves from scale degree

(1) 1 (to) 2
(2) 3rd

(1) ____ to ____ and common tones are kept as the bass descends a (2) ____ (*general interval*).

B♭:   IV   II

15 IV II⁶ and IV II may, for the most part, be used interchangeably. One difference in their use, however, is important to remember: IV II⁶ commonly occurs in both major and minor keys, whereas IV²

diminished

is generally found only in major keys. (Remember, II, a _____ triad in minor, is rarely found in root position.)

(1) **y**

(2) The spacing in V is incorrect. There is more than an octave between AT.

14 Consider problem **w**. Which of the two solutions (**x** *or* **y**) is correct? (1) _____ What is wrong with the incorrect solution? (2) ....

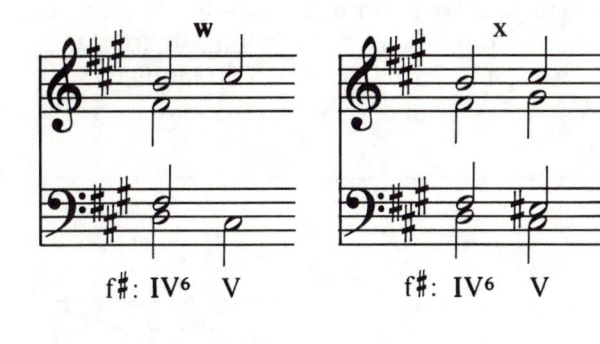

f#: IV⁶   V   f#: IV⁶   V

f#: IV⁶   V

15 Complete the AT for the following IV⁶ V connections. Be sure to avoid voice crossing and to use correct spacing in V.

G: IV⁶   V

16

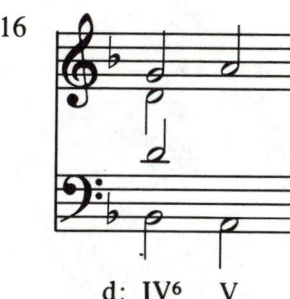

d: IV⁶   V

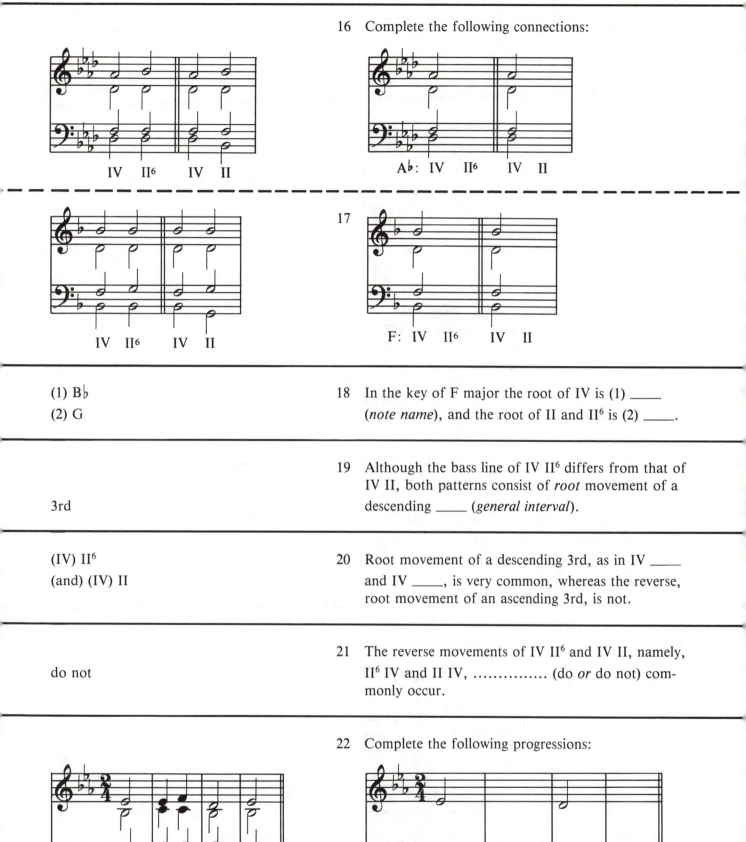

16 Complete the following connections:

IV II⁶ IV II

Ab: IV II⁶ IV II

17

IV II⁶ IV II

F: IV II⁶ IV II

(1) Bb

(2) G

18 In the key of F major the root of IV is (1) _____ (*note name*), and the root of II and II⁶ is (2) _____.

3rd

19 Although the bass line of IV II⁶ differs from that of IV II, both patterns consist of *root* movement of a descending _____ (*general interval*).

(IV) II⁶

(and) (IV) II

20 Root movement of a descending 3rd, as in IV _____ and IV _____, is very common, whereas the reverse, root movement of an ascending 3rd, is not.

do not

21 The reverse movements of IV II⁶ and IV II, namely, II⁶ IV and II IV, ... (do *or* do not) commonly occur.

22 Complete the following progressions:

Eb: I   IV II V⁷   I

12 In moving from a IV⁶ with doubled fifth to V, all stepwise voice leading is possible.
   Consider the problem below. What notes are to be added in the AT? ____ ____ (*Do not write the chord*.)

A C

13 Continuing with the problem from the previous frame, which of the two solutions below is correct?
   (1) ____
   What is wrong with the incorrect solution?
   (2) ....

(1) x

(2) The alto and tenor voices cross.

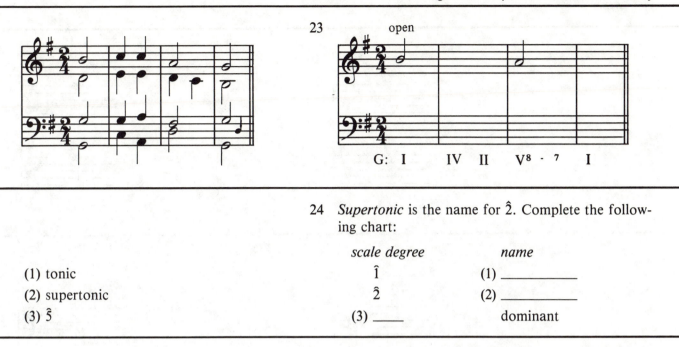

23

G: I   IV   II   V⁸ · ⁷   I

24 *Supertonic* is the name for $\hat{2}$. Complete the following chart:

(1) tonic

(2) supertonic

(3) $\hat{5}$

scale degree	name
$\hat{1}$	(1) _____
$\hat{2}$	(2) _____
(3) _____	dominant

25 Give the Roman numeral analysis of the following progression:

F: I I⁶ II II⁶ V⁷ I

(1) tonic
(2) dominant
(3) supertonic

26 Just as I I⁶ (and I⁶ I) and V V⁶ (and V⁶ V) prolong (1) _____ and (2) _____ harmony, respectively, II II⁶ (and II⁶ II) prolongs (3) _____ harmony.

voice exchange

27 As in I I⁶ (and V V⁶) a typical SB pattern in II II⁶, as illustrated below, is _____ _____.

D: II   II⁶

(Note: Since II and II⁶ do not generally have a soprano of $\hat{6}$, parallel 10ths between SB in II II⁶ are not common.)

9   When IV⁶ is used as a pre-dominant, the best voice leading is achieved by doubling the fifth of the chord, Î. By using this doubling, you will automatically avoid the problematic augmented 2nd in minor keys.

(1) **x**

(2) fifth

(3) **y**

(4) alto

Study the examples below. In example (1) ____, the correct doubling of the (2) _____ of IV⁶ provides smooth voice leading. In example (3) ____, doubling the third of IV⁶ results in faulty voice leading; there is an augmented 2nd in the (4) _____ voice.

g: IV⁶   V   g: IV⁶   V

10   Write the AT for each of the following IV⁶ chords, doubling the chord fifth in each case:

f#:   IV⁶

11

B♭:   IV⁶

third (*or* bass)

28 Study the AT voice leading in the example below. In order to attain a II⁶ with doubled _____ and to avoid parallel octaves, the AT must move by leap.

D: II   II⁶

29 Complete the AT. (*Be sure to double the third of II⁶ and to avoid parallel octaves.*)

B♭: II   II⁶

30

E: II   II⁶

31 (*Remember to double the root of II and be particularly careful to avoid parallel octaves.*)

A♭: II⁶   II

$\hat{4}$ $\hat{5}$

5 Write the outer voices for the following IV⁶ V connections. Use the typical soprano, ____ ____.

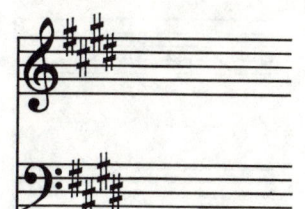

E: **IV⁶** V

(*Soprano may be written an octave lower.*)

6

g: **IV⁶** V

(*Soprano may be written an octave higher.*)

7

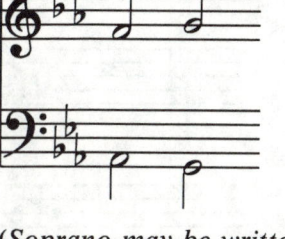

c: **IV⁶** V

(1) fifth

(2) is

8 The typical voice leading in IV⁶ V is illustrated below: Note that the (1) _____ (*chord member*) of IV⁶ is doubled and that the resulting voice leading (2) .... (is *or* is not) all stepwise.

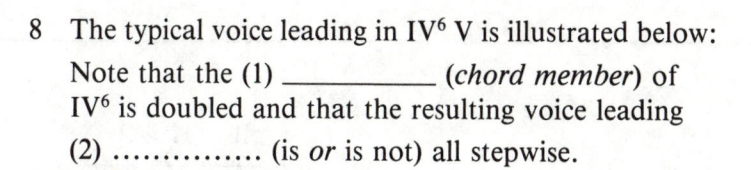

c: **IV⁶** V

32 Complete these patterns, using voice exchange in the SB:

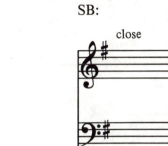

G: II   II⁶

33

E♭: II⁶   II

34

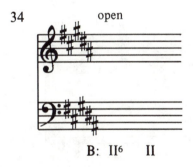

B: II⁶   II

35 Complete these progressions, using SB voice exchange in the prolongation of supertonic harmony:

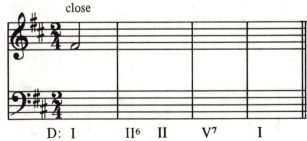

OR

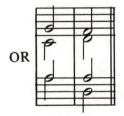

D: I   II⁶   II   V⁷   I

2 IV⁶ often functions as a *pre-dominant* chord, leading to V. Give the Roman numeral analysis of the following:

(1) I IV⁶ V$^{8-7}$ I

(1) E♭ :

(2) pre-dominant

In this example, IV⁶ is used as a (2) _____ chord.

---

3 Write the Roman numeral analysis of this example:

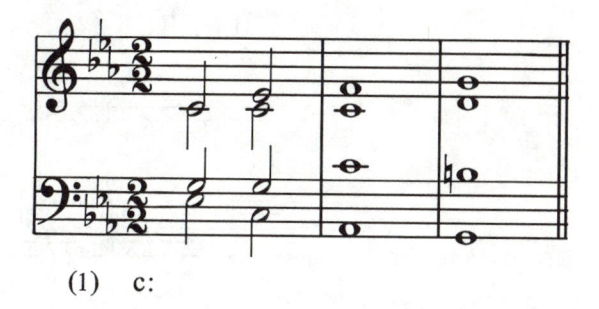

(1) I⁶ I IV⁶ V

(1) c:

(2) pre-dominant (chord)

IV⁶ functions as a (2) ....

---

4 As illustrated in example **x** (and in previous frames), the soprano most frequently occurring with IV⁶ V is $\hat{4}$ $\hat{5}$ (a soprano pattern which could never occur with root position IV to V because of the resulting parallel octaves with the bass). Note in example **x** that $\hat{5}$ is approached by step from above in the bass and by step from below in the soprano.

Write the most common soprano for example **y**:

(Soprano may be written an octave higher.)

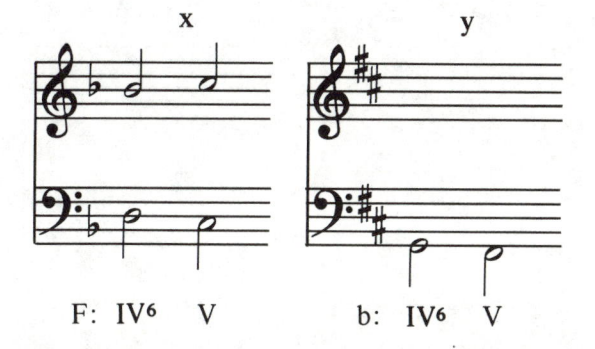

F: IV⁶ V   b: IV⁶ V

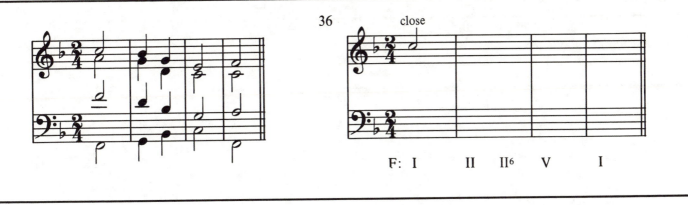

36

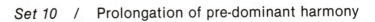

F: I   II   II⁶   V   I

---

37 Just as the SB voice exchange in I I⁶ may be connected by a passing ⁶₃ chord, so may the SB voice exchange in II II⁶.

Study the examples below. Both I I⁶ (in example **x**) and II II⁶ (in example **y**) are connected by a

(1) passing

(1) _____ ⁶₃ chord. Complete each Roman numeral analysis:

(2) VII⁶

(2) G: I   ___ I⁶   IV   V   I

(3) I⁶

(3) G: I   II ___ II⁶   V   I

VII⁶

38 As shown in the examples in the previous frame, the passing ⁶₃ chord used in connecting I and I⁶ is ____, and the passing ⁶₃ chord used in connecting II and II⁶ is I⁶. (Note: Almost any harmony may be prolonged with a passing ⁶₃ chord. ⁵₃ chords, because of their stability, are rarely used as passing chords.)

plagal

42 Sometimes a phrase ends with the progression IV I, which is termed a *plagal* cadence. The phrase below concludes with a _____ cadence.

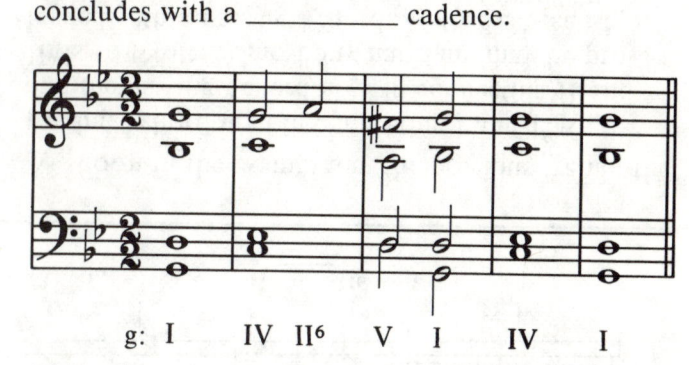

g: I   IV II⁶   V   I   IV   I

43 When a plagal cadence occurs, it often immediately follows a V⁽⁷⁾ I progression. Give the Roman numeral analysis of the following example, and label the cadence according to type.

A: I | II⁶ II | V⁷ I | IV | I ‖
$\underbrace{\qquad}$
plagal
cadence

44 Conclude the progression below with a plagal cadence, and complete the Roman numeral analysis:

IV   I

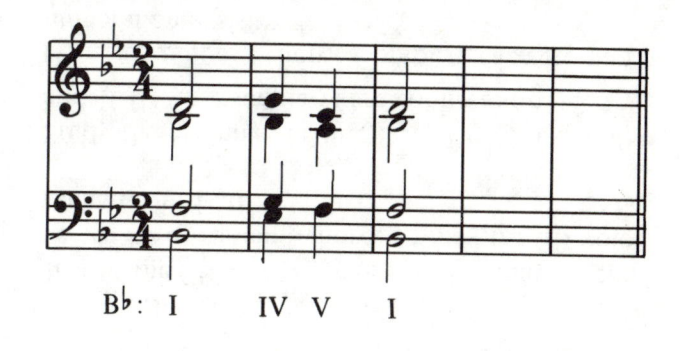

B♭: I   IV V   I

Set 15 / OTHER USES OF IV⁶

1 In addition to its use in prolonging tonic harmony, IV⁶ has a variety of other usages. We will consider a few of the most important in this set.

39 Complete the Roman numeral analysis of this progression:

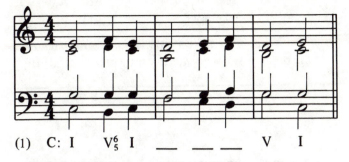

(1)   C: I   V$^6_5$ I   ___   ___   ___   V   I

(1) II^6 I^6 II

Although the passing chord between II^6 and II is a

(2) I^6

(2) ____, consisting of $\hat{1}$, $\hat{3}$, and $\hat{5}$, the chord does not have tonic function—it does not open or close a harmonic progression. Its function is to connect the II and II^6. Though in the overall key context $\hat{1}$, $\hat{3}$, and $\hat{5}$ are stable, in this immediate context they are active—their function is to lead to members of II.

40 In the example below connect the SB voice exchange with passing tones. (*Do not write the AT.*)

E♭:   II   I^6 II^6

41 Write SB voice exchange connected with passing tones for the following:

G: II^6 I^6 II

38 Write the Roman numeral analysis:

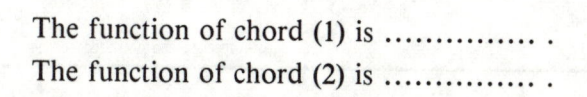

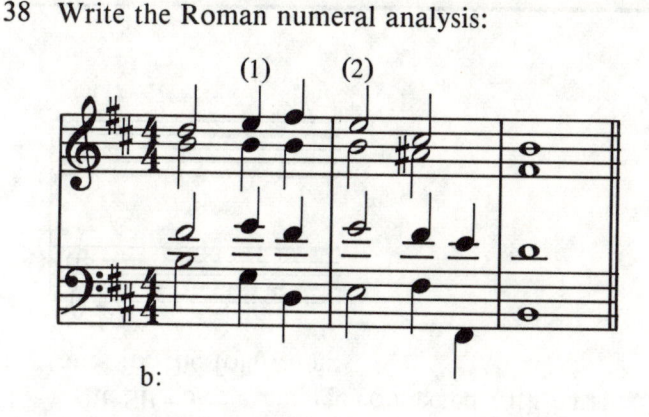

b:

I IV⁶ I⁶ | IV V⁸⁻⁷ | I ‖

(1) tonic prolongation

(2) pre-dominant

The function of chord (1) is ....

The function of chord (2) is ....

39 Write the following progression. Bracket the prolongation of opening tonic.

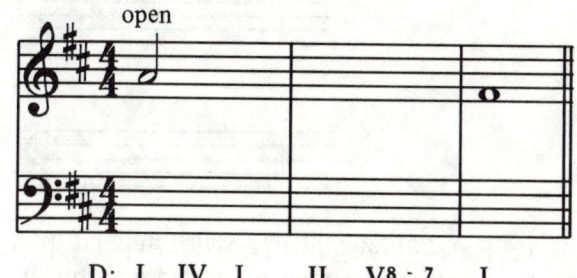

D: I IV I   II V⁸ ⁻ ⁷ I

40 Set this figured bass. First give the Roman numeral analysis and bracket the prolongation of opening tonic.

E♭: I IV⁶ I⁶ II⁶ V I

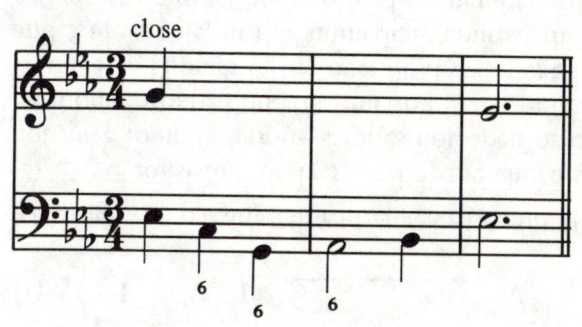

41 Phrases may end in a variety of ways. Cadence patterns that we have studied thus far are:

(1) authentic

(2) half

(3) deceptive

V⁽⁷⁾ I (1) _____ cadence

⟶ V (2) _____ cadence

V⁽⁷⁾ VI (3) _____ cadence

42 When the SB voice exchange of II II⁶ (or II⁶ II) is connected with passing tones, the passing I⁶ automatically has a doubled third. Complete the inner voices:

E♭: II   I⁶   II⁶

43

G: II⁶   I⁶   II

44 Write the following prolongations of supertonic harmony, using SB voice exchange:

close

F: II⁶   I⁶   II

45   close

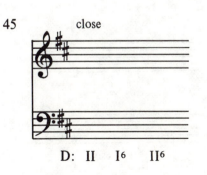

D: II   I⁶   II⁶

35 (*Hint: What is the typical setting?*)

I   IV⁶   I⁶

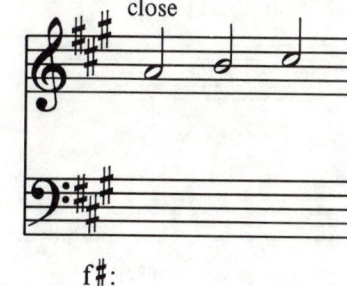

close

f#:

I   IV   I
*   *

(*Note:* *Using I⁶ would result in a doubled third.*)

36   open

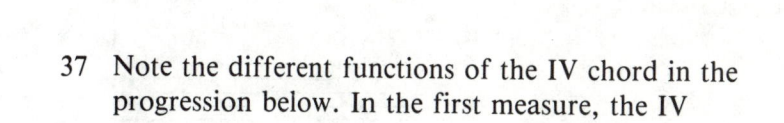

Bb:

(1) prolong

(2) pre-dominant

37 Note the different functions of the IV chord in the progression below. In the first measure, the IV chord is used to (1) _____ the opening tonic. In the second measure, the IV is used as a (2) _____ chord, leading to the dominant.

C: I   IV I   IV V⁷   I
        I

46 Complete the following progression using procedures outlined above. (*First write the outer voices; then fill in the AT, using the smoothest correct voice leading.*)

A: I V$^4_3$ I^6 II I^6 II^6 V$^{8-7}$ I

AT

47 When II I^6 II^6 or II^6 I^6 II with SB voice exchange are written in close spacing, faulty parallels are not a problem. However, when written in open spacing, with usual doubling, parallel perfect 5ths between II and I^6 are inevitable. In the example below parallel perfect 5ths occur between the .... voices.

G: II   I^6 II^6

close

48 The parallel perfect 5ths in the example in the preceding frame may be avoided in two ways:

1. By using _____ spacing (as shown in example **x**).

2. By doubling the third of II instead of the root (as shown in example **y**).

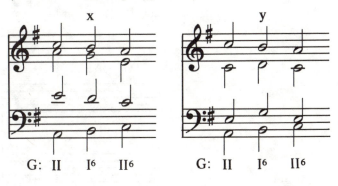

G: II   I^6 II^6 G: II   I^6 II^6

31

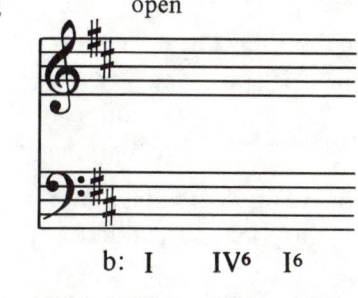

E♭: I   IV⁶ I⁶

32 open

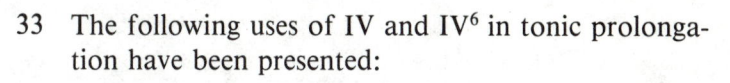

b: I   IV⁶ I⁶

33 The following uses of IV and IV⁶ in tonic prolongation have been presented:

(1) N

I IV I
I⁶ IV I⁶   Most often used with a(n) (1) ____
I IV I⁶   (P, N, *or* IN) soprano or a sustained $\hat{1}$
             in the soprano.

I IV⁶ I⁶   Typically used with a passing soprano,

(2) $\hat{3}$ $\hat{4}$ $\hat{5}$

(2) ____ ____ ____.

The best doubling is:

(3) root (*or* bass)

I and IV   (3) _____

(4) third (*or* bass)

IV⁶   (4) _____

(5) fifth

I⁶   (5) _____

34 Set the following soprano patterns using IV or IV⁶ to prolong tonic. (*Refer, as necessary, to the summary in the previous frame.*)

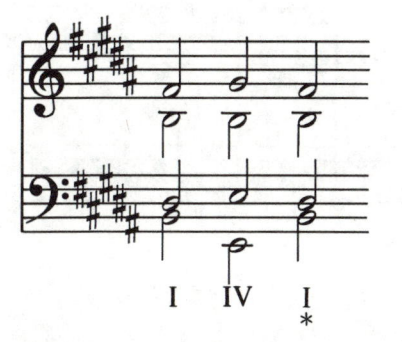

I   IV   I
              *

(*Note: *Using a I⁶ would take the bass out of range.*)

open

B:

OR

49 Complete the following, doubling the third of II:

B: II   I⁶   II⁶

(As we see here—and as later sets will confirm—voice leading considerations sometimes preclude the use of usual doubling.)

50 The following are important points for review:

The function of pre-dominant harmony is to lead from an (1) _____ _____ to the (2) _____.

(1) opening tonic
(2) dominant

Ways of (3) _____ pre-dominant harmony that have been introduced are:

(3) prolonging

   IV II⁶
   IV II
   II II⁶ and II⁶ II
   II I⁶ II⁶ and II⁶ I⁶ II

In IV II⁶ all voices are sustained but for the movement from a (4) ____ above the bass to a (5) ____ above the bass. In IV II the upper voice movement is the same as in IV II⁶.

(4) 5th
(5) 6th

The common SB pattern in II II⁶ and II⁶ II is (6) _____ _____. Usual doubling is the (7) _____ of II and the (8) _____ of II⁶.

(6) voice exchange
(7) root (*or* bass)
(8) third (*or* bass)

Sometimes a passing (9) ____ (*chord symbol*) connects the voice exchange in the prolongation of supertonic harmony. Correct voice leading is most easily achieved by using close spacing.

(9) I⁶

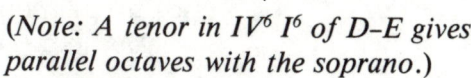

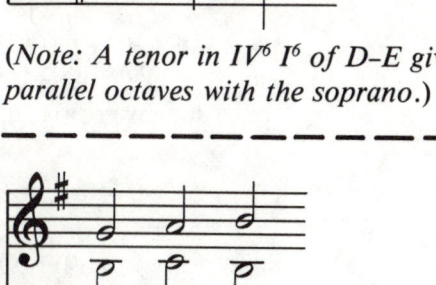

(*Note: A tenor in IV⁶ I⁶ of D–E gives parallel octaves with the soprano.*)

27 Complete the inner voices as directed above:

A: I   IV⁶   I⁶

28

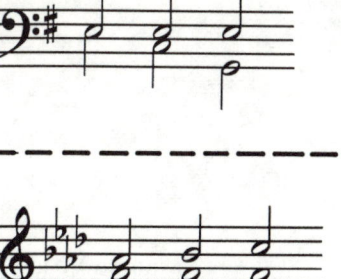

e: I   IV⁶   I⁶

29   close

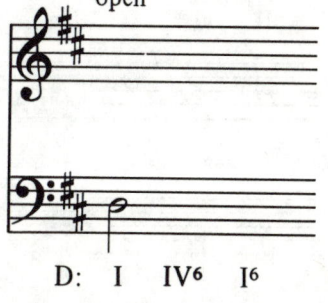

f: I   IV⁶   I⁶

30 Use this procedure in completing the following examples:

1. Write the bass line. (*Remember the correct direction.*)
2. Write the soprano that is typically used ($\hat{3}$ $\hat{4}$ $\hat{5}$).
3. Write the AT in the smoothest correct way. (*Double the third of IV⁶ and the fifth of I⁶. Keep the common tone in the same voice; use a neighboring pattern in the other voice.*)

open

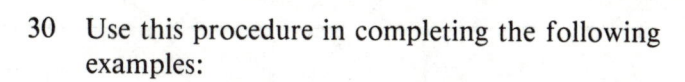

D: I   IV⁶   I⁶

(*SAT may be written an octave higher.*)

51 Set the following melodies, using prolongation of opening tonic and prolongation of pre-dominant harmony. Give the Roman numeral analysis of each. Remember to follow the usual doubling and voice-leading procedures.

c: I VII⁶ I⁶ IV II⁶ V⁽⁷⁾ I

open

52

B♭: I V$^4_3$ I⁶ II II⁶ V⁽⁷⁾ I

OR

V⁸⁻⁷ I

close

parallel
10ths

voice
exchange

53 Set this figured bass following procedures outlined above:

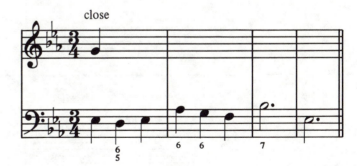

close

E♭: I V$^6_5$ I II⁶ I⁶ II V⁷ I

OR

V⁷ I

6
5   6 6   7

22 Write the outer voices for each. (*Use the typical soprano line.*)

(*only correct bass*)

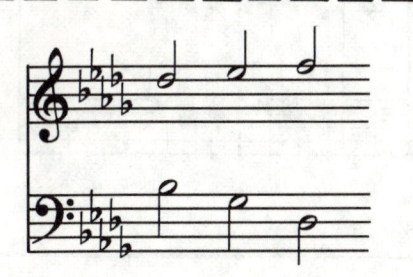

(*only correct bass*)

A: I   IV⁶   I⁶

23

bb: I   IV⁶   I⁶

---

24 The best doubling for IV⁶ (as the best doubling for VI) depends upon the way the chord is being used. The best doubling in I IV⁶ I⁶ is that which gives the smoothest correct voice leading. Note the smooth inner voice leading in the example below. The

(1) common tone

(1) _____ _____ is kept in the alto, and the tenor has a neighboring pattern of

(2) $\hat{5}$ $\hat{6}$ $\hat{5}$

(2) ___ ___ ___ (*scale degrees*).

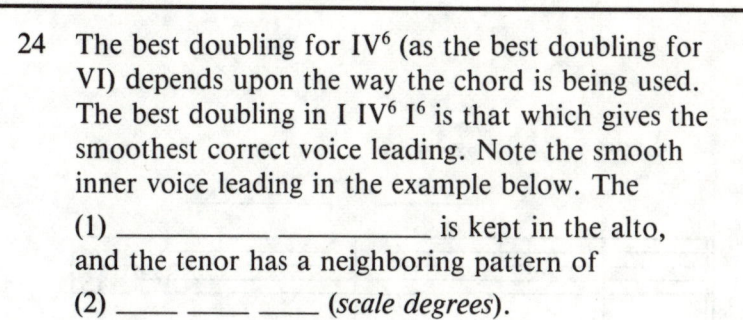

G: I   IV⁶   I⁶

---

25 Refer again to the example in the previous frame.

(1) third (*or* bass)

The (1) _____ of IV⁶ is doubled.

(2) fifth (*or* soprano)

The (2) _____ of I⁶ is doubled.

---

26 The smoothest voice leading in I IV⁶ I⁶ results from the following doubling:

I	root

(1) third

IV⁶ (1) _____

(2) fifth

I⁶ (2) _____

1 The VI chord has a variety of uses which will be covered in this and the following two sets. First we will consider the use of VI as a pre-dominant immediately preceding V in major keys.

IV, II, and II⁶

2 Although the most common pre-dominant chords are ____, ____, and ____, other chords may function as pre-dominants as well.

---

3 Give the Roman numeral analysis of the following:

(1) E♭ :

(1) I VI V I

In this example VI precedes and leads to V. It therefore functions as a (2) _____ chord.

(2) pre-dominant

---

4 Give the Roman numeral analysis of the example below:

(1)

(1) A♭: I VI V I

(2) pre-dominant
(3) dominant

VI functions as a (2) _____ chord, leading from the opening tonic to the (3) _____.

---

do not

5 VI and V .... (do *or* do not) have a common tone.

---

(1) contrary motion-nearest
(2) move the SAT (*or* upper voices) to the nearest chord tones in contrary motion to the bass.

6 The smoothest correct way to connect two triads that do not have a common tone (such as IV V and VI V) is the (1) .... connection. The procedure is to (2) ....

16 As shown in the previous frame, IV⁶ is used to connect I with I⁶. This bass pattern is *descending* and paired with a stepwise ascending soprano, $\hat3\ \hat4\ \hat5$. Complete the bass line for the following:

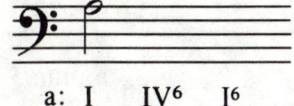

a: I   IV⁶   I⁶

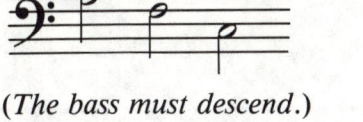

(*The bass must descend.*)

---

descending

17 I IV⁶ I⁶ is characterized by a _____ bass line.

18 Write the bass line:

E♭: I   IV⁶   I⁶

($\hat3$) $\hat4$ $\hat5$

19 The most common soprano for I IV⁶ I⁶, as illustrated below, is an ascending stepwise line, $\hat3$ ____ ____.

E♭: I   IV⁶   I⁶

---

20 Complete the soprano line:

c♯: I   IV⁶   I⁶

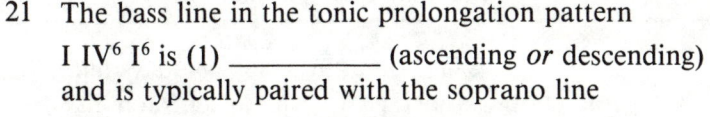

---

(1) descending

(2) $\hat3$ $\hat4$ $\hat5$

21 The bass line in the tonic prolongation pattern I IV⁶ I⁶ is (1) _____ (ascending *or* descending) and is typically paired with the soprano line (2) ____ ____ ____ (*scale degrees*).

7 Complete this connection, moving the upper voices to the nearest chord tones in contrary motion to the bass:

B♭: VI   V

---

parallel octaves between SB and parallel perfect 5ths between TB

8 What are the specific voice-leading errors in this connection? ....

E: VI   V

Rewrite it correctly:

E: VI   V

---

contrary motion-nearest

9 Complete the following. Remember that the smoothest correct connections of VI V are

....

F: VI   V

12

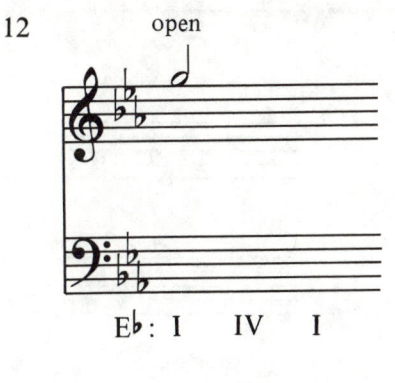

open

E♭: I   IV   I

13 (*Be careful to avoid parallel octaves in IV I⁶.*)

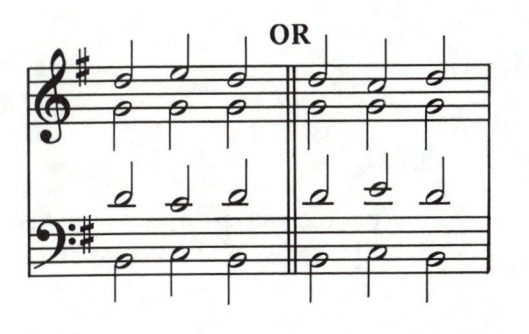

close

c: I   IV   I⁶

14 (*Keep the common tone in the same voice. Use neighboring patterns in the other voices.*)

OR

G: I⁶   IV   I⁶

15 IV⁶ is also used in prolonging tonic. Its most common usage is illustrated below. Give the Roman numeral analysis:

I IV⁶ I⁶

F:

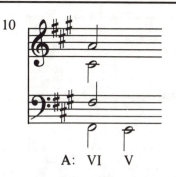

10

A: VI   V

11   As we will see in the next two sets, doubling in VI depends upon the way the chord is used; it depends upon the function of the chord and what precedes and follows it. When VI is used as a pre-dominant, the usual rule is to double the root. Complete the VI chord below, using correct doubling, and then connect VI to V:

close

G: VI   V

---

contrary

12   Complete the following connections. Double check each chord for correct doubling of the root and remember to move all upper voices in _____ motion to the bass. (*First write the bass.*)

open

E♭: VI   V

13

close

D: VI   V

7

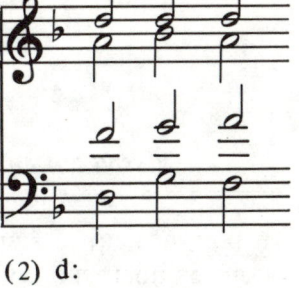

A♭: I   IV   I

8 Some other ways that IV is used in tonic prolongation are illustrated below. Write the Roman numeral
analysis of each:

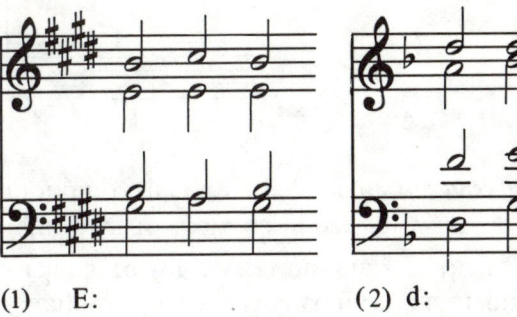

(1) E: _____   (2) d: _____

(1) I⁶ IV I⁶ (2) I IV I⁶

9 Note the smooth voice leading in the examples in
the previous frame. When a I⁶ precedes or follows
IV in a tonic prolongation pattern, the smoothest
voice leading is achieved by doubling the _____
(*chord member*) of I⁶.

fifth

10 The best doubling in I and IV is always the
(1) _____, and in the cases under consideration, the best doubling for I⁶ is the (2) _____.

(1) root
(2) fifth

11 Complete the following connections, using the
smoothest possible voice leading:

f: I⁶   IV   I⁶

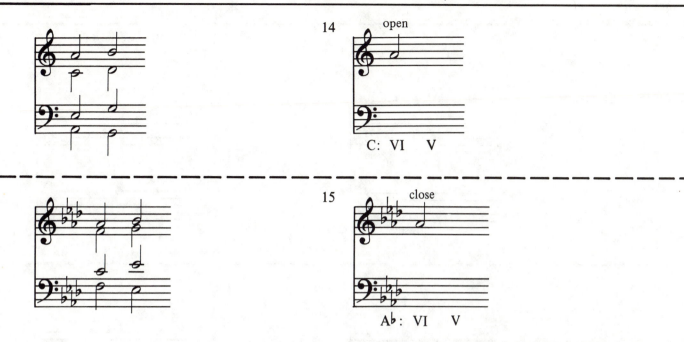

14 open

C: VI V

15 close

A♭: VI V

16 In previous frames the examples of VI as a pre-dominant have been in major keys. Using VI as a pre-dominant in minor keys is problematic. The reason for this is obvious in the example below. When the root of VI is doubled and the upper voices move up, in contrary motion to the bass (as they must to avoid faulty parallels), an augmented 2nd, in this case in the _____ voice, results. Because of the problematic nature of this progression, it is used less frequently and we do not deal with it here.

tenor

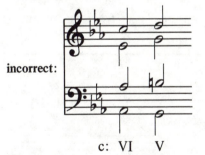

incorrect:

c: VI V

17 The frames below contain VI V I connections. As you complete these progressions, bear in mind the soprano scale degrees being used.

close

B: VI V I

3 The upper voice movement in I IV I may be
summarized:

$$\hat{5} \quad \hat{6} \quad \hat{5}$$
$$\hat{3} \quad \hat{4} \quad \hat{3}$$
$$\hat{1} \quad \hat{1} \quad \hat{1}$$

Complete the connection:

D: I   IV   I

4 In the succession I IV I, the function of IV is to
prolong   _____ tonic.

5 Complete the following tonic prolongation patterns:

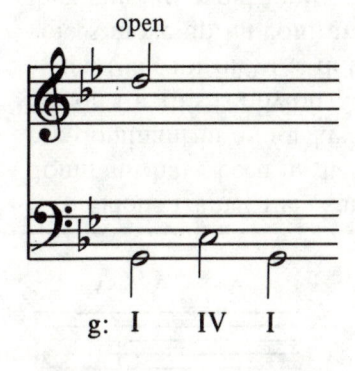

open

g: I   IV   I

6

close

e: I   IV   I

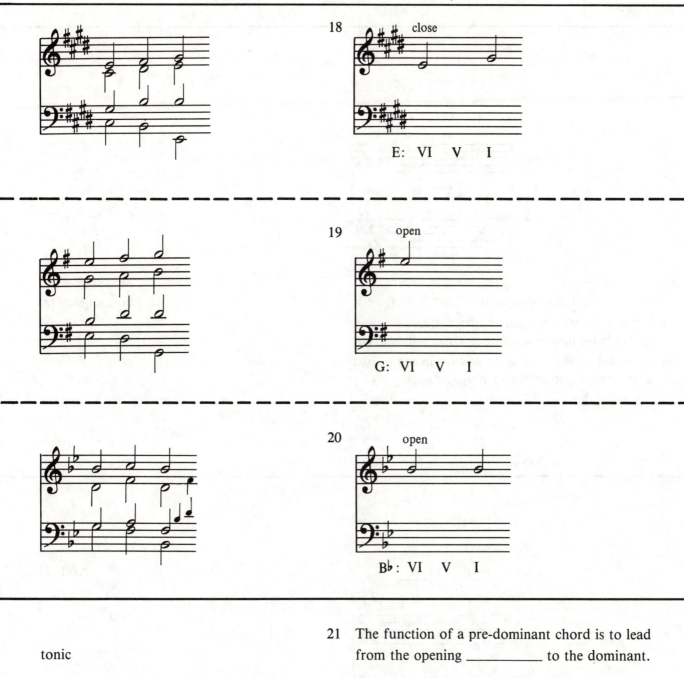

18 close

E: VI V I

19 open

G: VI V I

20 open

B♭: VI V I

tonic

21 The function of a pre-dominant chord is to lead from the opening _____ to the dominant.

two

22 As illustrated below, I and VI can be connected very smoothly because they have _____ (*how many*?) common tones.

G: I VI

(1) pre-dominant

1   While the most common use of IV is as a

(1) _____ chord, leading from the opening tonic to the dominant, there are other ways in which IV is used.

The example below illustrates the use of IV in tonic prolongation. Give the Roman numeral analysis:

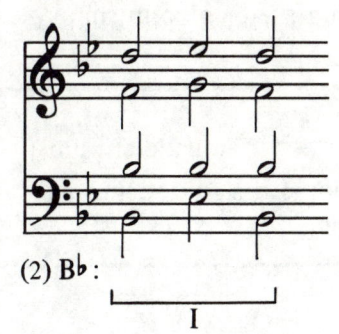

(2) B♭ :

(2) I IV I

---

(1) 1̂

(2) neighboring

(3) neighboring

2   I IV I is characterized by neighboring patterns in two of the upper voices. Note in the upper voices in the example below that the common tone, (1) ____ (*scale degree*), is kept in the same voice, and that 4̂ is a (2) _____ tone to 3̂, and 6̂ is a

(3) _____ tone to 5̂.

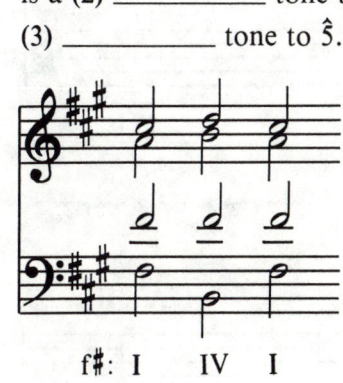

f♯: I   IV   I

23 Complete these connections, keeping the common tones between I and VI in the same voices:

F: I   VI

24

D: I   VI

25

A: I   VI

26 Write each of the following harmonic progressions in the smoothest correct way. Remember that in

ascend

moving from VI to V all upper voices _____ (ascend *or* descend). Bear in mind the soprano scale degrees being used.

F: I   VI   V   I

6. Set each figured bass. Give the Roman numeral analysis.

(1)

(2) *Use the typical soprano.*

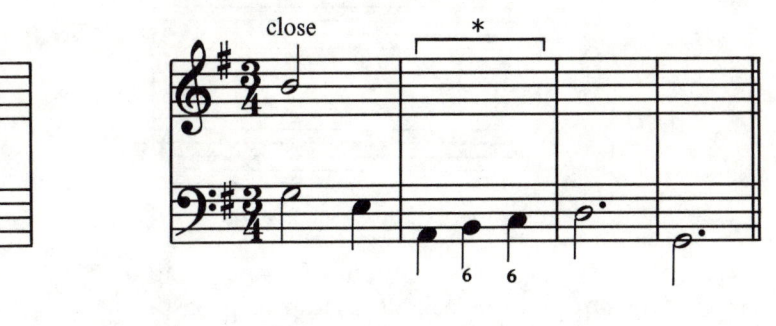

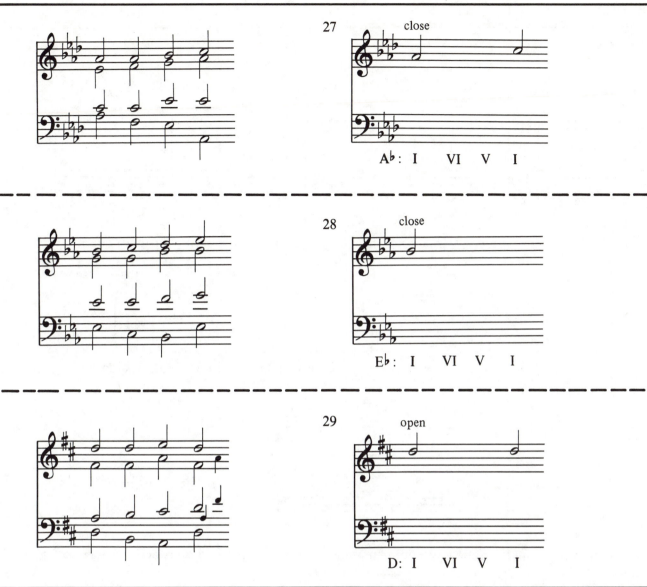

27   close

A♭: I   VI   V   I

28   close

E♭: I   VI   V   I

29   open

D: I   VI   V   I

---

30   Pre-dominant chords that have been introduced thus far are:

    IV
    II
    II⁶
    VI

Although these chords have different Roman numerals, as pre-dominant chords they have the same

(1) tonic

(2) dominant

function: They lead from the opening (1) _____ to the (2) _____ in a basic harmonic progression.

While it is important to realize the similarity of function of these chords, it is also important to know the different situations in which each is used.

The questions below will test your mastery of the material in Part 3. Complete the entire test, then check your answers with the correct ones on page 165. For each question that you miss, the corresponding material may be reviewed in the set whose number is given with the correct answer.

1. Using the chords IV, II, and II⁶, show (with Roman numerals) three ways that pre-dominant harmony may be prolonged:

   ____ ____   ____ ____   ____ ____

2. Give a four-voice illustration of prolongation of supertonic harmony. Use voice exchange in the SB. Provide the Roman numeral analysis.

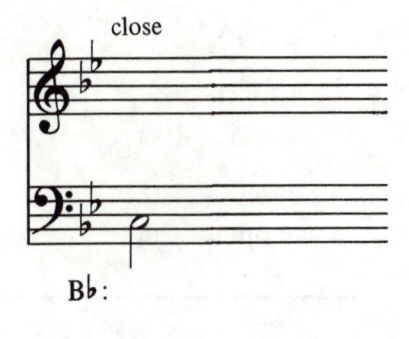

3. Set the following soprano for four voices. Choose the appropriate pre-dominant (IV, II, II⁶, or VI).

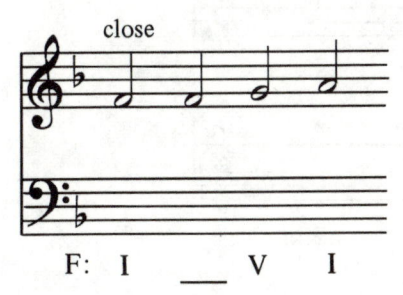

4. The deceptive resolution of V^7 is as follows:

   $$\text{upper} \left\{ \begin{array}{l} \hat{7} \text{ to } \underline{\quad} \\ \hat{4} \text{ to } \underline{\quad} \\ \hat{2} \text{ to } \underline{\quad} \end{array} \right.$$

   bass $\quad \hat{5}$ to ____

5. Write the following progressions. Describe the function of each VI chord.

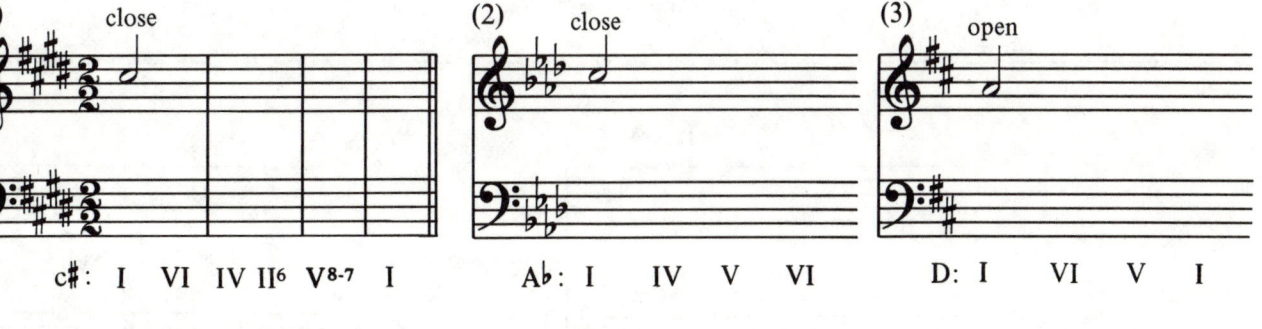

31 Obviously, there are scale degrees that some of the pre-dominant chords have in common, and there are some differences:

(1) $\hat{4}$, $\hat{6}$, and $\hat{1}$

IV contains (1) _____, _____, and _____.

(2) $\hat{2}$, $\hat{4}$

II and II⁶ contain (2) _____, _____, and $\hat{6}$ (though they rarely support $\hat{6}$ in the soprano).

(3) $\hat{6}$, $\hat{1}$, and $\hat{3}$

VI contains (3) _____, _____, and _____.

---

32 VI differs from IV and II⁶ in that, in leading to V, it is used in setting an *ascending* soprano. (Remember that in order to avoid faulty parallels, upper voices in VI V move in contrary motion to the bass; that is, they move _____ (up *or* down).)

up

---

33 On the other hand, IV and II⁶, in leading to V, are used in setting a *descending* soprano. (Remember that in order to avoid faulty parallels in IV or II⁶ to V, upper voices move in contrary motion to the bass; that is, they move _____ (up *or* down).)

down

II is generally used in setting either a descending soprano or a sustained (or repeated) soprano of $\hat{2}$.

---

34 In leading to V, VI is used in setting a(n)

(1) ascending

(1) _____ (ascending *or* descending) soprano;

(2) descending

IV and II⁶ are used in setting a(n) (2) _____ soprano.

---

35 Consider the soprano below. The problem is to set it with one of the basic harmonic progressions studied:

$$I \begin{bmatrix} IV \\ II \\ II^6 \\ VI \end{bmatrix} ? \; V \; I$$

How do we determine which pre-dominant chord to use? First, of the pre-dominant chords studied, only _____ and _____ contain $\hat{1}$ (the given soprano).

IV (and) VI

Bb: I   VI   II   V⁷   I

OR

VI in descending 5th progression, leading from opening tonic to II.

48 Set the following figured bass patterns. Give the Roman numeral analysis of each and describe the function of each VI chord.

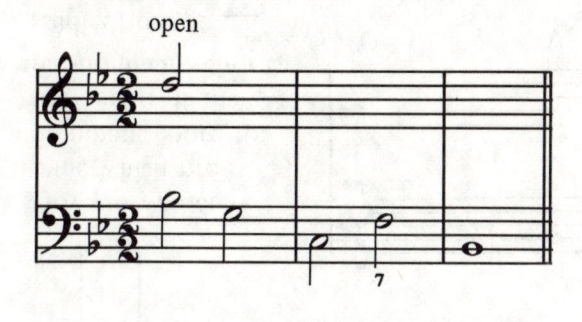

open

7

. . . .

Bb: I   VI   V   I

VI as pre-dominant.

49 close

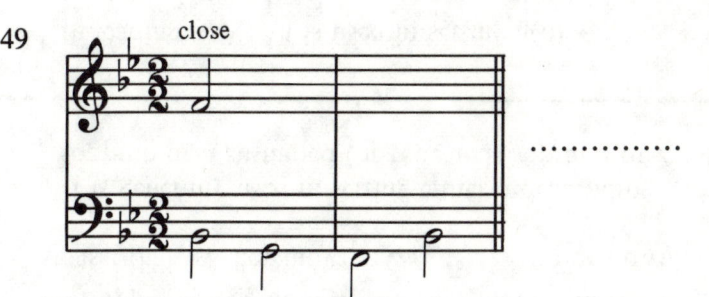

. . . .

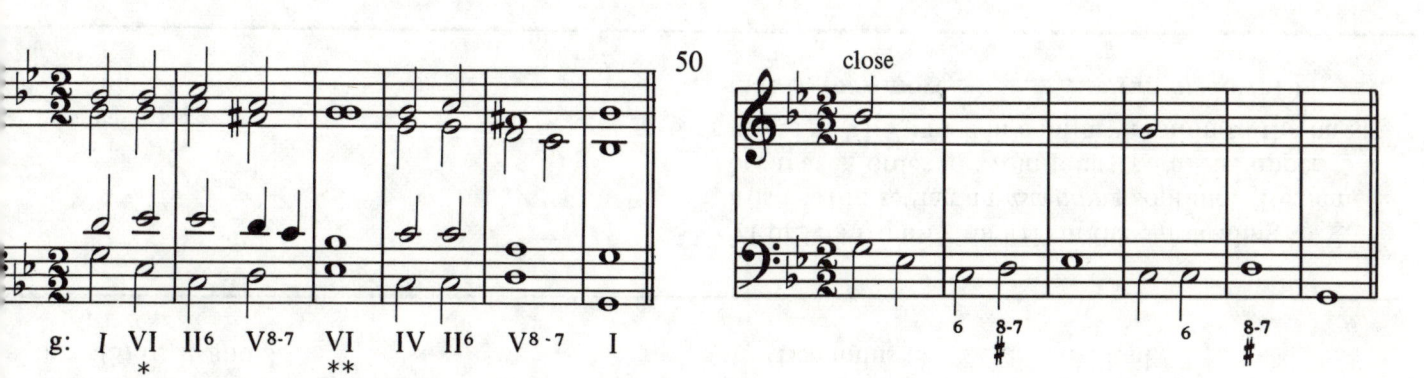

g: I VI II⁶ V⁸⁻⁷ VI IV II⁶ V⁸⁻⁷ I
       *   **

*VI in descending 3rd progression, leading from opening tonic to II⁶.
**VI as substitute for closing tonic (a deceptive cadence).

50 close

6   8-7   6   8-7
     #   #

. . . .

(1) VI

36 Now, continuing with the problem from the previous frame, which of these two pre-dominant chords may support an ascending soprano (Î 2̂) in leading to V? (1) _____ (See examples below.)

C: I IV V I   C: I VI V I

What is the error in the faulty example above?
(2) ....

(2) parallel perfect 5ths in the SB of IV V

---

37 Indicate which of the basic harmonic progressions listed in frame 35 may be used to set each of the following soprano lines (refer to the procedure given in previous frames, if necessary). Give the Roman numeral analysis and bass line for each.

G: I IV V I

(*Note: VI is not used in setting a descending soprano because it would result in parallel octaves and perfect 5ths between the bass and inner voices.*)

G:

D: I VI V I

(*Note: If IV were used, parallel octaves and perfect 5ths would result between the bass and inner voices. II and II⁶ are not used to support 6̂.*)

38
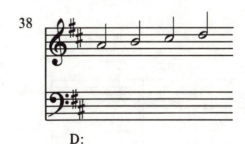

D:

45 Set the following figured bass. First give the Roman numeral analysis.

C: I I⁶ IV V VI IV II⁶ V I

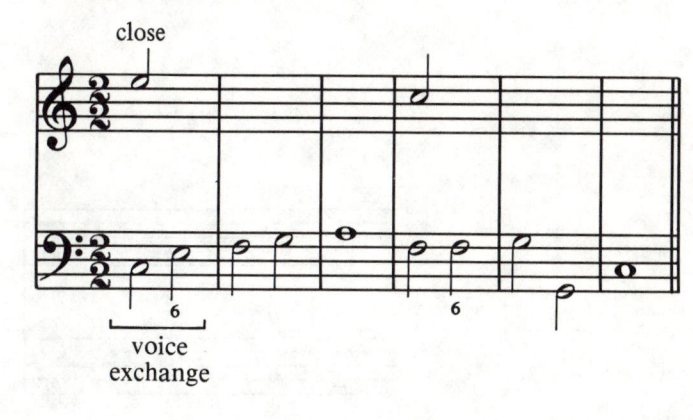

close

voice
exchange

6   6

46 In this and the previous two sets three different usages of VI have been introduced:

   1. VI as a pre-dominant.
   2. VI in descending 3rd and 5th progressions, leading from the opening tonic to IV, II⁶, or II.
   3. VI as a substitute for closing tonic.

(1) root

In usages 1 and 2 the (1) _____ of VI is doubled.

(2) third

In usage 3 the (2) _____ of VI is doubled.

Although usages 2 and 3 may occur within the same progression, VI does not generally occur as both a pre-dominant and a substitute for closing tonic within the same harmonic progression.

47 Give the Roman numeral analysis of the example below. Identify the function of the VI chords.

....

E: I VI | IV II⁶ | V⁸⁻⁷ | VI
   *   **
  IV II | V⁸⁻⁷ | I ‖

*VI in descending 3rd progression, leading from opening tonic to IV.
**VI as substitute for closing tonic (a deceptive cadence).

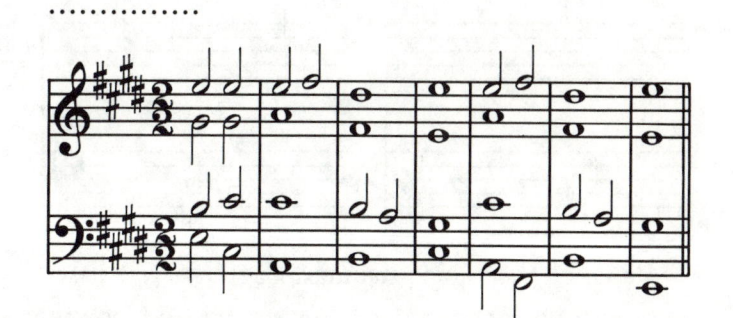

39

A:

I II(6) V I

(Note: Only II and II⁶ contain $\hat{2}$.)

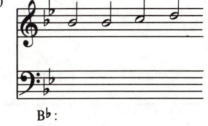

40

B♭ :

I VI V I

41 VI is different from IV and II⁶ (and II, as commonly used) in that it is used to support a(n)

(1) ascending

(1) _____ (ascending *or* descending) soprano in leading to V. An additional way in which VI differs from the other pre-dominants is that VI rarely leads directly to V⁷. Since VI does not contain $\hat{4}$, it cannot prepare the dissonant 7th of V⁷ by common tone.

Set 12 / VI IN DESCENDING 3RD AND 5TH PROGRESSIONS

1 More common than its use as a pre-dominant immediately preceding V is the use of VI illustrated below. Give the Roman numeral analysis:

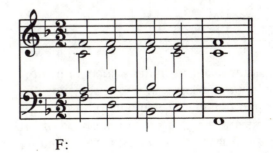

F:

I VI IV V I

41 Although VI can substitute for a closing tonic in a harmonic progression, VI is never a substitute for the *true* closing tonic. That is, a deceptive resolution will lead on to another harmonic progression that will conclude with a true closing tonic. Complete the Roman numeral analysis of the example below:

A: I VII⁶ I⁶
        I

|IV V VI IV|II V|I

42 As illustrated in the example in the frame above, a VI chord functioning as a substitute for closing tonic in a harmonic progression will usually be followed by a pre-dominant chord (IV, II⁶, or II) in leading on to the dominant and then to the true

closing tonic

_____ _____.

43 When a deceptive resolution occurs at the end of a phrase, in place of the expected authentic cadence, it is termed a *deceptive cadence*. A deceptive cadence does not give a feeling of closure; it will be followed by a harmonic progression leading to a(n)

authentic

_____ cadence.

44 Write the Roman numeral analysis of the example below:

(1) F: I V₃⁴ I⁶| II II⁶|V⁸⁻⁷|VI|
       II⁶ I⁶ II|V⁸⁻⁷|I‖

(1)

(2) deceptive

(3) authentic

Measures 3 and 4 form a(n) (2) _____ cadence.

The example concludes with a(n) (3) _____ cadence.

2 VI often leads, through a *descending 3rd bass* pattern, from an opening tonic to the predominant IV or II⁶. Give the Roman numeral analysis of each example below:

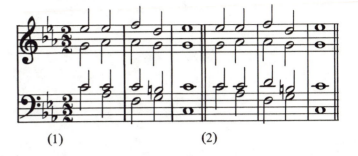

(1) c: I VI IV V I

(2) c: I VI II⁶ V I

(3) 3rds

In each case the bass moves in descending (3) _____ from the opening tonic to the pre-dominant.

3 Write the bass line for each of the following progressions:

b: I VI IV V I

4 A: I VI II⁶ V I

5 f: I VI II⁶ V I

6 E♭: I VI IV V I

descending 3rd

7 A common use of VI is in a _____ ____ bass pattern, leading from the opening tonic to IV or II⁶.

root

8 When VI is used as a pre-dominant (immediately preceding V), the best doubling is the _____. Likewise, in leading from the opening tonic to the pre-dominant IV or II⁶ (or II), the root of VI is doubled.

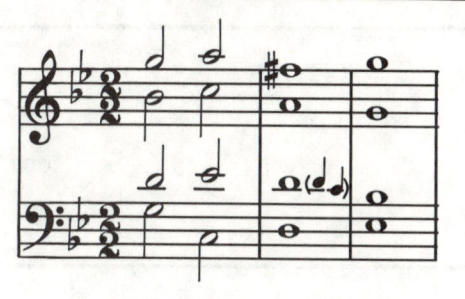

38

g: I   II⁶   V (8-7) VI

I   II⁶   V⁷   VI
     *   **

39   close

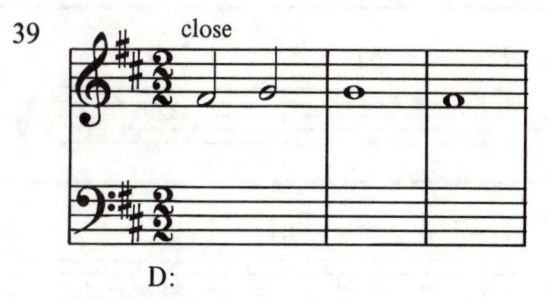

D:

(*Note: *II would result in faulty parallels between the bass and inner voices in I II.*
**Given a soprano of $\hat{4}$, V⁷ (which must be complete) must be used. II⁶ can lead to a complete V⁷, but IV cannot.)

I   II   V⁽⁷⁾   VI
     (or V⁸⁻⁷)

40

E♭ :

OR

I   II⁶   V⁷   VI

two

9 In I VI there is/are _____ (*how many?*) common tone(s). Complete this connection in the smoothest way:

B♭ : I   VI

two

10 VI and IV have _____ (*how many?*) common tone(s). Complete this connection. (*Keep the common tones in the same voices.*)

B♭ : I   VI   IV

11 Complete each of these connections in the smoothest way. (*Remember to keep the common tones in the same voices and to double the root of each chord.*)

open

f♯: I   VI   IV

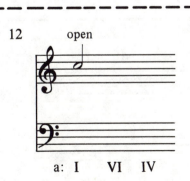

12   open   (*First write the bass.*)

a: I   VI   IV

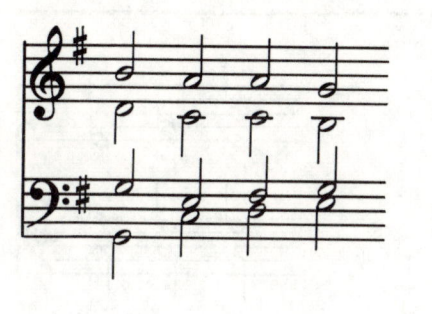

34

G: I   II⁶   V⁷   VI

35 Set the following figured bass patterns. Give the Roman numeral analysis of each.

I   IV   V⁸⁻⁷   VI

A: 8 - 7

36

I   II⁶   V⁸⁻⁷   VI

f♯:   6   8 - 7
              ♯

37 Set each of the following soprano lines for four voices, using a harmonic progression that consists of an opening tonic, a pre-dominant (IV, II⁶, or II), a dominant (V, V⁸⁻⁷, or V⁷), and a deceptive resolution of the dominant. Be sure to give the Roman numeral analysis of your setting. (*Hint: You may find trial and error to be necessary in some cases.*)

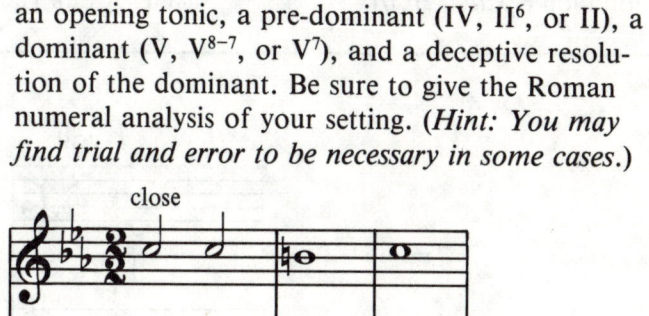

c: I   IV   V ⁽⁸⁻⁷⁾   VI

(*Note: *V⁷ cannot be used here. A V⁷, when used, must be a complete chord; and IV cannot, with good voice leading, lead to a complete V⁷.*)

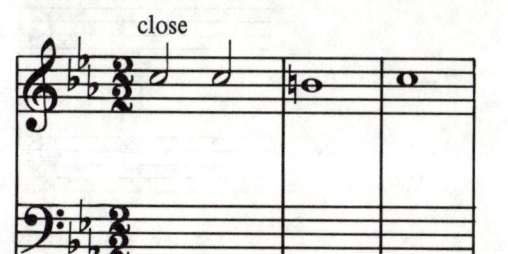

13

G: I   VI   IV

14   open

e: I   VI   IV   V   I

15   close

D: I   VI   IV   V⁷   I

IV (or) II⁶

16 A common usage of VI is in a descending 3rd bass pattern leading from the opening tonic to the pre-dominant ____ or ____.

one

17 VI and II⁶ have _____ (*how many?*) common tone(s). Complete the connection of VI II⁶ keeping the common tone in the same voice and moving the remaining voices stepwise. (*Remember to use correct doubling in II⁶.*)

B♭: I   VI   II⁶

30 Complete the following progressions. (*Bear in mind soprano scale degrees being used.*)

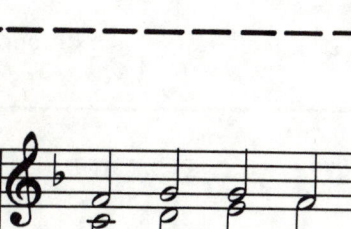

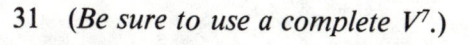

e: I   IV   V   VI

31 (*Be sure to use a complete V⁷.*)

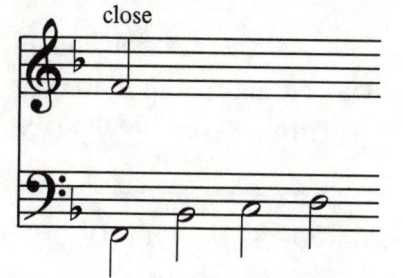

F: I   II⁶   V⁷   VI

32 (*First write the bass.*)

b: I.   IV   V   VI

complete

33 (*Remember: V⁷ must be a(n)* _____ (*complete or incomplete*) *chord.*)

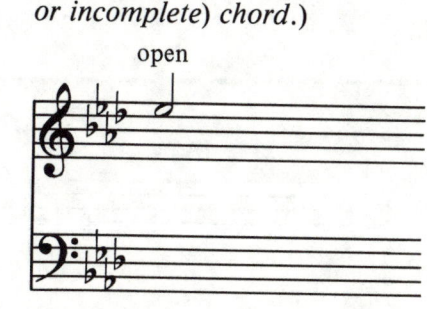

A♭: I   II   V⁷   VI

18 Complete each of these connections in the smoothest correct way. (*Double check each chord for correct doubling.*)

F: I VI II⁶

19

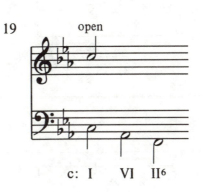

open

c: I VI II⁶

20 (*First write the bass.*)

close

d: I VI II⁶

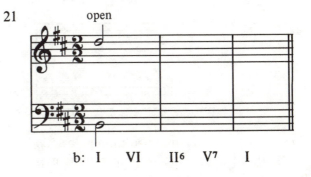

21

open

b: I VI II⁶ V⁷ I

Î

25 Write the following deceptive resolutions of V.

Remember, since VI is a substitute for I, ____ (*scale degree*) should be doubled.

E♭: V   VI

26

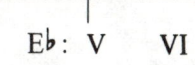

f♯: V   VI

27

c: V   VI

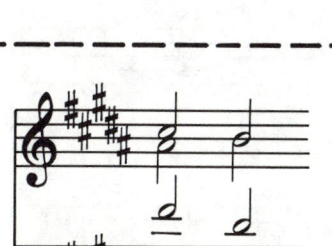

28

D: V   VI

29

B: V   VI

22

Eb: I   VI   II⁶   V⁷   I

OR

---

(1) diminished

23 In addition to leading from the opening tonic to IV or II⁶ in a descending 3rd bass pattern, VI may also *descend a 5th* (or ascend a 4th) and lead to II. This generally occurs only in major keys, since in minor keys II, a (1) _____ triad, is rarely used. Write the Roman numeral analysis of the following:

(2) F: I VI II V I   (2)

---

(1) common tone

(2) step

24 As illustrated below, the upper voice movement in VI II is identical to that of VI II⁶: The (1) _____ _____ is kept and the remaining voices move by (2) _____.

D: I   VI   II⁶   D: I   VI   II

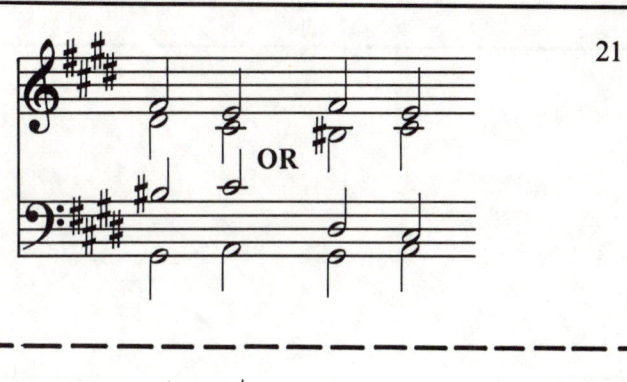

OR

21

c#: V⁷   VI

22

Ab: V⁷   VI

23 The V triad may also resolve to VI. Compare the voice leading in the examples below:

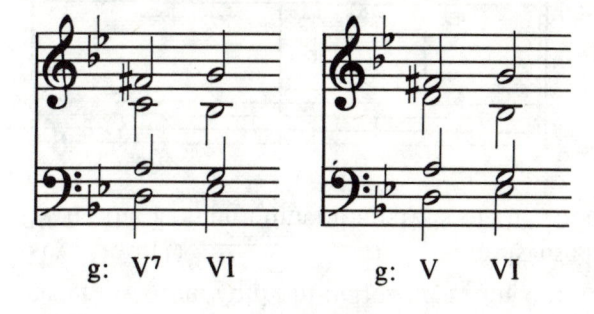

g: V⁷   VI   g: V   VI

The voicing in each chord of resolution is the same. The only difference between the two is that in V⁷ VI

(1) $\hat{4}$

(2) $\hat{5}$

it is (1) _____ that moves to $\hat{3}$. In V VI it is (2) _____ that moves to $\hat{3}$. (*It is important to follow this voice-leading procedure in resolving V to VI; otherwise, parallel octaves and/or perfect 5ths will result.*)

$\hat{7}$ $\hat{1}$

(1) $\hat{4}$ $\hat{3}$

$\hat{2}$ $\hat{1}$

$\hat{5}$ $\hat{6}$

24 The resolution of V⁷ VI is: (1) upper voices $\begin{cases} \hat{7} \underline{\quad} \\ \hat{4} \underline{\quad} \\ \hat{2} \underline{\quad} \end{cases}$

bass $\hat{5}$ _____

$\hat{7}$ $\hat{1}$

(2) $\hat{5}$ $\hat{3}$

$\hat{2}$ $\hat{1}$

$\hat{5}$ $\hat{6}$

The resolution of V VI is: (2) upper voices $\begin{cases} \hat{7} \underline{\quad} \\ \hat{5} \underline{\quad} \\ \hat{2} \underline{\quad} \end{cases}$

bass $\hat{5}$ _____

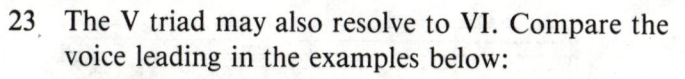

25 Complete the following:

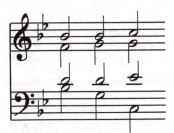

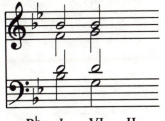

B♭: I   VI   II

(*Note: The bass from VI to II may also ascend a 4th.*)

26   open

A: I   VI   II

27   open

C: I   VI   II   V   I

y

28   Remember that the function of VI in the progressions being considered in this set is that of leading from the opening tonic to one of the pre-dominants, IV, II⁶, or II. Therefore, the order of the chords should not be reversed. Which setting of the given soprano below is correct? _____

A: I   IV   VI   I   VI   IV

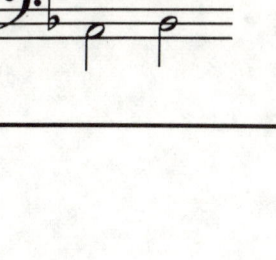

17

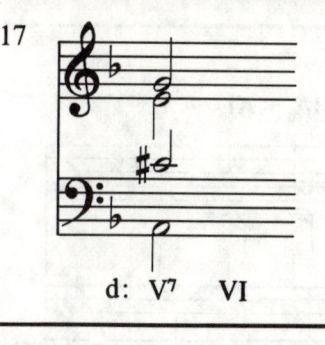

d: V⁷   VI

18 As you may have noticed in the previous examples, the V⁷ chords in V⁷ VI have been complete 7th chords.

An incomplete V⁷ does not permit as smooth a resolution to VI with doubled third (as illustrated in example **x**), and it can easily (and incorrectly) lead to VI forming parallel _____ (as shown in example **y**).

octaves

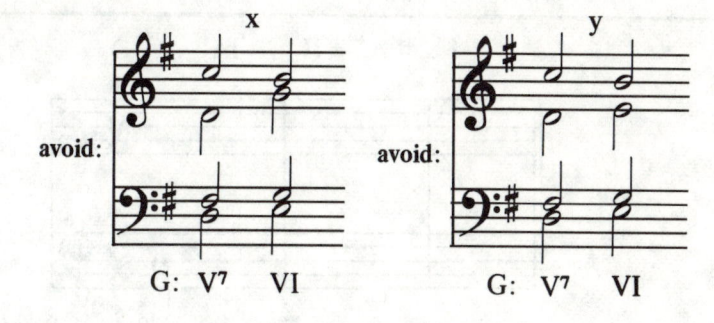

avoid: avoid:

G: V⁷   VI   G: V⁷   VI

19 Write the following deceptive resolutions of V⁷.

Remember, the V⁷ before VI should be _____ (complete *or* incomplete).

complete

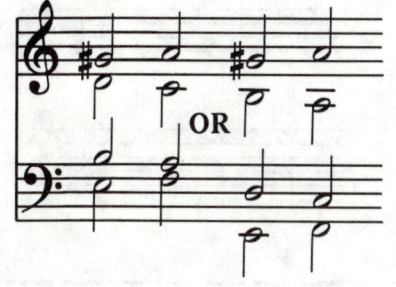

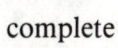

OR

a: V⁷   VI

20

F: V⁷   VI

29 VI may lead to a prolonged pre-dominant, as in the examples below. Give the Roman numeral analysis of each:

E: I VI | II⁶ II | V⁸⁻⁷ | I ‖

30

c♯: I VI | IV II⁶ | V | I ‖

I   VI   II⁽⁶⁾ V⁽⁷⁾   I

OR

V⁸⁻⁷   I

31 Set the following, using VI to lead from the opening tonic to the pre-dominant (IV, II⁶, or II). Conclude, then, with an authentic cadence. (*First give a Roman numeral analysis and write the bass line*.)

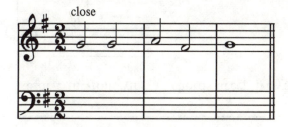

G:

I   VI   IV   V   I
           II⁶

(*Note: *II is not used in minor keys.
**V⁷ cannot be used with the given
soprano because 4̂ cannot be prepared.*)

32

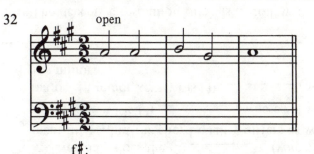

f♯:

(1) Î (and) Ŝ

(2) bass

(3) minor

(4) major

12 Although VI and I are very similar in that they both contain (1) _____ and _____ (*scale degrees*), VI provides a vivid contrast to I in its resolution of V or V⁷. Not only does the (2) _____ (*voice*) movement differ, but the chord quality differs as well. In major keys VI is (3) _____, whereas I is major. In minor keys VI is (4) _____, whereas I is minor.

---

(1) Î

(2) Ŝ

(3) Î

(4) Ĝ

13 The deceptive resolution of V⁷ is as follows:

upper voices
{
 7̂ to (1) _____
 4̂ to (2) _____
 2̂ to (3) _____
}

bass   5̂ to (4) _____

---

14 Resolve the following V⁷ chords deceptively:

f: V⁷   VI

15

E: V⁷   VI

16

B♭: V⁷   VI

33 Set the following figured bass patterns, using the smoothest correct voice leading. First give the Roman numeral analysis.

Bb: I VI II⁶ V⁸ ⁻ ⁷ I

34

e: I VI IV II⁶ V⁸⁻⁷ I

open

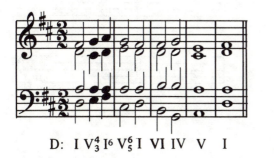

D: I V⁴₃ I⁶ V⁶₅ I VI IV V I

35

(1) $\hat{1}$
(2) $\hat{3}$
(3) $\hat{1}$

8 In example **x** resolve V⁷ to I. In example **y** resolve V⁷ deceptively (to VI).

Remember: $\hat{7}$ goes to (1) ____

$\hat{4}$ goes to (2) ____

$\hat{2}$ goes to (3) ____

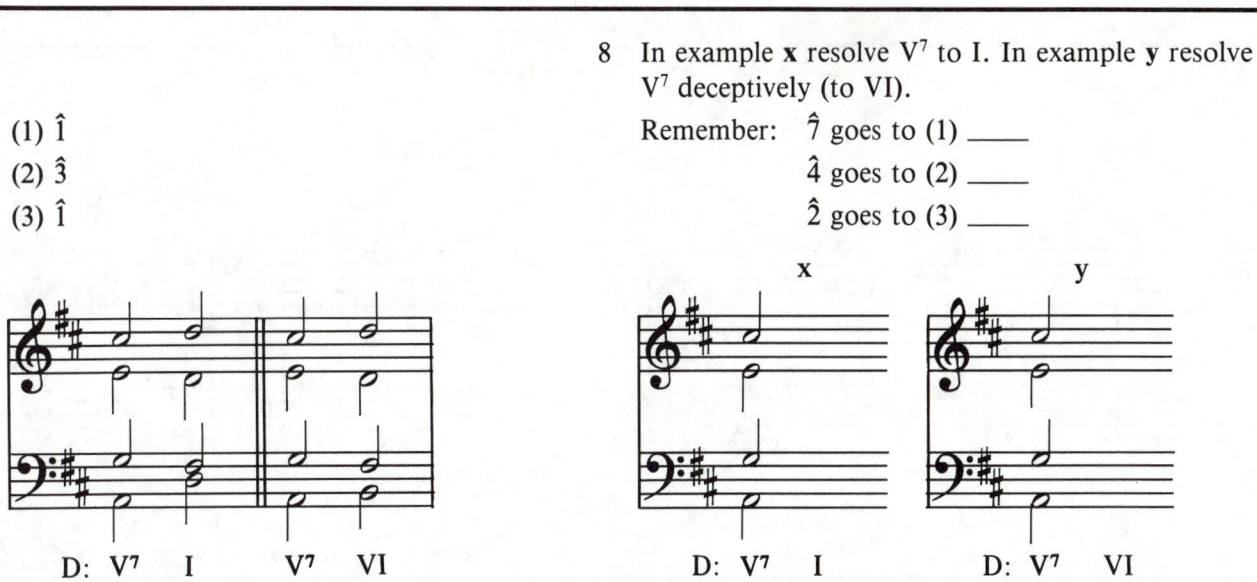

D: V⁷ I   V⁷ VI

D: V⁷ I   D: V⁷ VI

$\hat{1}$

9 When VI is used in place of the closing tonic, ____ (*scale degree*) is doubled.

---

10 Resolve V⁷ to VI as outlined above:

f#: V⁷   VI

$\hat{1}$

11 Sometimes in V⁷ I the leading tone in an inner voice does not resolve (as in example **x**). However, when V⁷ is resolved deceptively (as in example **y**), $\hat{7}$ must always resolve to ____.

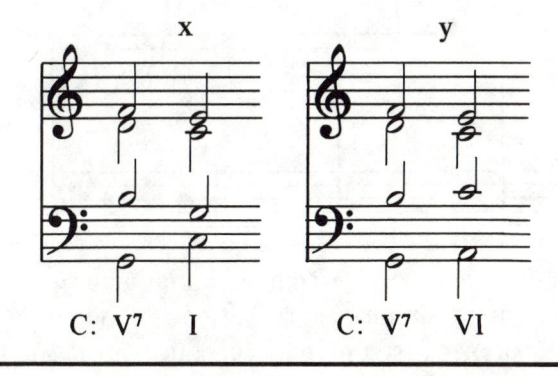

C: V⁷ I   C: V⁷ VI

1 Thus far we have discussed two uses of VI:

   1. As a pre-dominant in harmonic progressions in major keys: I VI V I.
   2. As a link in the movement from the opening tonic to the pre-dominant IV, II⁶, or II:

$$\begin{array}{c} \text{IV} \\ \text{I VI II}^6 \ \text{V}^{(7)} \ \text{I.} \\ \text{II} \end{array}$$

A very different way that VI may be used in both major and minor keys is as a *temporary substitute for the closing tonic* in a harmonic progression. Put another way, the dominant (V or V⁷) may resolve to VI rather than to _____.

I

(*Note: VI is not generally used as both a pre-dominant and a substitute for the closing tonic within the same harmonic progression.*)

---

(1) I

(2) VI

2 Study each progression below. In progression **x**, V⁷ resolves to (1) _____. In progression **y**, V⁷ resolves to (2) _____, a substitute for I.

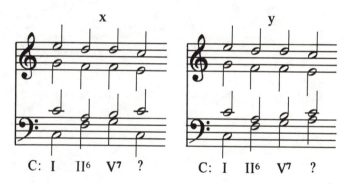

C: I II⁶ V⁷ ?   C: I II⁶ V⁷ ?

---

(1) two

(2) $\hat{1}$ and $\hat{3}$

3 VI and I have (1) _____ (*how many?*) common tones, namely (2) .... (*scale degrees*).

---

common

4 Because of the prominence of the soprano voice in a four-voice texture, VI is an especially effective substitute for I when it has $\hat{1}$ or $\hat{3}$ in the soprano, for these are the two _____ tones between I and VI.

5 Since I is the expected chord of resolution for a V or V⁷, when VI is used in place of I as the resolution of V or V⁷ the resolution is termed *deceptive*. In example **x** the *regular* resolution of V⁷ to I is illustrated. In example **y** the _____ resolution of V⁷ to VI is illustrated.

deceptive

6 Study the resolutions of V⁷ to I and V⁷ to VI below:

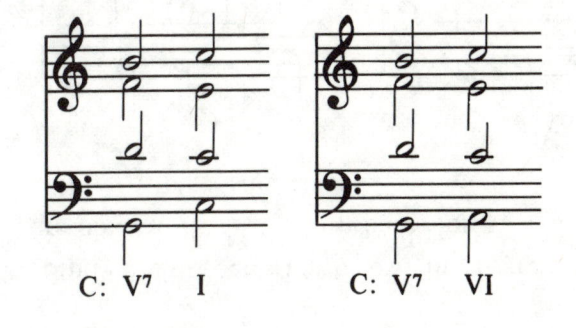

In these examples the tendency tones in V⁷ resolve identically:

$\hat{7}$ goes to (1) ____.

$\hat{4}$ goes to (2) ____.

In addition, $\hat{2}$ goes to (3) ____. The only difference in the resolutions is the (4) _____ (*voice*) movement. Note that the deceptive resolution of V⁷ results in a doubled third in the VI chord.

(1) $\hat{1}$
(2) $\hat{3}$
(3) $\hat{1}$
(4) bass

7 The doubled third in VI is a doubled $\hat{1}$.
It is easy to remember this doubling for this usage of VI: When VI is used as a substitute for I, double ____ (*scale degree*).

$\hat{1}$

Turn the book upside down now and continue to work on right-hand pages.

SUMMARY OF CHORD AND VOICE LEADING

Part 1 Pre-dominant chords: IV, II, II⁶

Set 1 / LEADING TO V

- A basic harmonic progression consists of the movement from an opening tonic, through a pre-dominant, to a dominant, and then to a closing tonic.

- The most common pre-dominant chords are IV, II, and II⁶.

- IV and II⁶ commonly occur in both major and minor keys. Root position II in minor keys, a diminished triad, occurs rarely.

- The root (or bass) of IV and II is doubled. The third (or bass) of II⁶ is doubled.

- The smoothest correct connections of IV V and II⁶ V are contrary motion-nearest. (The SAT move to the nearest chord tones in contrary motion to the bass.)

- The smoothest correct connections of II V are common tone-stepwise, though with some soprano patterns this type of connection is not possible (in which case the procedure is to move to the nearest chord tones, avoiding faulty parallels and allowing for correct doubling).

- IV may support $\hat{4}$, $\hat{6}$, or $\hat{1}$ in the soprano. II and II⁶ commonly have a soprano of $\hat{2}$ or $\hat{4}$ (but *not* $\hat{6}$).

Set 2 / LEADING TO V⁷

- In the connection of a pre-dominant chord to V⁷, the seventh of V⁷ ($\hat{4}$) is prepared by common tone. Other voices move according to the general voice-leading procedure: to the nearest chord tones that avoid faulty parallels, avoid an augmented 2nd in minor keys, and allow for correct doubling.
  (Note: IV in major and minor keys and II⁶ in minor keys will always move to an incomplete V⁷.)

- The seventh of V⁷ ($\hat{4}$) resolves down by step to $\hat{3}$ in the following I.

- Except when $\hat{7}$ is in the soprano, a complete V⁷ may resolve to either a complete or an incomplete I. A complete V⁷ with $\hat{7}$ in the soprano must resolve to an incomplete I. An incomplete V⁷ resolves to a complete I.

Set 3 / APPROACH FROM I

- The smoothest correct connections of I to each pre-dominant are:

  I IV—common tone-stepwise
  I II—contrary motion-nearest
  I II⁶—movement to the nearest chord tones, avoiding faulty parallels and allowing for correct doubling. (Remember: $\hat{6}$ in the soprano of II⁶—and II—should be avoided.)

Part 2   Prolongation of I

Set 4   /   I^6

- A basic harmonic progression often begins with a prolongation of the opening tonic, and a common way of prolonging tonic harmony is through the use of I^6.

- Two very common SB patterns in I I^6, or I^6 I, are parallel 10ths and voice exchange.

- The root of I is doubled and either the root or fifth of I^6 is doubled, depending upon which gives the smoothest voice leading.

- In connecting I to I^6, I^6 to IV or II^6, and in all other connections throughout this book, unless otherwise indicated, the *smoothest* correct voice leading is to be used.

Set 5   /   VII^6 AND V^6 (1)

- VII^6 is most commonly used as a passing chord in the prolongation of tonic harmony.

- A typical SB pattern in I VII^6 I^6, or I^6 VII^6 I, is voice exchange. Another common soprano is $\hat{1}$ $\hat{7}$ $\hat{1}$.

- VII^6 is also used as a neighboring chord to both I and I^6 (I VII^6 I and I^6 VII^6 I^6).

- The third of VII^6 is doubled.

Set 6   /   VII^6 AND V^6 (2)

- V^6 most commonly occurs as a neighboring chord to I (I V^6 I) in the prolongation of tonic harmony.

- V^6 is also used as an incomplete-neighboring chord to I (I^6 V^6 I).

- Either the root or the fifth may be doubled in a V^6, depending upon which gives the smoothest correct voice leading. The leading tone (the third) must never be doubled.

- It is important to understand the difference in function between VII^6 and V^6, and V and V^7. VII^6 and V^6 are used as passing, neighboring, or incomplete-neighboring chords in the prolongation of opening tonic harmony. Root position V and V^7 lead to the closing tonic in a harmonic progression.

Set 7 / INVERSIONS OF V⁷ (1)

- Whereas the function of root position V^7 is to lead to the closing tonic in a harmonic progression, inversions of V^7 are used to prolong the opening tonic.

- Inversions of V^7 are complete chords, and in their resolution to I or I^6, the active tones resolve, $\hat{7}$ to $\hat{1}$ and $\hat{4}$ to $\hat{3}$. (See below for the single exception to the latter.)

- V^6_5 is most commonly used as a neighboring chord to I (I V^6_5 I), and is also used as an incomplete-neighboring chord (I^6 V^6_5 I).

- V^4_3 typically occurs as a passing chord between I and I^6, or I^6 and I, with a SB parallel 10th pattern. It is sometimes used as a neighboring chord to I (I V^4_3 I) or I^6 (I^6 V^4_3 I^6).

- In I V^4_3 I^6 with a soprano moving in parallel 10ths ($\hat{3}$ $\hat{4}$ $\hat{5}$) with the bass, $\hat{4}$ does not resolve down to $\hat{3}$. This is the only case in which the non-resolution of the seventh ($\hat{4}$) is permissible. In all other cases, $\hat{4}$ in V^7 or inversion resolves to $\hat{3}$.

- V^4_2 is commonly used as an incomplete-neighboring chord to I^6 (I V^4_2 I^6) and also as a neighboring chord to I^6 (I^6 V^4_2 I^6).

- In all of these tonic prolongation patterns, the smoothest AT connections are usually common tone-stepwise.

Set 8 / INVERSIONS OF V⁷ (2)

No new chord usages or voice leading.

Set 9 / MORE ELABORATE PROLONGATION

- Inversions of V^7, VII^6, and V^6 may be preceded by a pre-dominant chord. Some typical usages are:

```
              I
I  IV  VII⁶  or, with soprano  5̂ 6̂ 7̂ 1̂
              I⁶

    IV
I  or  V⁴₂  I⁶
    II⁶

         V⁶
I  II  or  I
         V⁶₅
```

- As is the case with root position V^7, when an inversion of V^7 is preceded by a pre-dominant chord, the seventh (of the inversion of V^7) must be prepared by common tone.

- Just as V may be converted to V^7 with the introduction of a passing seventh in an upper voice (V^{8-7}), V may be converted to V^4_2 with the introduction of a passing seventh in the bass voice ($V-^4_2$).

- The progression V I or V^7 I at the end of a musical phrase is termed an authentic cadence. The ending of a phrase on V is called a half cadence. (Note: V^7 is too unstable to be used at a half cadence.)

Part 3   Other $^5_3$ and $^6_3$ Functions (1)

Set 10   /   PROLONGATION OF PRE-DOMINANT HARMONY

- Just as opening tonic harmony may be prolonged, so may pre-dominant harmony (though pre-dominant prolongation is usually not as extensive as tonic prolongation).

- Common ways of prolonging pre-dominant harmony are as follows:

IV II⁶	One voice moves from a 5th to a 6th above the bass, while all other voices remain stationary.
IV II	The upper voice movement is the same as in IV II⁶.
II II⁶ and II⁶ II	The typical SB pattern is voice exchange. The usual doubling rules apply: the root of II, the third of II⁶.
II I⁶ II⁶ and II⁶ I⁶ II	A passing I⁶ (with resulting doubled third) connects the voice exchange in the prolongation of supertonic harmony. Correct voice leading is most easily achieved by using close spacing.

Set 11   /   VI AS PRE-DOMINANT

- VI is used as a pre-dominant in major keys, leading directly to V in a basic harmonic progression (I VI V I).

- When used as a pre-dominant, VI has a doubled root.

- The smoothest correct connections of VI V are contrary motion-nearest.

- In the connection of I VI, both common tones are kept, and the remaining upper voice moves stepwise.

- VI differs from IV and II⁶ (and the most common usages of II) in that it is used to support an ascending soprano in leading to V.

- VI rarely leads directly to V⁷.

Set 12 / VI IN DESCENDING 3RD AND 5TH PROGRESSIONS

- A common use of VI is in a descending 3rd bass pattern, leading from an opening tonic to the pre-dominant IV or II⁶:

$$\begin{matrix} & & \text{IV} & \\ \text{I} & \text{VI or } & \text{V}^{(7)} & \text{I} \\ & & \text{II}^6 & \end{matrix}$$

- In a similar usage, VI may descend a 5th (or ascend a 4th) and lead to the pre-dominant II: I VI II V⁽⁷⁾ I.

- In these progressions the root of VI is doubled.

- The smoothest correct connections of VI to IV, II⁶, and II are common tone-stepwise.

Set 13 / VI AS SUBSTITUTE FOR I

- VI may be used as a temporary substitute for the closing tonic in a harmonic progression. When V or V⁷ resolves to VI rather than I, it is termed a deceptive resolution. If this resolution occurs at the end of a phrase in place of the expected authentic cadence, it is called a deceptive cadence.

- The deceptive resolution of V⁷ (which should be a complete chord) is:

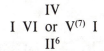

$$\begin{array}{ll} \text{upper} & \left\{\begin{array}{cc} \hat{7} & \hat{1} \\ \hat{4} & \hat{3} \\ \hat{2} & \hat{1} \end{array}\right. \\ \text{voices} & \\ & \\ \text{bass} & \begin{array}{cc} \hat{5} & \hat{6} \\ \text{V}^7 & \text{VI} \end{array} \end{array}$$

- The deceptive resolution of V is:

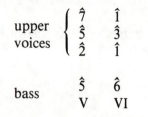

- Note in both cases above that the third of VI, $\hat{1}$, is doubled.

- VI is never the substitute for the true closing tonic in a harmonic progression. A deceptive resolution will lead on to another harmonic progression that will conclude with a true closing tonic.

Part 4   Other $\frac{5}{3}$ and $\frac{6}{3}$ Functions (2)

Set 14   /   IV AND IV⁶ IN TONIC PROLONGATION

- The chord succession I IV I is a prolongation of tonic harmony characterized by neighboring patterns in two of the upper voices, with the common tone kept in the other upper voice: $\hat{5}$ $\hat{6}$ $\hat{5}$
$\hat{3}$ $\hat{4}$ $\hat{3}$
$\hat{1}$ $\hat{1}$ $\hat{1}$

- Additional ways that IV is used in tonic prolongation are: I⁶ IV I⁶ and I IV I⁶. Common soprano lines contain neighboring patterns or a sustained $\hat{1}$.

- The typical use of IV⁶ in prolonging tonic is I IV⁶ I⁶, having a descending bass paired with a stepwise ascending (passing) soprano, $\hat{3}$ $\hat{4}$ $\hat{5}$.

- When IV⁶ is used to prolong tonic, the smoothest correct voice leading results from doubling the third of the chord.

- In prolongation patterns with IV and IV⁶, I⁶ has a doubled fifth.

- The ending of a phrase with the progression IV I is termed a plagal cadence. This is often immediately preceded by a V⁽⁷⁾ I progression.

Set 15   /   OTHER USES OF IV⁶

- IV⁶ may function as a pre-dominant, leading to V, typically with a soprano of $\hat{4}$ $\hat{5}$.

- When IV⁶ is used as a pre-dominant, the best voice leading is achieved by doubling the fifth of the chord and moving to V with all stepwise voice leading. (Care should be taken to avoid voice crossing and spacing errors.)

- A Phrygian cadence (a special type of half cadence) is characterized by the movement, in minor keys, from IV⁶ to V, paired with a soprano of $\hat{4}\ \hat{5}$.

- In the connection of I to the pre-dominant IV⁶ (with doubled fifth), a common tone is kept, but a leap in one of the inner voices is unavoidable.

- IV⁶ may prolong subdominant harmony. A typical SB pattern in IV⁶ IV or IV IV⁶ is voice exchange.

- IV⁶ may be used in the prolongation of dominant harmony, as a passing chord connecting V with V⁶₅.

- The soprano typically used with V IV⁶ V⁶₅ I is $\hat{5}\ \hat{4}\ \hat{4}\ \hat{3}$.

- With this usage of IV⁶ the smoothest correct voice leading is achieved by doubling the third.

Set 16 / III AND VII

- A typical use of III is as support for $\hat{7}$ in a descending soprano line ($\hat{1}\ \hat{7}\ \hat{6}$), in leading from I to IV.

- The root of III is doubled.

- I and III have two common tones which are kept in their connection.

- The smoothest correct connection of III IV is contrary motion-nearest.

- When the descending line $\hat{1}\ \hat{7}\ \hat{6}$ is used in minor keys, $\hat{7}$ is not raised and III is a major chord.

- A common use of III and VII is in a progression consisting of a series of descending 5ths: I IV VII III VI II V I.

- In writing the series of descending 5ths for four voices, the root of each chord is doubled. In major keys this results in a doubled leading tone in VII (which is permissible because VII does not lead to I, and the leading tone does not resolve).

- When the series of descending 5ths is written in minor keys, $\hat{7}$ is not raised in either VII or III (both are, therefore, major triads), but it is raised, as usual, in V.

Part 5. $\frac{6}{4}$ Chords

Set 17 / THE CADENTIAL $\frac{6}{4}$

- The cadential $\frac{6}{4}$ occurs above a bass of $\hat{5}$. Its function is to prolong dominant harmony at a cadence through the delaying of dominant chord tones in the upper voices.

- The symbol $V\left(^{6-5}_{4-3}\right)$ reflects this function and gives the specific voice leading in the resolution of the cadential $\frac{6}{4}$ to the dominant triad: The 6th above the bass resolves to the 5th above the bass; the 4th above the bass resolves to the 3rd above the bass.

- The bass of a cadential $\frac{6}{4}$ is doubled, and in the resolution of the $\frac{6}{4}$ to the dominant triad, the doubled bass note is kept as a common tone.

- The cadential $\frac{6}{4}$ may also resolve to V^7. The specific voice leading is given in the symbol $V\left(^{8-7}_{6-5}_{4-3}\right)$. All upper voices in the cadential $\frac{6}{4}$ move down by step.

- The cadential $\frac{6}{4}$ always occurs on a beat that is metrically stronger than the beat of its resolution.

- One of the most common pre-dominant chords, IV, II, or II⁶, typically precedes the cadential $\frac{6}{4}$.

- In the connection of the pre-dominant to the cadential $\frac{6}{4}$ the smoothest correct voice leading is used. The 4th above the bass (the principal active tone in the cadential $\frac{6}{4}$) is either prepared by common tone, if preceded by IV ($\hat{1}$ $\hat{1}$), or approached by step from above, if preceded by II or II⁶ ($\hat{2}$ $\hat{1}$).

Set 18 / $\frac{6}{4}$ CHORDS IN TONIC PROLONGATION

- There are three types of $\frac{6}{4}$ chord that are typically used to prolong tonic harmony. Each is named according to the function of its bass:

    Passing $\frac{6}{4}$—I V$^6_4$ I⁶ or I⁶ V$^6_4$ I, often with SB voice exchange, or with the soprano $\hat{1}$ $\hat{7}$ $\hat{1}$

    Stationary $\frac{6}{4}$—I IV$^6_4$ I, with neighboring patterns in two upper voices: $\begin{matrix}\hat{5}\ \hat{6}\ \hat{5}\\ \hat{3}\ \hat{4}\ \hat{3}\end{matrix}$

    Arpeggio $\frac{6}{4}$—I I⁶ I$^6_4$ or I I$^6_4$ I⁶

- In each of these $\frac{6}{4}$ chords the bass is doubled.

- Passing and stationary $\frac{6}{4}$ chords contain active tones which lead to and from the stable tones of tonic.

- The arpeggio $\frac{6}{4}$ is composed entirely of the stable tones within tonic harmony.

Part 6   7th Chords (Other than V⁷)

Set 19   /   STRUCTURAL TYPES

No new chord usages or voice leading.

Set 20   /   THE SUPERTONIC 7TH CHORD (1)

- The supertonic 7th chords, II^7, II^6_5, II^4_3, and II^4_2, are pre-dominant chords.

- All supertonic 7th chords have the same preparation and resolution pattern. The seventh, $\hat{1}$, is prepared by common tone in the preceding chord (usually I) and is then resolved down by step to $\hat{7}$ in the following dominant harmony.

- II^6_5 (which is a complete chord) is typically used in the harmonic progressions I II^6_5 V I and I VI II^6_5 V I.

- There are some noteworthy differences between the usage of II^6_5 and that of II^6:

  II^6_5 may have a soprano of $\hat{2}$, $\hat{6}$, or $\hat{1}$, whereas II^6 generally has a soprano of $\hat{2}$ or $\hat{4}$, but not $\hat{6}$.

  A common soprano in II^6_5 V is $\hat{2}$ $\hat{2}$; a common soprano in II^6 V is $\hat{2}$ $\hat{7}$.

  While II^6 may lead to either V or V^7, II^6_5 generally leads to V and not V^7.

- Care should be taken in connecting I^6 to II^6_5, for this connection is particularly susceptible to faulty parallels in major keys.

- Another important usage of II^6_5 is in the tonic prolongation pattern I II^6_5 V^4_2 I^6.

Set 21   /   THE SUPERTONIC 7TH CHORD (2)

- II^7 is most commonly used in the harmonic progression I II^7 $V^{(7)}$ I.

- In order to avoid faulty parallels, II^7 in major keys often occurs as an incomplete chord with the fifth omitted and either the root or the third doubled.

- In minor keys II^7 is more often a complete chord, though it may occur as an incomplete chord.

- All inversions of II^7 are complete chords.

- The dominant to which II_5^6 or II^7 leads may be prolonged by a cadential $_4^6$. The dissonant $\hat{1}$ is kept in the same voice and its resolution delayed.

- The most characteristic usage of II_3^4, the least common of the supertonic 7th chords, is in the harmonic progression $I\ II_3^4\ V^{(7)}\ I$.

- II_2^4 (which never precedes a root position dominant) is used in the tonic prolongation pattern $I\ II_2^4\ V_5^6\ I$.

- Supertonic harmony may be prolonged by the movement of II^7 to II_5^6 or II_5^6 to II^7, typically with a SB pattern of voice exchange. II^7 and II_5^6 may be connected by means of a passing I^6.

Set 22 / THE LEADING TONE 7TH CHORD (1)

- The leading tone 7th chord prolongs tonic harmony.

- Leading tone 7th chords, which are dim 7th chords in minor keys and dim-min 7th chords in major keys, are written as complete chords.

- The regular resolution pattern for leading tone 7th chords is to a I or I^6 with doubled third:

   $\hat{6}$ to $\hat{5}$
   $\hat{4}$ to $\hat{3}$
   $\hat{2}$ to $\hat{3}$
   $\hat{7}$ to $\hat{1}$

- VII^7 leads to I. VII_5^6 and VII_3^4 lead to I^6.

Set 23 / THE LEADING TONE 7TH CHORD (2)

- A fairly common exception to the regular resolution pattern of the leading tone 7th chord allows for normal doubling of the root in the tonic chord. If $\hat{2}$ occurs above $\hat{6}$ (forming a 4th) it may resolve to $\hat{1}$ rather than to $\hat{3}$.

- Typical uses of VII^7 and its inversions are:

   VII^7 (like V_5^6)   Neighboring chord to I ($I\ VII^7\ I$)
                             Incomplete-neighboring chord to I ($I^6\ VII^7\ I$)

   VII_5^6 (like V_3^4)   Passing chord between I and I^6 ($I\ VII_5^6\ I^6$)
                             Neighboring chord to I^6 ($I^6\ VII_5^6\ I^6$)

   VII_3^4 (like V_2^4)   Neighboring chord to I^6 ($I^6\ VII_3^4\ I^6$)
                             Incomplete-neighboring chord to I^6 ($I\ VII_3^4\ I^6$)

   VII_2^4 Rarely occurs

- In minor keys the I (or I^6) which precedes VII^7 (or inversion) should have regular doubling. In the connection of tonic to leading tone 7th chord, stepwise voice leading in all upper voices will be possible, allowing smooth introduction of the seventh and other dissonances.

- In major keys the I (or I^6) that precedes VII^7 (or inversion) may have regular doubling. If however, the use of regular doubling would result in faulty parallels, the third of I or I^6 is doubled instead.

Part 7 Diatonic Modulation

No new chord usages or voice leading.

Can't Find Your Mistake?

Have you ...

- kept voices within their respective ranges?

- used correct doubling in each chord?

- used correct spacing in each chord?

- avoided AT leaps of a 5th or more?

- used the *smoothest* (to the nearest chord tones) correct voice leading?

- avoided faulty parallels?

- avoided a melodic aug 2nd (between $\hat{6}$ and $\hat{7}$ in minor keys)?

- resolved the leading tone (where necessary)?

- prepared the seventh of V^7 (or inversion) by common tone, when V^7 (or inversion) is preceded by a pre-dominant chord?

- resolved the seventh of V^7 (or inversion) down by step?

- prepared or smoothly introduced (as appropriate) and resolved dissonances in the supertonic and leading tone 7th chords and in the cadential $^6_4$?

- used the typical soprano, voice leading, chord usage, or chord succession?

ANSWERS TO TEST COVERING PART 1

1. (1) (IV)   root $\hat{4}, \hat{6}, \hat{1}$ (maj and min)
   (2) II⁶   third $\hat{2}, \hat{4}$ maj and min
   (3) II   root $\hat{2}, \hat{4}$ maj   (Set 1)

2. (1) pre-dominant   (2) dominant   (Set 1)

3. (1) CMN   (4) CMN
   (2) CTS   (5) CMN
   (3) CTS   (Sets 1 and 3)

4. (1) $\hat{4}$
   (2) prepared (by) common tone   (3) chord tones
   (4) parallels   (5) aug 2nd
   (6) correct doubling   (Set 2)

5. (1)

(2)

OR

(3)

(Sets 1–3)

6. (1)

a: I   II⁶   V⁽⁷⁾   I

(2)

b: I   IV   V⁽⁷⁾   I

(Set 3)

ANSWERS TO TEST COVERING PART 2

1. (1) root (*or* bass)   (Set 4)
   (2) third (*or* bass)   (Set 5)
   (3) root (or) fifth   (Sets 4 and 6)
   (4) complete   (Set 7)

2.

(Set 4)

3. (1) passing   (Sets 5 and 7)
   (2) parallel 10ths   (Set 7)
   (3) voice exchange   (Set 5)

(4)  (5)

(Sets 5 and 7)
SAT may be written an octave lower.

4. (1)

I V⁶₅ I
N

(2)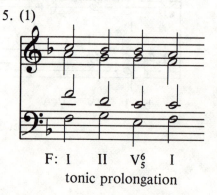

a: I V⁴₂ I⁶
   IN

(Sets 7 and 8)

5. (1)

F: I II V⁶₅ I
tonic prolongation

(2)

B♭: I IV VII⁶ I⁶
tonic prolongation   (Set 9)

6.

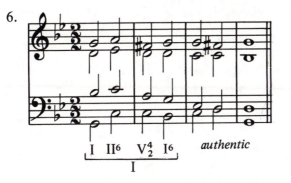

I II⁶ V₂⁴ I⁶   *authentic*

$\lfloor\underline{\quad\quad}\rfloor$
I

(Set 9)

7.

D: I V₃⁴ I⁶ V₅⁶ I   II⁶ V⁽⁷⁾ I

or, simply

(Set 8)

ANSWERS TO TEST COVERING PART 3

1. IV II⁶   IV II   II II⁶   II⁶ II   (*Any three of these in any order is correct.*)

(Set 10)

2.

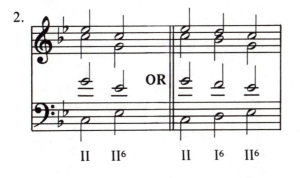

II   II⁶   II   I⁶   II⁶

SAT may be written an octave lower.   (Set 10)

3.

VI

(Set 11)

4. ($\hat{7}$ to) $\hat{1}$
   ($\hat{4}$ to) $\hat{3}$
   ($\hat{2}$ to) $\hat{1}$
   ($\hat{5}$ to) $\hat{6}$

(Set 13)

5. (1)

VI in descending 3rd pro-
gression, leading from
opening tonic to IV.

(Sets 10 and 12)

(2)

VI as substitute for
closing tonic.

(Set 13)

(3)

VI as pre-dominant

(Set 11)

6. (1)

e: I II⁶ V⁸⁻⁷ VI

(Set 13)

(2)

G: I VI II I⁶ II⁶ V I

(Sets 10 and 12)

ANSWERS TO TEST COVERING PART 4

1. (1)

pre-dominant

(Set 15)

(2)

passing chord in dominant prolongation

(Set 15)

(3)

tonic prolongation

(Set 14)

2.

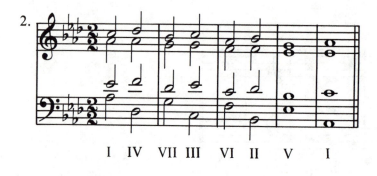

I   IV   VII   III   VI   II   V   I

(Set 16)

3.

I   IV   I
I

OR

(Set 14)

4.

c: I   III   IV   IV⁶   V

(Sets 15 and 16)

5. (1) Phrygian   (Set 15)
   (2) deceptive   (Set 13)
   (3) authentic   (Set 9)
   (4) plagal   (Set 14)
   (5) half   (Set 9)

ANSWERS TO TEST COVERING PART 5

1. (1) tonic   (Set 18)
   (2) tonic   (Set 18)
   (3) dominant   (Set 17)
   (4) tonic   (Set 18)

2.

cadential

(Set 17)

3.

stationary

OR

(Set 18)

4.

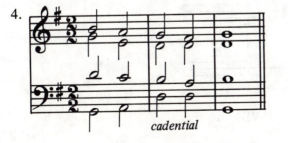

cadential

(Set 17)

5.

arpeggio

(Set 18)

6.

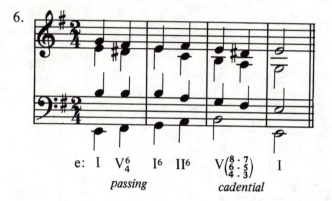

e: I   V⁶₄   I⁶   II⁶   V($\begin{smallmatrix}8\text{-}7\\6\text{-}5\\4\text{-}3\end{smallmatrix}$)   I

passing   *cadential*

(Sets 17 and 18)

ANSWERS TO TEST COVERING PART 6

1.

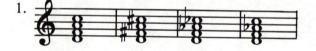

(Set 19)

2. (1) min   (2) dim-min
   (3) dim-min   (4) dim

(Set 19)

3. (1) IV⁶₅   (2) II⁴₂

(Set 19)

4. (I) II⁶₅ V I *or* (I) II⁷ V⁽⁷⁾ I *or* (I) II⁴₃ V⁽⁷⁾ I
   Note: The dominant may be prolonged by a cadential ⁶₄

(Sets 20 and 21)

5. (I) II⁶₅ V⁴₂ I⁶ *or* (I) II⁴₂ V⁶₅ I

(Sets 20 and 21)

6. (1)   (2)

VII⁷ I   VII⁴₃ I⁶

(Set 22)

7.

VII$^4_3$　I^6

(Set 23)

8. (1)

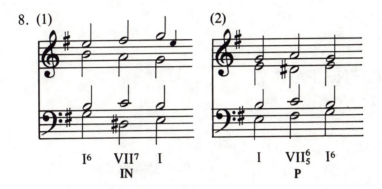

I^6　　VII^7　I
　　　IN

(2)

I　VII$^6_5$　I^6
　　P

(Set 23)

9.

I　II$^6_5$　V　　I

(Set 20)

10. (1)

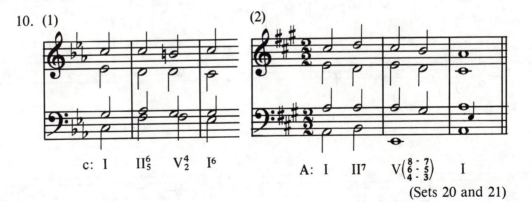

c:　I　　II$^6_5$　V$^4_2$　I^6

(2)

A:　I　II^7　V$\left(^{8\ -\ 7}_{^6\ -\ 5}_{4\ -\ 3}\right)$　I

(Sets 20 and 21)

11. (1)   (2)

(Sets 20 and 21)

ANSWERS TO TEST COVERING PART 7

1. (1) diatonic   (2) common
   (3) opening   (4) pre-dominant
   (5) (I, I⁶,) II, II⁶, IV, IV⁶, VI   (6) (I, I⁶,) II⁶, IV, IV⁶
   (7) opening tonic

(Sets 24 and 25)

2. (1) A E c♯ D b
   (2) g E♭ c F d

(Set 24)

3. (1) f♯: IV VI I   (2) f♯: IV   (3) B♭: III VI
     A: II IV VI   b: I   d: I IV
   (4) B♭: V VI I III
     F: I II IV VI

(Set 24)

4. (1)   (2)

(Set 25)

5. (1)   (2)

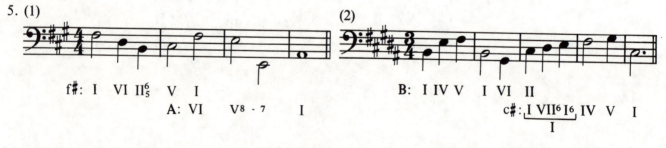

(Set 25)

BASIC HARMONIC PROGRESSIONS: SCHEMATIC OVERVIEW

This chart is a schematic overview of the ways in which chords may be ordered to form the basic four-stage progression

$$\text{OPENING TONIC} \ - \ \text{PRE-DOMINANT} \ - \ \text{DOMINANT} \ - \ \text{CLOSING TONIC}$$

as studied in this book. The alternatives within each stage are shown in separate columns. The opening tonic stage may consist of two or more prolongations strung together, with the final chord in one of the stated chord successions becoming the initial chord in another (or a repetition of the same) succession. Boxes contain explanations of the constraints on flow from one stage to the next. Except as limited by these constraints, any of the alternatives in a column may progress to any of the alternatives in the next column to the right. Thus, horizontal alignment from one column to the next has no significance. Special symbols are defined as follows:

symbol

$\begin{Bmatrix} x \\ y \\ z \end{Bmatrix}$ *Any one* of x, y, or z may be chosen.

$x \quad y$ Chord symbols x and y may exchange positions.

(x) The figured bass symbol x may or may not be present. For example, $I^{(6)}$ means I or I^6. (The *large* parentheses used in connection with the cadential $^6_4$ indicate that *voice leading* is shown by the figured bass symbols.)

OPENING TONIC	LINK (OPTIONAL)	PRE-DOMINANT	DOMINANT	CLOSING TONIC
I	III	II	$V^{(7)}$	I
I _ I^6	from I only to IV only	in major only	$V\begin{pmatrix} 8-7 \\ 6-5 \\ 4-3 \end{pmatrix}$	I $IV\binom{6}{4}$ I
$I^{(6)} \begin{Bmatrix} VII^6 \\ V^4_3 \\ IV \end{Bmatrix} I^{(6)}$	VI	II^6	from $\begin{Bmatrix} II^{(6)} \\ II^7 \\ II^6_5 \\ IV \end{Bmatrix}$ only	VI
	from I only	IV		substitute for I from $\begin{Bmatrix} V^{(7)} \\ V\begin{pmatrix} 8-7 \\ 6-5 \\ 4-3 \end{pmatrix} \end{Bmatrix}$ only
$I^{(6)} \begin{Bmatrix} V^6_{(5)} \\ VII^7 \end{Bmatrix} I$	to $\begin{Bmatrix} IV \\ II^{(6)} \\ II^6_5 \end{Bmatrix}$ only	IV^6 ①②		
		VI ①②	V IV^6 V^6_5	
$I^{(6)} \begin{Bmatrix} V^4_2 \\ VII^6_5 \\ VII^4_3 \end{Bmatrix} I^6$	IV VII III VI	in major only	to I only	
	from I only to II only	II^7		
I IV^6 I^6		II^6_5 ②		
I _ V^6_4 _ I^6		II^4_3 ①		
I IV^6_4 I		IV $II^{(6)}$		
I I^6 I^6_4		IV _ IV^6 ①②		
I III IV $I^{(6)}$		II _ II^6		
I IV VII^6 $I^{(6)}$		II^7 _ II^6_5 ②		
I $\begin{Bmatrix} IV \\ II^6_{(5)} \end{Bmatrix} V^4_2 I^6$		II _ I^6 _ II^6		
I II $V^6_{(5)}$ I		II^7 _ I^6 _ II^6_5 ②		
in major only		① IV^6, VI, and II^4_3 are approached from I only.		
I II^4_2 V^6_5 I		② IV^6, VI, and II^6_5 lead to V only, not to V^7.		

NOTES

NOTES

NOTES

NOTES

NOTES

NOTES